TRAVEL DEMAND MANAGEMENT AND ROAD USER PRICING

Travel Demand Management and Road User Pricing
Success, Failure and Feasibility

Edited by

WAFAA SALEH
Edinburgh Napier University, UK

GERD SAMMER
University of Bodenkultur, Austria

ASHGATE

Published by
Ashgate Publishing Limited
Wey Court East
Union Road
Farnham
Surrey, GU9 7PT
England

Ashgate Publishing Company
Suite 420
101 Cherry Street
Burlington
VT 05401-4405
USA

www.ashgate.com

British Library Cataloguing in Publication Data
Travel demand management and road user pricing : success,
    failure and feasibility. - (Transport and society)
    1. Transportation demand management 2. Congestion pricing
    I. Saleh, Wafaa II. Sammer, Gerd
    388.3'1

Library of Congress Cataloging-in-Publication Data
Saleh, Wafaa.
    Travel demand management and road user pricing : success, failure and feasibility / by
Wafaa Saleh and Gerd Sammer.
        p. cm. -- (Transport and society)
        Includes index.
    ISBN 978-0-7546-7303-3
    1. Urban transportation policy. I. Sammer, Gerd. II. Title.

HE305.S26 2009
388.4'13142--dc22

                                                                                            2008045424

ISBN 978 0 7546 7303 3
e ISBN 978 0 7546 8906 5

Mixed Sources
Product group from well-managed
forests and other controlled sources
www.fsc.org Cert no. SA-COC-1565
© 1996 Forest Stewardship Council

Printed and bound in Great Britain by
MPG Books Ltd, Bodmin, Cornwall.

Contents

PART II   INTERNATIONAL EXPERIENCES WITH TDM MEASURES

List of Figures

List of Tables

List of Contributors

Professor Kay W. Axhausen is Professor of Transport Planning, Institute of Transport Planning and Systems, at the Eidgenössische Technische Hochschule, (ETH) Zurich. Before that he worked at the Leopold-Franzens Universität, Innsbruck, Imperial College London and the University of Oxford. He has been involved in the measurement and modelling of travel behaviour for the last 25 years contributing especially to the literature on stated preferences, micro-simulation of travel behaviour, valuation of travel time and its components, parking behaviour, activity scheduling and travel diary data collection. He was the chair of the International Association of Travel Behaviour Research (IATBR) and is an editor of *Transportation*.

Professor Phil Blythe is Professor of Intelligent Transport Systems and Director of the Transport Operations Research Group at Newcastle University. He leads one of the most committed and innovative teams of multi-disciplinary ITS researchers in Europe. His research portfolio covers a wide range of areas where ITS has been applied to transport, including: road to vehicle communications, road user charging and toll systems; ITS for assistive mobility, smartcards and RFID, wireless/smartdust technologies and future intelligent infrastructure. His forward-looking research attempts to bridge the technology-policy gap in terms of what technologies may evolve to meet future policy objectives or indeed influence future policy thinking. He has led and advised a major number of research initiatives/ projects in the area of road user charging, info-mobility, smartcards and wireless networks in both the UK and Europe.

Professor Giulio Erberto Cantarella has a Civil Engineering degree in Transportation from the School of Engineering of the University of Naples Federico II. Since November 1999 he has been Professor in the School of Engineering at the University of Salerno. His research activity has mainly regarded: choice modelling for transportation system users through models derived from random utility theory or with fuzzy utility, or regressive ANN models; models and algorithms for travel demand assignment to congested transportation networks, under stationary conditions or with day-to-day or within-day dynamics; methods for transportation network design both with discrete and continuous variables; methods for urban network traffic monitoring and control; macro or micro-scopic models for transportation terminal analysis.

Professor Peter Clinch is an environmental economist at University College Dublin. Since 2003 he has been, concurrently, Jean Monnet Professor of European Environmental Policy and Professor of Planning. He was appointed by the European Union to the Jean Monnet Chair in 2003 in recognition of his research and scholarship in this field and, in 2006, was made an Honorary Member of the Royal Town Planning Institute for distinguished contributions to planning. Professor Clinch is editor of the international journal *Planning Theory and Practice* and a member of the editorial board of the *Journal of Environmental Planning and Management* (both Taylor and Francis).

Professor Jonas Eliasson is Professor of Transport Systems Analysis and Director of the Centre for Transport Studies at the Royal Institute of Technology in Stockholm. His main research focus is methodology for decision support for transport planning, in particular transport modelling and cost-benefit analysis. Research topics include integrated land use-transportation modelling, activity-based modelling, road pricing, travel time variability and stated preference valuation. He has been involved in a large number of applied analyses of transport investments and policy measures. He was the project manager for the design of the Stockholm congestion charging system, and later chaired the expert panel summarizing the extensive evaluation of the system. Currently, he is involved in the ongoing evaluation and refinement of the Stockholm congestion charges, and also provides expert advice for several other cities considering introducing congestion charging. He is also currently the chairman of the committee responsible for the transport modelling and cost-benefit analyses for the National Transport Investment Plan.

Dr. Joel P. Franklin is Assistant Professor in the Department of Transport and Economics at the Royal Institute of Technology, Stockholm, Sweden. He received a MS in Civil and Environmental Engineering in 1998 at the University of California, Davis, and a PhD in Urban Design and Planning in 2006 at the University of Washington, Seattle. Dr. Franklin also has prior experience as a transport consultant in Sacramento, California. His research involves the application of advanced quantitative methods to the evaluation of transport policies with respect to broad social goals such as social equity and urban sustainability, with particular emphasis on non-parametric methods and on the relationship between transport accessibility and land development. In his current post he teaches transport-related courses in policy, economics, and geographic information systems, and he serves as director of the International Master Programme in Transport Systems.

Dr. Antonio Gschwender presently assigns his time to professional work, academic work, board games, music, and being a husband. He works at the public transport authority in Santiago, Chile, and teaches public transport planning at the Universidad de Chile, where he collaborates in research as well. He worked in the early design phase of Transantiago (2001–2003) at the Chilean Transportation Planning Office (Sectra).

Dr. Ha Hai Nam is currently a lecturer at the Posts and Telecom Institute of Technology (Vietnam) exploring a range of topics from pervasive computing to smart graphics. He received his PhD in Computing Science at Newcastle University in 2008. For his doctorate he explored different ways of automating the lighting design process using both perception-based and example-based approaches. As a research associate at Newcastle University, he was involved in a number of projects such as Ask-IT (an EU-funded project), Document Management System (funded by Medical Research Centre, UK) Immersive Video, Head Shaping.

Dr. Anders Karlström is Associate Professor in Economics and Transport at the Royal Institute of Technology, Stockholm, Sweden. In his work he uses a spectrum of theoretical, econometric, and computational tools with a focus on 'applied micro'. He has applied econometric tools to give insight and quantitative guidance to inform decisions on institutions and policies in various fields, in particular in the fields of labour economics and transport economics. His research activities include modelling activity-based transport demand, land-use, spatial computable general equilibrium, infrastructure and labour market productivity, and dynamic discrete choices.

Dr. Andrew Kelly is an environmental economist specializing in, climate and energy modelling, transport modelling, economics and policy, and air emissions modelling and policy formation. Dr. Kelly is a director of AP EnvEcon an environmental economics focused research firm in Ireland. As part of his current work Dr. Kelly is leading a national integrated assessment modelling project encapsulating air quality and greenhouse gas emissions modelling and policy formation. This work also includes the development of national level capacity for assessment of transport emissions and the effectiveness of both technical and non-technical policy measures.

Dr. Jonas Larsen is a lecturer in the Department of Environment, Society and Spatial Change at Roskilde University, Denmark. He co-authored *Performing Tourist Places* (Ashgate 2004), *Mobilities, Networks, Geographies* (Ashgate 2006) and *Tourism, Performance and the Everyday: Consuming the Orient* (Routledge 2009).

Professor David Levinson holds the RP Braun/CTS Chair in Transportation in the Department of Civil Engineering at the University of Minnesota. His research focuses on transportation policy, planning and deployment, transportation and land use interactions, and travel behaviour. He has authored or edited five books on transport: *Financing Transportation Networks*, *Assessing the Benefits and Costs of Intelligent Transportation Systems*, *Access to Destinations*, *The Transportation Experience*, and *Planning for Place and Plexus: Metropolitan Land Use and Transport*. He is also the editor of the *Journal of Transport and Land Use*.

Professor Hong K. Lo is Professor of Civil Engineering at the Hong Kong University of Science and Technology. He specializes in dynamic transportation system modelling, traffic control, network reliability, and public transportation analysis. He is managing editor for the *Journal of Intelligent Transportation Systems*, Editor (Asia/Pacific) for *Journal of Transport and Land Use*, and serves on the editorial boards of several international journals, including *Transportation Research Part B*, *Transportmetrica*, *Journal of Advanced Transportation*, *ASCE Journal of Urban Planning and Development*, and *International Journal of Sustainable Transportation*.

Dr. Stefano de Luca obtained a Civil Engineering degree in Transportation at the University of Naples Federico II. In 2003 he got a PhD degree in Transportation Engineering at the University of Rome La Sapienza. Since 2004 he has been Assistant Professor of Transportation Planning at the School of Engineering of Salerno. His research activity has mainly regarded: choice modelling for transportation system users through models derived from random utility theory or regressive ANN models; models and algorithms for travel demand assignment to congested transportation networks under stationary conditions; macro or micro-scopic models for transportation terminal analysis.

Dr. Juan Carlos Muñoz is Associate Professor at the Department of Transport Engineering and Logistics, Pontificia Universidad Católica de Chile (PUC). His areas of interest include transport networks, transit operations, logistics, and optimization, where he has published in the key journals in the field. He was personal adviser to the Minister of Public Works, Transport and Telecommunications (2003–2004) during the final design phase of Transantiago. He was also one of the 12 experts asked to provide guidance and suggestions for the plan in March 2008.

Dr. Patrick Olivier is a Senior Lecturer at Newcastle University UK. With an undergraduate degree in physics and a doctorate in computational linguistics he feels very much at home in an interdisciplinary research centre such as the Informatics Research Institute. He has spent most of his research career conducting both theoretical and applied research at the intersection of artificial intelligence, computer graphics and human-computer interaction.

Professor Juan de Dios Ortúzar is Professor and Head of the Department of Transport Engineering and Logistics, Pontificia Universidad Católica de Chile (PUC). He has taught and researched in travel demand modelling, particularly discrete choice model applications, since 1973. He has published more than 70 papers in journals and is co-author of the best selling *Modelling Transport* (Wiley 2001).

Dr. Chih Wei Pai got a BSc degree in computing in Taiwan. He obtained his MSc degree in Transport Engineering from Newcastle University and a PhD degree (with focus on motorcycle safety) from Edinburgh Napier University. His main research area is road safety using advanced econometric models. His PhD research findings have been published in several highly-respected journals such as *Accident Analysis and Prevention*, *Traffic Injury Prevention*, and *Safety Science*.

Dr. Wafaa Saleh is a Senior Lecturer in Transportation in the School of Engineering and the Built Environment, Edinburgh Napier University. Her research and teaching areas include transport modelling, travel demand management, modelling travel behaviour and forecasting, transport and the environment, transport safety, transport management in developing countries and traffic engineering. She has published extensively in the area of travel demand management.

Professor Gerd Sammer is Professor of Transport Planning in the Department of Landscape, Spatial and Infrastructure Sciences at the Institute for Transport Studies, University for Natural Resources and Applied Life Sciences, Vienna (Universitaet für Bodenkultur Wien). From 1990 to 1994 he was the head of the Institute for Transport Studies and Road Construction at the Graz University of Technology in Austria. He has also been Honorary Professor at the Széchenyi István College Györ in Hungary since 1997. He is a civil engineer with specialization in transport planning. His key qualifications comprise the fields of transportation analysis and forecasting, planning and scenarios techniques for urban, regional and interurban transport problems, techniques of cost-benefit- and sustainable-development-analysis, behavioural modelling, stated response analysis as well as mode choice. He is author and co-author of over 100 papers and contributions to books in different languages.

Dr. Pushpendra Singh received his PhD in mobile computing at the INRIA Research Lab, Rennes, France in 2004. He developed a framework to provide fault tolerance to applications running on mobile devices. After the PhD, he joined inter-disciplinary research at the Department of Psychology at the University of Portsmouth, where he worked on developing mobile device based adaptive speech remediation software for Japanese English speakers. He joined the Informatics Research Institute, Newcastle University in December, 2005 as a research associate and worked on real-time visualization of 3D Data on mobile devices and prototyping and evaluation of ubiquitous computing environments. He is currently a research engineer in the ARLES research group at INRIA, Paris-Rocquencourt.

Barbara W.Y. Siu received her BEng in civil engineering and is about to finish her doctoral degree in transportation engineering from the Hong Kong University of Science and Technology. Her research interests include travel time reliability, travel behaviour modelling, integrated transportation network supply and demand management, network planning over time, spatial interaction of transportation and land-use.

Dr. Kathryn Stewart is a Lecturer in Transportation in the School of Engineering and the Built Environment at Edinburgh Napier University. Her ongoing research is on traffic assignment modelling examining the network effects of road tolls and she is involved in projects on dynamic traffic assignment and micro-simulation modelling.

Nebiyou Tilahun is a PhD candidate in the Civil Engineering Department at the University of Minnesota. His research interests are in travel behaviour, transportation planning and transportation economics.

Professor John Urry is a Distinguished Professor of Sociology, Lancaster University; Fellow of the Royal Society of Arts; Founding Academician, UK Academy of Social Sciences; Chair RAE Panels (1996, 2001); Honorary Doctorate, Roskilde University. He has published around 40 books and special issues, and approximately 100 refereed articles and 80 chapters. He is currently Director of the Centre for Mobilities Research. Recent books include *Sociology beyond Societies* (2000), *The Tourist Gaze* (2002), *Performing Tourist Places* (2004), *Mobilities, Networks, Geographies* (2006), *Mobilities* (2007), *After the Car* (2008).

Craig Walker has an MSc in Transport Engineering and Planning from Edinburgh Napier University. This follows a BA in Urban Geography and a MLitt. in Strategic Studies, from the University of Aberdeen. He is now a Transport Management Consultant with Faber Maunsell/AECOM in Edinburgh and continues to be interested in road traffic accident statistics and projects.

Weihong Guo (Amy) received her MSc in Transport Engineering and Operations from Newcastle University. She is currently in the final stage of completing a doctorate in Intelligent Transport Systems. Her PhD thesis is entitled 'Use of a New Methodology to Investigate the Effectiveness of a Pervasive and Intelligent Future Traveller Information System in Encouraging Public Transport Use'. Her main research interests are in the field of applying emerging technologies to improve the efficiency of transport networks, with particular interests in the area relating to smartcard applications, traveller information systems and travel behaviour. She is a researcher in the Transport Operations Research Group at Newcastle University.

Acknowledgements

This book presents a number of contributions on specific research agendas relevant to TDM measures as discussed at the Third International symposium on success and failure of travel demand management measures which was organised at the Transport Research Institute (TRi) at Napier University in Edinburgh. We would like to thank Napier University for supporting the Symposium. The editors would also like to acknowledge the support they received from their academic institutions while preparing the contents of this book.

We would also like to express our gratitude to the invited authors for their contributions. Finally we are grateful to the reviewers who had to read and often reread the chapters and provided advice and guidance on the presented work.

The contents of this book reflect the authors' views and do not necessarily reflect the views of any other organisations or individuals who have supplied or committed data or other resources.

Chapter 1

Travel Demand Management and Road User Pricing: Success, Failure and Feasibility

Wafaa Saleh and Gerd Sammer

Traffic congestion and associated problems have become a major worry for transport planners, politicians and the public. These transport-related problems require immediate attention, particularly as many past policies have failed to deal with them adequately. The traditional approach of 'predict and provide' for dealing with traffic congestion is no longer viable. That is, it is no longer feasible that the forecasts of vehicle usage are accommodated by building more roads; it is widely accepted that unrestrained demand for travel by car cannot be sustained. Measures taken to address the problems have therefore shifted to 'predict and manage' or travel demand management (TDM).

TDM measures are sets of policies with the primary objective of influencing the travel behaviour of individuals through voluntary reduction or restriction on private vehicle use and ownership and the provision of travel alternatives. TDM measures are often referred to as 'push and pull' measures and can include regulatory, pricing, planning or persuasive policies. These policies attempt to modify the temporal and spatial dimensions of travel, mode choice and perhaps even the decision to travel. The objective of such measures is to encourage individuals to either make their trips outside peak times, by a different mode or to find another way of carrying out the trip purpose. Applying such measures can result in a more efficient transport system, improved environmental conditions and improvements in safety as well as revenue generation, which may be earmarked for investment in the transport system. TDM can generate positive effects on health and in the long term can also effect a change in spatial development of land use.

TDM can broadly be categorized as fiscal and non-fiscal measures. Non-fiscal measures that can be adopted by planners and policy makers include traffic calming and access controls and restrictions, parking management and control, public transport improvements, road space reductions, urban traffic management and control systems, traffic bans/restrictions, and travel awareness campaigns. Fiscal measures can include parking charges, workplace parking levies, fuel taxes, vehicle excise duty, car ownership permits, public transport subsidies, priority measures for walking and cycling and road-user charging.

During the 2005 symposium pricing measures, in particular road user pricing, dominated the research agenda. This is not unexpected since there is a growing interest in pricing measures, which gained a lot of popularity and support over recent years for a number of reasons. Firstly, there is the growing level of traffic congestion combined with delays to public transport, and the failings of non-pricing measures and policies in achieving evident impacts on traffic congestion and other related urban problems. Secondly, the legislation, technological, implementation and political issues associated with pricing systems have been recognized and almost resolved. Moreover, there are now a number of pricing schemes implemented in the world and a growing number of interested cities and decision makers who are showing greater interest and willingness to adopt pricing policies in order to resolve transport problems. A lot of studies and research programmes have been devoted to studying the impacts of such pricing systems. Finally, pricing measures seem to be more attractive to decision makers since they are more effective in achieving their objectives and particularly in generating a stream of revenues, which could then help in the implementation of other TDM measures. All of these factors contributed to the fact that pricing measures are, and will continue to be in the near future, the most important TDM measures. But we should not forget that pricing measures are still not popular, therefore the implementation needs strong arguments to convince the public.

Theory and sociopolitical goals of pricing imply that the extent of the charges imposed on an individual should reflect the costs they impose on others and on the environment, thus helping to reduce negative externalities of traffic. Various terms have been used as well as road pricing, e.g. road user charging, congestion charging, congestion pricing, road tolling, variable pricing, etc., all of which generally reflect the same principle. The execution of the theoretical principles of congestion charging into practice however is complex and will hardly, if ever, be met in reality (Saleh 2005). This is because the pricing structure has to reflect the actual costs the motorists impose on the system according to time, distance and place and/or other applicable variables. In order to realize the theoretical framework, the system has to be flexible and easy to alter in the future as and where appropriate. Although that is theoretically possible to determine, it is political acceptance and practicality that might prove very difficult, if not unfeasible. The danger therefore is that pricing regimes might turn, in the majority of cases, into another imposed toll or fixed charge for travellers and a means of generating further revenues for the local authorities.

Therefore, the aim should be to develop, implement and monitor the performance of integrated TDM plans and policies, underpinned by a package of measures which aims to manage road congestion and improve the performance of the transport system. An integrated programme of TDM pricing and non-pricing measures should therefore be devised in order to assist local authorities and cities in developing appropriate schemes that meet their local objectives, solve the local transport problems and would be politically and publicly feasible. There shouldn't be more interest in pricing measures just because they generate revenues. With other complementary TDM measures, which try to avoid undesirable side effects, pricing might provide the optimum solutions to transport problems. The research and investigations of non-pricing, as well as pricing measures should be continued.

The outcome of the 2005 TDM symposium has informed the debate on TDM, including road user charging, on what went right and what went wrong over the past decades (Saleh 2007). The researchers succeeded in obtaining a general acceptance that pricing mechanisms should play a role in TDM, but that this should be through the 'old' use of parking charges and tolls as well as the 'new' use of road user charging; we are doing things 'right' in developing useful new methods, and in creating a body of evidence which is beginning to consider what works and what doesn't. We had also been successful in persuading the public that induced traffic is a real phenomenon which is now genuinely believed.

Where had we gone wrong then? We went wrong in that some of the work we produced was too simplistic and/or too theoretical and ignored the dynamics of behavioural response, the undesirable impacts of TDM measures and the political acceptance and implementation processes. Many so called 'proofs' were flawed or were based on flawed assumptions with some questionable evidence being used as model inputs. There is a need for more research into practical applications and real cases and more emphasis to be directed towards empirical investigations. We haven't always shown sufficient understanding of 'the bigger picture' and lacked interest in and learning from the international experiences with TDM. We do not demonstrate that we appreciate future *needs* and *implications* on societies, equity issues, transport systems and the environment.

The symposium closing remarks recommended that transport academics should provide more encouragement and support to politicians in an attempt to reduce the gap between academics and politicians. The discussions of the symposium recommended in particular the need to carefully investigate both the desirable as well as the non-desirable impacts of TDM measures, to investigate further implications of all pricing measures and to validate the models we use to assess and test our policies. For example measures of parking pricing and public transport fare structures and subsidies could well be underutilized. Furthermore, recommendations included the need for further engagement with the international experiences in the area of TDM. Impacts of complementary measures such as high occupancy policies are also of relevance. Finally, more attention and research should be directed towards the future interventions such as provision of driver information and ITS and their wider impacts on transport systems and societies, including safety and the environment. These drawbacks are explored within this book, with each chapter offering a handling of one of the issues discussed.

The Chapters

The book contains a number of contributions which address some of the recommendations of the 2005 TDM symposium. Each of the chapters reports on findings and results of theoretical and practical work in the area of travel demand management, including pricing measures.

The first part of the book focuses on investigations of the impacts of TDM measures. The chapter by Sammer (2008) argues that, in general, only short-term easy to observe effects are taken into account in the evaluation of TDM measures. These include for example, a move from car traffic to more environmentally friendly modes of transport, effects upon revenues, and time savings due to the decreasing number of traffic jams as well as short-term impacts on the environment. Long-term effects on the other hand such as land use problems, effects upon the local economy and value-added in the region, are methodologically difficult to determine. Other examples include the choice of a different destination, a switch to non-motorized traffic, the choice of a different route and rat running, reduced travel demand and boundary effects. The boundary effects, for example, due to a toll cordon, and a redistribution of effects with social, health and economic consequences are hardly ever covered.

There are three possible reasons for such oversight according to Sammer: Lack of knowledge of these side effects, difficulties with the methodology and the intentional omission of the undesirable results. Two case studies have been used to present the argument: an urban congestion pricing in Graz and a parking management scheme for private car parks in the Vienna region. The chapter concludes that measures of travel demand management have a considerable demand-managing effect, both on short-term and long-term positive effects on traffic environment etc.; but the analysis shows too, that such measures can have considerable side effects which are often neglected.

The third chapter by De Luca and Cantarella (2008) discusses the gap in research and development work in TDM investigations and predictions. The authors recognize that increases in travel demand can no longer be faced through a supply-side approach only, due to constraints on the available budget as well as natural resources. Hence, modern transport policies also follow a demand-side approach, trying to influence amount and pattern of demand flows. That is, the appraisal of TDM measures requires a travel demand analysis including careful segmentation of users into categories and trip purpose; estimates of demand elasticity through choice models, regarding for example, the number of trips, time of day, destination, mode and route, and their relationship with features of transportation supply as described by level of service attributes.

Moreover, the authors point to the increasing relevance of choice model assessment. For example travel demand analysis is commonly based on random utility theory and, over the years, most effort in literature has been devoted to generalized choice model formulations introducing more parameters, but less attention has been paid to choice model validation and comparison against real data. The chapter argues that it is evident that a very sophisticated choice model actually only slightly outperforms a simpler one. The authors propose a general procedure to validate a choice model against real data and to compare its effectiveness with other models not necessarily specified through the same approach. Numerical examples referring to a real case are also reported.

Kelly and Clinch (2008) investigate changes in parkers' profile for the argument of any (negative) impacts on a TDM scheme to increase on-street parking charges in Dublin City. In an ex-ante and ex-post real case study, which is rare in practice, the documentation of such social profile analysis for a case of significant change provides a vital reference in the literature. The study provides important evidence for understanding the impact of a new tariff and pricing structure on the characteristics or 'profile' of those parking in an area, for example, casual versus frequent users and users of varying social class, which are very crucial. These considerations are important as a given tariff may disproportionately price certain groups out of the service.

Using data from a large-scale study, utilizing revealed and stated preference survey data relating to on-street parking, Kelly and Clinch consider profiling data from two 1,000 plus face to face surveys in a central on-street parking area before and after an actual citywide change in the price of on-street parking in Dublin, Ireland. Following the 50% price increase in on-street parking zones in Dublin city, there was just over a 4% drop in parking events in the case study area, and a 16.5% drop in average parking duration. However, the survey data from the same case study site show little change in the characteristics of those parking in the area. The noticeable changes consisted of a slight reduction in the most infrequent parkers and a reduction in city and suburban commuters relative to those travelling from further afield. Overall, at this price change level the 'profile impact' in terms of changes in demand was expectedly small with no major shifts.

Stewart (2008) addresses the theoretical issue of extending the formulation for stochastic system optimisation (SSO) pricing schemes to include marginal user cost (MUC), such that total perceived network travel costs for all classes are minimised, and presents an objective function for MUCSSO. To achieve such a flow pattern under an MUCSSO assignment link tolls are applied, which may differ for each user class. Marginal social cost price tolling is examined for differing user classes, and then the possibility of reduced (or minimal) revenue tolling strategies to produce the same effect are investigated.

Stewart argues that it might be politically desirable to allow for toll exemption for one or more MUCs, and the possibilities of producing toll sets that apply to less than the total number of user groups, but still result in the MUCSSO flow pattern being achieved are considered. The chapter claims that the methods used to derive toll sets are equally applicable to any stochastic assignment method.

Axhausen et al. (2008) present an investigation into the relentless trend of the falling cost of travel; this trend has created a world in which travellers mix local and non-local interactions easily, be it face-to-face or mediated by the various forms of telecommunication. The implications of this change of scale have not yet been fully discussed, as the most relevant literature in sociology generally skirts around its practical implication. The chapter discusses the interaction between social capital creation, travel and transport policy and outlines how transport policy has to overcome its limitations.

The discussions show that the current spatial distribution of social capital limits the speed with which citizens can adjust their behaviour in response to policy initiatives currently contemplated to achieve the policy goals of the reduced social exclusion, fewer greenhouse gas emissions and improved welfare. The expected impact on these structures may very well make the citizens unwilling to see these policies adopted in the first place. Transport policy makers will have to enlarge the scope of their policy making and find new partners if they want to be successful in their core mission: the provision of a transport system which provides the services needed for everyone at minimum social cost.

Weihong et al. (2008), provide a vision of future travellers' information systems (FTIS) by envisioning a link to pervasive computing technologies. A newly invented technique, immersive video, is applied to investigate user perceptions of the envisaged FTIS and the impact on individual travel choices. The design and development of immersive video are presented in detail. Initial results suggest that although the demand for such a vision of FTIS could be high, other travel demand management schemes must be considered as a coordinating tool to significantly influence individual mode choices.

The second part of the book presents a number of international experiences with TDM measures and their impacts. The chapter by Saleh et al. (2008) presents an investigation of the impacts of the provision of driver information using variable message signs (VMS), a specific type of ITS, on accident rates and severities on Scottish trunk roads. VMS alerts drivers to road works, weather conditions, accidents and expected delays as well as relaying generic road safety messages, and VMS signs are now present on many major roads in most countries. It had been claimed that the VMS have resulted in consistent reductions in speed and lowered accident rates, however not with much conclusive evidence. Furthermore, previous research suggested that while a reduction of speed was observed as a result of a sign that urges reduced speed, there was concern for an increase in speed thereafter, hence increased risk. The net safety effects of such message systems were rather inconclusive in the literature.

In Chapter 8, Saleh et al. use accident data, flow data location and accident rates at a number of VMS sites in central and north east Scotland before and after the installation of VMS to investigate effectiveness of VMS on accident reductions. The authors argue that there is evidence of some improvement in accident severities at VMS locations and also evidence of an increase in accident rates at these sites after installation of VMS.

Muñoz and Ortuzar and Gschwender (2008) investigate public transport management and operation and impacts on the performance of the bus system in Santiago de Chile. The system has been completely in private hands since the late 1970s, and in full deregulation during the 1980s, which eventually left the city with a very inefficient system, undignified treatment of passengers and a high accident rate. On top of all this the system is characterized by a high level of noise and environmental pollution due to bad maintenance of petrol engines, and a high rate of accidents due to both careless driving and (less-often) failure of brakes due to poor maintenance.

The Chilean government decided to intervene, developing the entire public transport system, integrating the well-reputed but not heavily used underground (Metro, a public company) and the private buses, based on a structure of trunk and feeder services (purposely designed), a modern bus fleet, integrated fares-paid by touchless smart cards and a high-tech centralized control system. It also developed an entirely new industry structure that was franchised through an international call for tenders, with operating contracts awarded to ten national and international firms. The new, integrated public transport system, known as 'Transantiago', went into operation on 10 February 2007. The chapter attempts to provide an objective account of the project history and discusses what lessons can be learned from this traumatic process.

Siu and Lo (2008) consider both transportation supply and demand management (TS-DM) measures, to underpin the development of an effective transportation management strategy. The authors, using the transportation infrastructure provision as the supply and the travelling public as the demand, assess demand management policies. They argue that synergy can be achieved in solving congestion problems when TS-DM strategies are developed jointly in an integrated manner, utilising a bi-level formulation to determine the time-dependent TS-DM strategy.

In the model, the upper level contains the TS-DM strategy as the decision variable whereas the lower level problem captures the time-dependent equilibrium residential/ employment location choices of travellers in the form of a combined model. This study then compares the benefit of the optimal mixed TS-DM strategy versus the traditional strategy of pure demand management. Using a small network example, they demonstrate that the integrated TS-DM strategy is a promising way for designing and managing transportation network over time, creating win-win outcomes for both the network operator and road users.

Nebiyou and Levinson (2008) estimate differences in willingness to pay a toll on a current trip in a stated preference context based on people's actual previous experience. The analysis is based on the I-394 MnPASS High Occupancy/Toll (HOT) lane project recently implemented in the Minneapolis/St. Paul region. The subjects in the study had been assigned a trip to complete and recorded their experiences. Then, respondents were asked to choose between a free alternative and the use of HOT lanes under different travel time and toll combinations in a stated preference survey. The analysis groups the travellers into subscribers and non-subscribers of the MnPASS (electronic toll collection transponder) system and further groups them into categories based on trip departure time (AM peak, PM peak and off-peak) and their previous experience (delayed or not). The findings suggest an increased willingness to pay among subscribers who were late in the PM rush hour. They also found some evidence that individuals who were late during the AM peak have a lower willingness to pay as compared to their on-time counterparts.

Finally, Franklin, Eliasson and Karlström (2008), deal with the new congestion pricing systems in Stockholm, one of the most ambitious systems in the sense that the congestion charges apply to the entire urban core. The system is now in place long enough to measure some real effects of congestion pricing on daily travel patterns, particularly with regard to how they affected people of different income level and gender. The analysis also comprises the benefits and burdens of the congestion charges on those who adjusted travel behaviours and those who did not, using a welfare analysis.

The outcome shows for the travel pattern that route and mode changes were far from a simple adaptation strategy. The fact that hardly anyone of the discretionary trips was obviously not 'replaced' in a simple one-to-one fashion may be an important observation. The assumption cannot be kept up that there is a more or less fixed number of trips to be made, and that the effect of the charges can be categorized only into 'mode change', 'departure time change' and 'destination change'. For discretionary trips, the adaptations seem to be much more multi-faceted, to the point that it is hard to say what really happened. The welfare analysis of morning commute trips found that the distribution of benefits and burdens due to paying the toll, enjoying travel time savings, or adjusting to it by changing travel mode, did not show significant differences among income group. The un-tolled were the only group with a net benefit. However, this group represents nearly 90% of the population, an overwhelming majority.

References

Axhausen, K.W., Urry, J. and Larsen, J. (2009), 'The Network Society and the Networked Traveller', in Saleh, W. and Sammer, G. (eds), *Travel Demand Management and Road User Pricing: Success, Failure and Feasibility* (Aldershot: Ashgate).

Muñoz, J.C., Ortuzar, J. de D. and Gschwender, A. (2009), 'Transantiago: The Fall and Rise of a Radical Public Transport Intervention', in Saleh and Sammer (eds).

De Luca, S. and Cantarella, G.E. (20098), 'Validation and Comparison of Choice Models', in Saleh and Sammer (eds).

Franklin, J.P., Eliasson, J. and Karlstroem, A. (2009), 'Travellers' Responses to the Stockholm Congestion Pricing Trial: Who Changed, Where Did They Go, and What Did It Cost Them?', in Saleh and Sammer (eds).

Kelly, J.A. and Clinch, J.P. (2009), 'On-Street Parking Pricing: *Ex Ante Ex Post* Profile Analysis following a 50% increase in On-Street Parking Charges in Dublin City', in Saleh and Sammer (eds).

Tilahun, N.Y. and Levinson, D.M. (2009), 'Unexpected Delay and the Cost of Lateness on I-394 High Occupancy/Toll Lanes', in Saleh and Sammer (eds).

Saleh, W. (2007), 'Success and failure of travel demand management: Is congestion charging the way forward?', Special Issue of *Journal of Transportation Research Part A*.

Saleh, W. (2005), 'Road user charging: Theory and practice'. *Journal of Transport Policy* Vol. 12 (5) pp. 773–76.

Saleh, W., Walker, C. and Pai, C.W. (2009), 'Variable Message Signs: Are They Effective TDM measures?', in Saleh and Sammer (eds).

Sammer, G. (2009), 'Non Negligible Side Effects of Traffic Demand Management', in Saleh and Sammer (eds).

Siu, B.W.Y. and Lo, H.K. (2009), 'Integrated Network Improvement and Tolling Schedule: Mixed Strategy versus Pure Demand Management', in Saleh and Sammer (eds).

Stewart, K. (2009), 'Modelling Impacts of Tolling Systems with Multiple User Classes', in Saleh and Sammer (eds).

Weihong, A.G., Blythe, P., Olivier, P., Singh, P. and Ha, H.N. (2009), 'An Evaluation of Future Traveller Information System and its Effectiveness in Demand Management Schemes', in Saleh and Sammer (eds).

PART I
Travel Demand Management:
Investigation of Impacts

Chapter 2
Non-Negligible Side Effects of Traffic Demand Management

Gerd Sammer

1. Introduction

Travel Demand Management (TDM) is one of the most cost effective measures to steer travel demand in a desirable direction. From a transport policy point of view, steering traffic in a desirable direction involves some organizational measures, for example distance-based road pricing or the management of parking fees, which reduce the demand for car traffic and move traffic in the direction of more environmentally-friendly public and non-motorized modes of transport. Compared to infrastructure measures the cost of TDM measures is comparatively lower while the effects upon the demand are possibly higher. This advantageous cost-benefit-ratio looks even better if all effects which are relevant for a 'traditional' cost-benefit-analysis are considered.

An analysis of relevant surveys shows that in general only short-term and easy to observe effects are taken into account for the evaluation. Examples of these include a move from car traffic to more environmentally friendly modes of transport, effects upon revenues, time savings due to the decreasing number of traffic jams, and the short-term impact upon the environment. Long-term effects on the other hand are hardly ever covered. Such effects include, for example, land use problems, effects upon the local economy and value-added in the region or effects which are methodically difficult to determine such as the choice of a different destination, a switch to non-motorized traffic, the choice of a different route and rat running, reduced travel demand, boundary effects, for example due to a toll cordon, and a redistribution of effects with social, health and economic consequences. The same is also true for some obviously negative effects which might spoil the image of successful measures. In general such effects are often assumed to be not dominant; therefore they are considered as side effects. However, they are rather long-lasting and should not be forgotten in the course of conscientious scientific work.

One may well ask for the reasons of such negligence regarding the side effects. Three important categories of causes can be determined:

- Lack of knowledge of these side effects: Given that it is difficult, time-consuming and costly to include them, they are hardly ever covered in transport studies which are used as a base for traffic management measures nor in before-and-after-evaluation studies; thus are they rarely mentioned in literature.

- Difficulties with the methodology: To include the so-called side effects in a survey, data gathering and analysis methods are required which go beyond the commonly used methods and are more complicated, time consuming, and costly. This is particularly true when stated response techniques are used. (Sammer 2003, Lee-Gosselin 2003).
- Undesirable results: At least some of the so-called side effects have negative consequences. This means that there is little or no incentive to determine such effects in a before-and-after-analysis, particularly if such an analysis is time consuming and costly. The pressure to succeed is particularly high in the case of expensive real-life demonstrations of certain measures since at the end of the survey these measures are meant to be pushed as a success.

In this contribution the statements made are evaluated with the help of two case studies; firstly, an urban congestion pricing scheme in Graz and secondly a parking management scheme for private car parks in the Vienna Region. These two cases are presented in the following sections.

2. Case Study: Urban Congestion Pricing in Graz

The case study about urban congestion pricing for the city of Graz was carried out within the framework of the European Research Project TransEcon (TransEcon-consortium 1996–1998).

2.1 Transport related background information about Graz

The city of Graz is the capital of the Austrian province of Styria. The conurbation of Graz has a population of 365,000 people. A total of 230,000 people live in the city itself and 135,000 in the surroundings. The car-ownership rate of the conurbation is 538 cars/1000 residents for the year 2006. Public transport comprises trams, buses, and a commuter rail system. The city of Graz uses the slogan 'Gentle Mobility' for its transport policy which includes the promotion of walking, cycling, and the use of public transport while trying to limit motorized private transport by traffic calming, parking charges and limited access for cars to the city centre. Concentric zones similar to the skins of an onion define the priority of the modes in the road network of Graz.

- Zone 1 comprises the heart of the city centre. This zone is a pedestrian precinct. The passage of public transport and cycles is assured. Motorized traffic is limited to loading activities from 6:00 until 11:00.
- Zone 2 lies concentrically around the first zone. It is freely open to public transport and cycles. Throughout the day traffic is only permitted for

'authorized persons' (30km/h speed limit). Permitted vehicles are loading/
unloading vehicles, taxis, cycles, residents' cars with permission to park
(permission to park in limited parking zones), and disabled persons'
vehicles.

• In Zone 3 access is assured for motorized traffic for the whole day. All
parking areas are paid parking (limited to 1.5 to 3 hours maximum parking
duration). Parking for longer periods is generally only possible in public
garages. All streets with the exception of priority streets are subject to a 30
km/h speed limit. Public transport can pass without constraints (thanks to
the provision of bus lanes, tram rails) and has priority at traffic lights.

• Zone 4 comprises the suburbs and newly-built areas. Apart from paid
parking which is only provided at several points in central areas, this zone is
very much identical to Zone 3 in terms of traffic organization. Development
in this zone is concentrated in serviced areas along public transport routes.

• Zone 5 is the surrounding countryside. Current plans are to provide
attractive public transport routes with rail rapid transit, bike-and-ride, and
park-and-ride facilities.

This zonal traffic model gives top priority to non-motorized and public transport. It
limits car transport in the city centre to business and residential traffic. Thus, most
of the commuter traffic is forced to transfer to non-motorized and public transport.
It should be mentioned that in recent years the problem of exceeding particle
emissions was raised. Therefore congestion pricing is periodically discussed.

2.2 Description of congestion pricing scenarios

The scenarios comprise the investigation of the influence of the introduction of a
toll cordon surrounding the central area of Graz. This area covers Zones 1, 2, and
3 and is shown as area A in Figure 2.1. The border of area A shows the location of
the toll cordon.

2.2.1 Base scenario   The toll has to be paid when a vehicle is crossing the toll
cordon in the direction of the city centre. During the off-peak period, a vehicle is
charged €1.15 (Table 2.1), which is equivalent to a single multi-trip ticket for the
public transport network. A monthly toll ticket is also available for €33.00. During
the peak periods from 7:00 to 8:00 a.m. and from 5:30 to 6:30 p.m., vehicles are
charged the double price of €2.30. In conjunction with the cordon toll measure the
following concomitant measures are included in the base scenario:

• Provision of additional multi-storey car parks at the toll border with a
parking fee of €3.50 per hour;

• Significant improvements in the capacity of public transport (regular
intervals of three minutes for all tram lines);

• Overall cycle path network with high quality parking facilities;

- Extension of the paid parking area to Zone 4 (area B in Figure 2.1) with a maximum parking time of three hours, except for residents.

Table 2.1   Toll fees

Toll fee per vehicle entering	Off peak period	€ 1.15/vehicle entry
	Peak periods	€ 2.30/vehicle entry
Toll fee per month independent of frequency of entering the cordon	Off peak period	€ 33.00/month
	Peak periods	€ 66.00/month

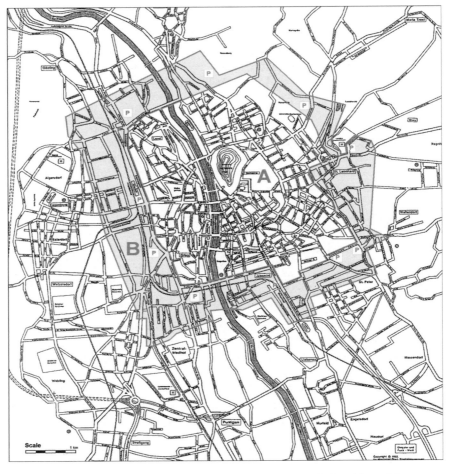

Figure 2.1   City map of Graz with the toll and extended paid parking zone

Note: The border of Zone A describes the toll cordon and includes the Zones 1, 2 and 3 mentioned in Section 2.1. The area B indicates the extension of the paid parking zone and is part of Zone 4.

In total, five scenarios were investigated. Two additional toll scenarios deal with different toll fees, one with a fee 50% higher than the base scenario and one with a reduction of 50%, in order to gain information about the demand elasticity regarding the toll level. Another scenario was defined to investigate the effect of a toll cordon at the city border. That is the border between Zone 4 and Zone 5 described in section 2.1. The last scenario called 'shopping bonus' was developed to compensate for the undesirable side effects of the base scenario.

2.2.2 Scenario shopping bonus This scenario was developed in order to avoid the negative side effects identified in the basic scenario. People who pass the toll cordon by public transport get the price for the ticket refunded if they go shopping in the toll area.

2.3 Methodology of the analysis

2.3.1 General considerations The estimation of future travel behaviour is undoubtedly not a simple, one-dimensionally explicable type of individual behaviour, especially if one important goal is the identification of supposed but unknown behavioural side effects. It is rather a host of objective and subjective aspects that combine and create comparatively complex, subjective situations of choice in each individual case (Brög 1981, Brög and Erl 1981; Sammer et al. 1998). Such a task calls for a suitable research approach, thus a 'situational approach based on an interactive interview technique' was used. This approach integrates socio-demographic, economic, supply-related and situational variables. It provides a considerably better insight into the aspects affecting travel behaviour than purely formal mathematical models with the assumption of known variables. This is especially due to the fact that in this concept emphasis is placed on a consistent disaggregation in all phases of the analysis in order to take the individual case fully into account. The scope for action that actually exists is determined for each individual decision unit (here: the individual trip as part of a trip chain); against the background of this subjective choice situation the possible reactions are estimated compared to alternative options. The situational approach proceeds on the assumption that the individuals are given a certain scope for action ('objective' situations) by their environment. This scope for action is determined by:

- the hypothetical assumption of the scenarios of the toll cordon;
- the constraints and freedom derived from the social demography of the individual and the other members of his/her household;
- the social values, norms and opinions regarding the areas relevant to travel behaviour.

Each individual experiences these 'objective' situations in a specific way. Individually different 'subjective' situations (consisting of variables from all three areas mentioned, i.e. the transport related environment, the socio-demography and the social values) are created. These 'subjective' situations differ from the 'objective' ones by incomplete, consciously or unconsciously distorted perceptions. The degree of deviation depends on the individual person and his/her specific experience. In these subjective situations, individual decisions are taken. In order to create a model of travel behaviour, it is necessary to reconstruct the chain of 'objective situation – personal perception – subjective situation – individual choice – behaviour'. If one wishes to influence travel behaviour, it is possible to intervene at any point in this chain to accomplish this. Consequently, such an analysis structure makes it possible to determine the probable individual reactions to measures with the help of the individual explanations of travel behaviour.

2.3.2 Survey procedure

Changes in travel behaviour resulting from the proposed measures were determined with the aid of a combined stated adaptation (Lee-Gosselin 2003, Sammer 2003) and in-depth-interview technique. This technique is based on two surveying steps: a mixed postal and telephone household survey and in-depth interviews (Figure 2.2).

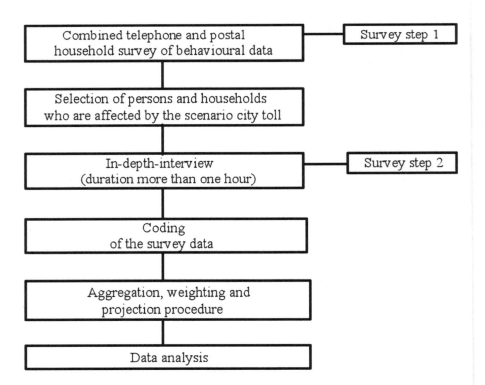

Figure 2.2   Survey procedure

In order to familiarize the respondents with the subject matter and to make them feel relaxed, at first the currently used modes of transport of each family were determined with a kind of card game, and the trips of the various family members previously ascertained in a written survey were depicted and memorized. All trips were analysed in regard to the motives for the use of a specific mode of transport. In this context the conditions on one specific day were of less interest than the generally valid reasons for the choice of a means of transport by the respondent.

The respondents were then asked to plan a new daily schedule. Figure 2.2 shows the procedure for the survey. If a person's trip is affected by the measure considered here (i.e. the person passes the toll cordon), the person has the following possibilities to react:

- abandon the trip, if possible. This is only a valid option for trips without a subjective necessity or if the chore can be undertaken by someone else. A commuter trip, for instance, cannot be abandoned;
- use a different mode of transport, for example public transport or cycle etc. This reaction of the interviewee is only possible if all activities outside the home are still possible in spite of using a different mode of transport;
- park the car outside Area A and change to a different mode of transport for the rest of the trip (i.e. walk, public transport);
- choose another destination outside the limited area; this is only possible if there is a destination of equal value outside the limited area;
- choose a route which does not cross the toll cordon, if the destination is not within the cordoned area;
- accept to pay the toll.

The aggregation of individual behavioural results was achieved with a so-called classification procedure (Sammer 1982). This means that the trips covered in the in-depth survey were divided into behaviourally homogenous strata with regard to possible reactions. For each stratum, the reaction probability is known as the mean value. The strata were then weighted. The strata were defined according to the following characteristics:

- trips of residents and non-residents of Graz;
- trips within the toll cordon, originating there, leading there and completely outside the toll cordon;
- trips subdivided according to the mode, i.e. pedestrian, bicycle, public transport, car driver and car passenger trips.

Since an analysis of combinations of the three strata was not possible due to the relatively small random sample of only 297 trips, a method was applied to ensure that the distribution within the categories of each stratification group was the same as in the parent population (Sammer and Fallast 1990). The parent population of all trips for those behaviourally homogenous strata is approximately known due to a survey based on a large sample. The reactions in the consolidated sample were aggregated and/or grossed up to the total population.

2.3.3 Traditional stated preference technique   For methodological reasons the base scenario was analysed with the 'traditional' stated preference technique (Lee-Gosselin 2003). The objective was to test the hypothesis that the traditional stated preference technique is not appropriate to identify complex travel behaviour reactions ('behavioural side effects'), which occur in a congestion pricing scenario. The behavioural reactions occur between modes but the respondents were current car users. Three alternatives were provided: car, park-and-ride, and public transport. The respondents were asked to make 10 separate choices (ranking tasks) between three hypothetical mode alternatives.

The hypothetical alternatives were characterized by various levels of attributes presented to the respondents. Each alternative had two attributes, total travel time and cost of the journey. In this context, the journey means the total journey to and from the city centre so that the return trip was also taken into account. Each attribute had three levels. The levels were calculated as percentage shares (per cent change in time/cost) of a base value. However, absolute values were presented to the respondents. The levels were -20% (decrease), 0% (no change), and +20% (increase). There was one exception, however: the levels for the cost of the car were 0%, +50%, and +100%.

In order to make the choice seem more realistic, the attributes (travel time and cost) were customized or tailored to the actual trip. The base values play a very important role in the stated preference exercise since the attribute values presented to the respondents were absolute. Total travel time means average door-to-door time, including in-vehicle time, walking time and waiting time. The base value for the cost of public transport was based on the price of the most economical ticket type (e.g. season ticket). Out-of-pocket costs (fuel and other variable costs, parking charge) were considered when the cost of the car was calculated. The parking charge was not included as a separate attribute; instead, the parking charge at the destination (if any) was added to the fuel cost. The base values for park-and-ride cost and total travel time were estimated in the same way as the base values for cars and public transport.

Ten stated preference games were presented to each respondent, of which the first one was a reference question using the base values. In addition, three extreme cases were presented, one in favour of each mode. The respondents were asked to rank the alternatives from best to worst. The sample size was 110 persons and 1120 trips.

Figure 2.3 shows the possible behavioural reactions. While the traditional stated preference technique allows for only two options – the use of a different mode of transport or the use of the car and accepting to pay the toll – the stated adaptation approach on the basis of an interactive in-depth survey permits coverage of all possible reactions. From the methodological point of view warning lights should flash in our heads since no respondent refused the alternative in the traditional stated preference game, even if respondents showed a different behavioural reaction when the adaptation technique was used.

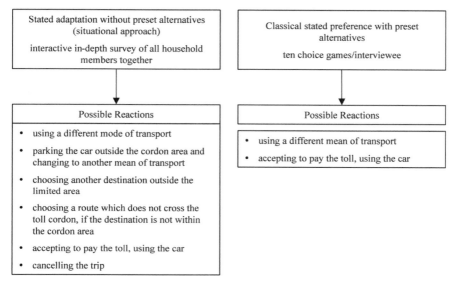

Figure 2.3   Behavioural reaction to congestion pricing for car users; comparison of two different approaches

2.4 Behavioural reaction to urban congestion pricing

In total, 54% of the car user trips are not affected by the toll cordon, because the users do not pass this cordon on their trip. In Figure 2.4 the behavioural reaction of all affected car users is recorded on the base of the two different techniques. The traditional stated preference technique shows a considerably different result compared with the stated adaptation approach: 15% of the affected car trips are shifted to public transport, while for 85% of the trips the car is still used and the toll paid. The stated adaptation method shows a bigger variety of reactions: the share of public transport use is 3.7 percentage points lower than in the other model, the share of car trips is 16.6 percentage points lower. In total, a completely different reaction is shown for 20% of the trips: 7.2% of the trips are omitted, for 7% a changed car route is used, 3.8% show a different destination and in 2.3% of the cases a trip by bicycle or on foot is preferred to the car use.

If one considers the results of the base scenario for the shopping traffic the percentage share of behavioural reactions which cannot be determined with the help of the traditional 'stated preference technique' is considerably higher (Figure 2.5). When it comes to shopping trips affected car users seem less inclined to switch to different modes of transport: slightly less than 4% of car users opt

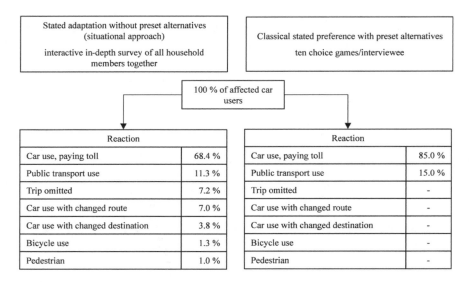

Figure 2.4   Behavioural reaction of car users to congestion pricing, comparison of two different approaches (weekday traffic)

Stated adaptation technique without preset alternatives (situational approach)

100 % of affected car users for shopping trips

Reaction	
Car use, paying toll	69.8 %
Public transport use	3.9 %
Trip omitted	13.1 %
Car use with changed route	0.9 %
Car use with changed destination	11.5 %
Bicycle use	-
Pedestrian	0.8 %

24.6 % less shopping trips in congestion pricing area

Figure 2.5   Behavioural reaction to congestion pricing for shopping trips by car (weekday traffic)

for public transport, about 70% stick to their cars and pay the toll. More than a quarter of the affected car users react in a way which cannot be identified by the traditional 'stated preference technique': 13% of the trips are omitted altogether and are deduced from the scenario. Shopping activities connected with these trips

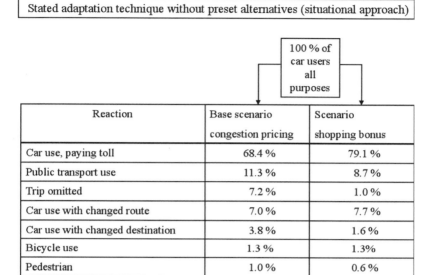

Reaction	Base scenario congestion pricing	Scenario shopping bonus
Car use, paying toll	68.4 %	79.1 %
Public transport use	11.3 %	8.7 %
Trip omitted	7.2 %	1.0 %
Car use with changed route	7.0 %	7.7 %
Car use with changed destination	3.8 %	1.6 %
Bicycle use	1.3 %	1.3%
Pedestrian	1.0 %	0.6 %

Figure 2.6   Behavioural reaction to congestion pricing for car users, comparison of two scenarios (weekday traffic)

are either organized in a different way or abandoned completely. Slightly less than 12% of car users pick another destination for their shopping trip outside the toll cordon. Within the toll cordon one can expect about 25% fewer shopping trips made by car users. From an environmental point of view this is desirable, but in the long run this can lead to a move of shops from inside the toll cordon to areas at the outskirts of the city. As far as spatial planning is concerned, this leads to some negative urban sprawl.

A comparison of the base scenario with the scenario 'shopping bonus' (see Sections 2.2.1 and 2.2.2) shows that undesired side effects can be largely compensated for by the introduction of a 'shopping bonus' (Thaller 2000). While the share of deduced traffic is 11% of all affected trips of car users in the base scenario, this share sinks to about 3% in the 'shopping bonus' scenario (Figure 2.6). This allows the conclusion that suitable concomitant measures can help to prevent at least part of the negative side effects of a city toll.

The analysis of the modal shift shows that a limitation of the choice alternatives to a shift to public transport and park & ride, as is generally done by the traditional 'stated preference technique', does not permit a sufficiently clear presentation of the behavioural reactions to a city toll (Figure 2.7) since there is also a shift to non-motorized transport and some trips are completely omitted.

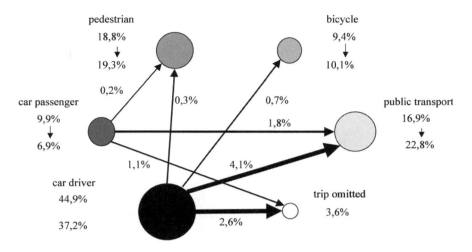

**Figure 2.7   Behavioural reaction to congestion pricing, modal shift
(weekday traffic)**

2.5 Interpretation

The results of the analysis show clearly that the introduction of a city toll leads to the generally known positive effects such as the switch away from cars to more environmentally friendly modes of transport, a reduction in the number of traffic jams, and a reduction of exhaust gas and greenhouse gas emissions but also to undesirable side effects. Some of these are:

- Reduced traffic can lead to some consumer loss; in the example just considered this economic loss equals about 5% of the toll revenues in the base scenario.
- Due to the deduced traffic and a switch from shopping destinations at the city centre within the toll cordon to other destinations at the outskirts, downtown shops and enterprises suffer a loss in turnover and revenues.
- In the long run this is likely to lead to the move of at least some shops and companies from their current location to the outskirts which has an undesired decentralization effect and strengthens the car-oriented areas at the outskirts.
- Given that the toll is limited to certain areas of the city, the effect of the toll cordon upon the cost of the users is an uneven one and a border area is created; as a consequence of changed route choices there will be more car traffic at the border of the toll cordon which means more traffic jams there and thus an undesirable effect upon the environment.

Specific concomitant measures like the 'shopping bonus' considered in our example help to avoid at least some undesirable side effects. Suitable methods of analysis are required to identify them. Traditional types of analysis, such as the stated preference technique are frequently unable to do so.

3. Case Study: Parking Management Scheme for Private Car Parks

One of the most effective traffic demand management measures is on-road parking management (paid parking zones, limitation of parking duration, residents' parking privilege, environment-oriented parking fees etc.). A big problem arises due to the limitation of these regulations to public space. In many developed cities the share of private parking slots, especially those of shopping centres and commuter car parks, exceeds those on public roads. This fact makes parking management schemes less effective and calls for new instruments to limit car traffic to a level that helps to avoid congestion. The extension of parking management strategies to private car parks seems to be an appropriate solution.

To investigate the impacts of this solution, a study was conducted for the Vienna Region (Klementschitz et al. 2005; Sammer et al. 2007), to evaluate the impacts on traffic demand and to identify any side effects. The case study has the objectives to analyse both the reaction of car users to various types of parking management for parking slots in private car parks and the long term effects upon the operators of such private car parks. The survey is focused mainly on car parks available for customers of shopping centres and leisure facilities but parking slots for commuters of large companies with 50+ slots are also included. As far as the reactions of car users to the parking management of parking slots on private ground are concerned, the following are of particular interest: change of modes of transport, switch to different trip destinations in alternative areas without off-road parking management, moving away from paid parking zones to free of charge public road spaces in the vicinity and abstaining from the trip. Also, the long term effect of an obligatory management of private parking slots upon the choice of site by the operators and developer is of particular interest. For example, a relocation of facilities to the surrounding area of cities without parking management in private car parks would be counterproductive. This would mean that in the long run, companies move out of city centres which would lead to increasingly car-oriented spatial structures and to a growing use of cars.

3.1 Transport related background information about the study area

The study area covers the city of Vienna and the surrounding area, which belongs to three Austrian provinces and represents a conurbation of about 2.7 million inhabitants and is called Vienna Region. The city of Vienna is at the centre of the conurbation. The car ownership rate is over 450 cars/100 residents in the city itself and 600 cars/1000 residents in the surrounding area. The transport infrastructure consists of an excellent public transport service (rapid transit, underground, tram, bus) with an integrated ticketing system on a low price level and a dense network of motorways. Within the second ring road of the city of Vienna the whole public space is subject to a parking management scheme (paid parking zones, limitation of parking duration, residents' parking privilege).

3.2 Description of scenarios for a private car park management scheme

In the framework of this case study, four options for parking management schemes for private car parks were investigated:

- obligatory pay parking schemes for users of shopping centres and other privately owned large car parks (obligatory parking fee for customers);
- obligatory pay parking scheme for shopping centres by way of parking slot fees per offered space levied by the operator. The revenues are handed to a regional authority (e.g. in form of an environmental protection or council accessibility tax);
- obligatory limitation of car trips to shopping centres by a defined trip quota, depending on air pollution;
- obligatory limitation of the maximum number of parking slots, depending on the accessibility by public transport and/or on air pollution.

In this chapter the first two options are addressed to show the negligible side effects which require a specific analysis technique for their identification. The general results for all 4 options are recorded in the research report (Klementschitz et al. 2005; Sammer et al. 2007)

3.2.1 Scenario obligatory parking fees for customers of shopping centres   The size of the obligatory parking fee depends on the characteristics of the site:

- location of the site: city centre, outskirts or industrial area;
- kind of business enterprise: shopping centre, office and administration building, business enterprise, leisure facility.

The fee for short-term parking of customers usually ranges from €0.80 to €1.80 per hour, depending on the location. These user-related fees have a direct impact upon the travel demand of customers as well as the location policy of the operator in the long term. The scenario is divided into two sub-scenarios. This is necessary because during the interview car users spontaneously mentioned that the introduction of parking fees would make them use parking slots on public roads , because such slots are easily available in the vicinity of the chosen destination without any fee (sub-scenario A). In such cases respondents were given the additional information (sub-scenario B) that the same parking fee would be levied for public parking slots, too. The original situation without any parking fee on public roads in the vicinity of the shopping centres is defined as sub-scenario A.

3.2.2 Scenario with obligatory parking space levy for operators of large private car parks   This charge ranges from €20 to €60/month and parking slot, depending on the location and the type of operation (see above) and should be paid to the organization maintaining the road, earmarked for environmental protection. This kind of parking management indirectly controls the travel demand of car users, depending on the fraction of the charge which the car driver has to bear. This kind of charge primarily affects the operator by minimizing the offer of parking slots either to avoid excess capacities or to influence the choice of location in the long run.

3.3 Methodology of analysis

The analysis had the objective to determine the impact of the different types of parking management defined in section 3.2 on the travel behaviour of car users and on the reaction of the operators of shopping centres and other business enterprises. To achieve this it was necessary to use interview techniques which made it possible to determine the behaviour of car users and operators. For this case study the stated adaptation technique (Sammer 2003; Lee-Gosselin 2003) was used as part of an interactive in-depth-survey, both for car users and for operators.

3.3.1 Survey of car users   Telephone interviews were conducted with car users. Initially, respondents were asked whether they had used the car during the last few days to reach a shopping, leisure or work destination. In order to get a realistic idea of the behavioural change, respondents should recall real life destinations. Those people who mentioned that they had been on such trips were asked in detail about their travel behaviour to these destinations. Then the car drivers were asked about the various scenarios. A total of 229 trips were discussed with the stated-adaptation technique (Table 2.2).

Table 2.2   Sample for the travel behaviour survey

gross sample	709 respondents
net sample (people who had been on relevant trips and were prepared to participate in the interview)	144 respondents
	229 trips

3.3.2 Survey of operators of shopping centres and business enterprises   To ascertain the reaction of operators to the various options, a qualitative interactive in-depth-interview was conducted with each of them in their office. A semi-structured questionnaire was used to have a standardized framework but at the same time to capture all possible reactions and their reasons with open-ended questions.

A total of 25 operators were interviewed, all of them active in the Vienna Region considered in this survey (Table 2.3).

Table 2.3   Sample of operators of various enterprises

Type of enterprise	net sample
shopping centres	11 respondents
leisure facilities	6 respondents
business enterprises	4 respondents
office buildings	4 respondents
Total	25 respondents

3.4 Reaction to the introduction of obligatory parking fees for customers of shopping centres

As mentioned before the behavioural reaction of car users going to a shopping centre is split into two sub-scenarios.

3.4.1 Sub-scenario A obligatory parking fees for customers of shopping centres with no paid parking zone in their vicinity in comparison with sub-scenario B with paid parking zone in their vicinity   Figure 2.8 shows the behavioural reaction of car users on shopping trips for sub-scenario A compared to sub-scenario B. The introduction of parking fees for car parks of shopping centres will lead to some evasive action and make 23% of car drivers look for parking slots in neighbouring streets, if a sufficient number of free of charge parking slots are available. A significantly lower share of 22% of drivers accepts the introduction of the parking fee. The percentage shares for other reactions are also significantly lower than the respective percentage shares in sub-scenario B. Such reactions are the choice of a different shopping destination, the use of other modes of transport, the complete omission of the shopping trip, etc. It needs to be stressed that such a differentiation of the behavioural reactions cannot be identified and demonstrated by traditional stated preference techniques.

3.4.2 Sub-scenario B obligatory parking fees for customers of shopping centres with paid parking zones in their vicinity   In the analysis the reaction to parking fees from 0.80 €/h to 1.80 €/h for shopping centres was ascertained. A fairly wide variety of options are possible (Figure 2.9).

Car users react in a very sensitive way to parking fees: the higher the parking fee in well developed urban areas the more likely car users will switch to alternatives, such as public transport or walking. At a parking fee of €1.80/h 16% of respondents pick another shopping destination where no fees are levied and 36% do no longer frequent the original shopping destination if they have to pay parking fees there.

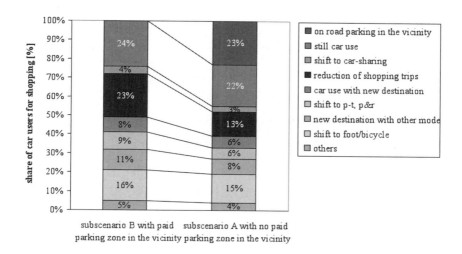

Figure 2.8   Comparison of the behavioural reaction of users of cars for shopping purposes to an obligatory pay parking scheme (parking fee per hour €1.80) for shopping centres in the Vienna Region for sub-scenario A and B

Note: Sammer et al. (2007).

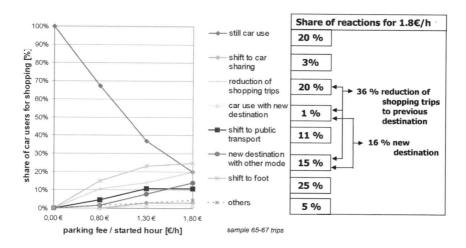

Figure 2.9   Behavioural reaction of cars for shopping purposes to obligatory pay parking schemes for shopping centres in the city of Vienna (weekday traffic)

Note: Sammer et al. (2007).

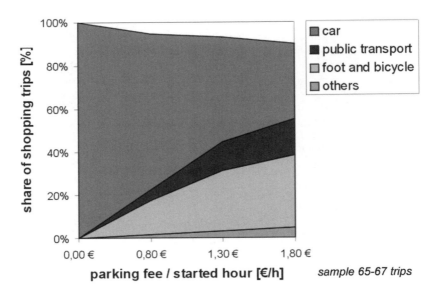

Figure 2.10   Change of modal split for shopping purposes as a result of obligatory pay parking schemes for shopping centres in Vienna

Note Sammer et al. (2007)

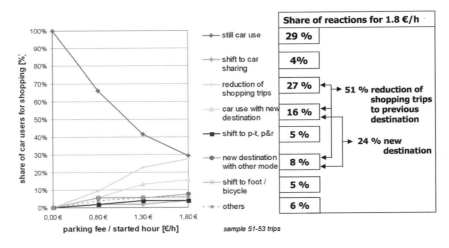

Figure 2.11   Behavioural reaction of users of cars for shopping purposes to an obligatory pay parking scheme for shopping centres at the outskirts of Vienna

Note: Sammer et al. (2007)

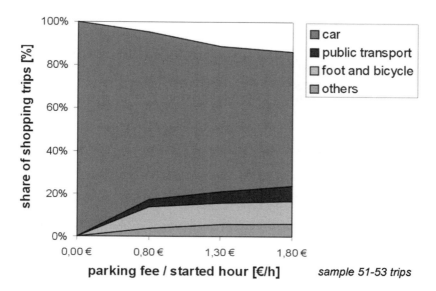

parking fee / started hour [€/h]   *sample 51-53 trips*

Figure 2.12   Change of modal split for shopping purposes as a result of an obligatory pay parking scheme for shopping centres at the outskirts of Vienna

This means a risk for the competitive situation of shopping centres, which levy parking fees compared to those which do not.

Figure 2.10 shows the effect of the reaction of car drivers upon the modal split. It is obvious that the elasticity of car trips is high: With rising parking fees the number of car trips decreases rapidly to be replaced by walking or cycling. This means that the introduction of parking fees could significantly contribute to the reduction of car use.

The effect of parking management close to shopping centres at the outskirts of cities in conurbations upon the demand for car traffic is significantly lower, as Figures 2.11 and 2.12 demonstrate. But the number of car trips for collective purchases instead of several trips for smaller purchases increases.

3.4.3 Reaction of the operators   About 50% of the operators of shopping centres react in a negative way to the obligatory introduction of parking fees for parking slots (Table 2.4). They argue that this would be damaging to the image of the shopping centre and they hold the opinion that it would be difficult to explain such measures to customers. All operators would refund the parking fees to their customers in such a case. This means that the control effect upon the demand for car trips would be lost. It might be possible to compensate for such refunding by combining parking management with the levy of an obligatory parking slot charge on operators.

Table 2.4   Opinion of operators and developers about obligatory pay parking scheme (OPPS) for shopping centres

Share of responses	
50 %	loss of image → difficult argumentation to customers
100 %	refund of parking fee → loss of control effect for traffic demand → combination of OPPS with parking space tax
90 %	influence over decisions on location → problem at boundary of zones with different fee level → equal treatment of all locations is important

3.5 Reaction of operators and developers to parking space levy for shopping centres

The introduction of a charge or levy per parking slot ('traffic generation charge') for operators of shopping centres has no direct effect upon the travel demand of car users. Such a measure leads operators of private car parks to choose and plan carefully and to opt for a fairly low number of parking slots within their option. One can only expect such shortages to have indirect and few controlling effects upon the travel demand, which is recorded in Table 2.5.

As far as the operators are concerned the effects are the same ones as for the other options. Therefore the introduction of this measure only makes sense in a large spatially and functionally coherent catchment area of a conurbation. Only thus distortions of competition and consequently migrations to other locations can be avoided. This measure is particularly useful in combination with an obligatory parking fee, because it helps to prevent operators from refunding parking fees, a step which would prevent the parking fee from having a controlling effect upon traffic demand.

3.6 Interpretation

The results of the analysis lead to the following interpretation regarding the effects of parking management of private parking slots. It is necessary to differentiate between short-term and long-term effects. The objective of any such measures is the control of car travel demand to avoid congestions and negative impacts upon the environment. The results indicate the likelihood of some probably undesirable side effects which might be compensated for in part by concomitant measures. It is necessary to bear in mind that the behavioural elasticities which could be observed indicate the maximum potential of behavioural changes. For reasons of methodology the stated adaptation analysis used is based on the assumption that respondents are fully informed about and aware of alternative options and the issues involved. It can be proved that in reality people are generally not that well informed and aware of their options (Sammer 2006).

Table 2.5   **Opinion of operators and developers about parking space levy for shopping centres**

Share of responses	
73 %	influence over the decision on location → problem at boundary of zones with different tax level → equal treatment of all location is important
100 %	passing the cost to customers
27 %	jeopardizing of existing location of shopping centres
64 %	reductions of number of parking spaces

Obligatory parking fees for customers have a high control effect upon car travel demand and are highly suitable if the private parking slots account for a certain amount, at least one third, of all parking slots. For the measure to be effective it is necessary that parking facilities on public roads in the vicinity of such private paid parking zones are also subject to the same parking management as far as the level of the parking fee is concerned. The control effect is considerably lower if the operators of shopping centres refund the parking fees to their customers. This can be offset by an obligatory charge for traffic generation per parking slot which the municipal authorities levy on operators (a so-called 'traffic generation charge').

One has to bear in mind that a considerable number of car users opt for other shopping destinations if comparable shopping centres which do not charge parking fees are within convenient reach. This non-negligible side effect can mean that shopping centres and enterprises with considerable customer traffic which do charge parking fees are at a disadvantage. To uphold free competition it is necessary to have the same basic rules and regulations for all private car parks in a spatially and functionally coherent area, but a graduation of parking fees depending on the quality of the development of the site and the ease of access by alternatives modes of transport (public and non-motorized) is recommended. One can also argue in favour of such a graduation on the basis of the different behavioural elasticities of car users depending on the location of the site in relation to the city centre.

Another non-negligible side effect was identified. In the long run, operators of shopping centres and leisure facilities consider moving such centres, facilities, and enterprises to other areas unless the same parking rules apply to all public and private parking facilities within a spatially and functionally coherent customer catchment area. Such a migration would mean that in the long run such facilities and enterprises choose sites at the outskirts of cities which would lead to an undesirable urban sprawl and the counterproductive effect of longer car trips. To avoid such unwanted side effects obligatory parking fees for private car parks have to be introduced in large spatially and functionally coherent catchment areas. From an administrative point of view it would seem advisable to apply this rule only to private car parks of a minimum size, for example 50 parking slots.

The introduction of a levy per offered parking slot for operators has no direct effect upon the travel demand. But this measure should be considered in addition to the introduction of obligatory parking fees for visitors to shopping centres. Operators of shopping centres mentioned their intention to refund the parking fees to all customers. The charge would probably limit this refunding thus supporting the steering effect upon visitors who come by car. This measure would have the additional effect that shopping centres would be made more accessible by public and non-motorized means of transport and that more attention would be paid to such alternative means of transport when selecting new sites for shopping centres.

4. Conclusions

The two case studies support the hypothesis mentioned in the beginning that measures of travel demand management, particularly those which internalize the external costs of car users with the help of road pricing or parking fees, have a considerable demand-managing effect. But the analysis shows, too, that such measures can have considerable side effects. These side effects fall into two main categories.

In the short run there will be undesired side effects upon the shopping traffic, which is far more flexible than commuter traffic. Such side effects are the reduced shopping traffic and the choice of new shopping destinations, for example shopping centres without parking fees and road tolls. In general this leads to a shift of shopping traffic away from the city centre towards the periphery and outskirts of cities where no charges are levied. Particularly affected are shopping centres in areas which are subject to a charge and close to their border (e.g. toll cordon).

In the long run some decentralization is likely because shopping centres move to the periphery of conurbations if no adequate measures are taken to prevent this. *What could be considered as adequate measures then?* Whenever charges are levied on car users in the form of road-pricing or parking fees for public or private car parks the borders within which these measures apply should be drawn in a fair way. This means that the line of demarcation has to be drawn very carefully to avoid unfair competition between shopping centres within and without the charge area. Payment of compensation, for example in the form of a shopping bonus, is also an option to prevent the shopping traffic from looking for different destinations.

The analysis of undesired side effects requires special methodologies. Quite a number of generally accepted methods, such as the traditional stated preference technique are unable to identify such effects. These findings lead to the conclusion that there are quite a number of unidentified side effects of TDM measures which have not yet been discovered. In particular the social effects of road tolls and parking fees are interesting areas for further research because well-researched findings in such areas are rare so far.

References

Brög, W. (1981), 'Individuelles Verhalten als Basis verhaltensorientierter Modelle', in *Schriftenreihe der Deutschen Verkehrswissenschaftlichen Gesellschaft* No. B57, Verkehrsnachfrage-Modelle (Köln: Deutschland).

Brög, W. and Erl, E. (1981), 'Die Anwendung eines Individualverhaltensmodelles unter Berücksichtigung haushaltsbezogener Aktivitätsmuster', *Socialdata*, (München: Deutschland).

Klementschitz, R., Sammer, G., Stark, J., Weber, G., Stöglehner, G., Dittrich, D. and Bittner, L. (2005), 'Instrumente zur Steuerung des Stellplatzangebotes für den Zielverkehr (Projekt – INSTELLA), [Instruments to control the parking supply and demand at the destination], Teil 1: Analyse nationaler und internationaler Anwendungsbeispiele [Part 1: Analysis of national and international applied examples] und Teil 2: Befragung der Verkehrsteilnehmer und Operatoren sowie Maßnahmenempfehlungen [Part 2: Survey of transport users and operators and recommended measures]', im Auftrage der Stadt Wien, der Länder Burgenland und Niederösterreich: Wien.

Lee-Gosselin, M.E.H. (2003), 'Can you Get There From Here? Reflections on Stated Response Survey Quality and Innovation', in P.R. Stopher and P.M. Jones (eds), *Transport Survey Quality and Innovation* (Oxford: Elsevier), pp. 331–45.

Sammer, G. (2003), 'Ensuring Quality in Stated Response Surveys', in Stopher and P Jones, (eds), pp. 365–75.

Sammer, G. and Thaller, O. (2003), 'Road Pricing in Österreich – Über unerwünschte Wirkungen fragen Sie Ihren Arzt oder Apotheker [Road Pricing in Austria – Ask your doctor or chemist about undesirable side effects]', in *Wettbewerbselement Kundenorientierung in der Transportwirtschaft*, OEVG Spezial, Band 53, Festgabe zum 70. Geburtstag des Präsidenten des OEVG, Herrn Prof. Peter Faller, Wirtschaftsuniversität Wien, 67–81, (eds). Kummer, S., Gürtlich, G.H. and Riebesmeier, B.

Sammer, G., Fallast, K., and Wernsperger, F. (1998), 'Potential Estimate for the Acceptance of A New Motorised Bicycle in Urban Traffic: Methodic Aspects and Results', in J.D. Ortuzar, D. Hensher, and S. Jara-Diaz, *Travel Behaviour Research: Updating the State of Play* (Oxford: Elsevier) pp. 317–38,

Sammer, G. (1982), 'Untersuchung zur Verkehrsmittelwahl im Personenverkehr, Heft 179 der Schriftenreihe Straßenforschung, Kommissionsverlag Forschungsgesellschaft für das Straßenwesen', Wien, Österreich.

Sammer, G., Stark, J. and Klementschitz, R. (2007), 'A Parking Management Scheme for Private Car Parks – A Promising Approach to Mitigate Congestion on Urban Roads?', in Proceedings of the World Road Congress of the World Road Association PIARC, 17–21 September 2007, Paris.

Sammer, G., Gruber, Ch. and Röschel, G. (2006), 'Quality of Information and Knowledge about Mode Attributes in Mode Choice', Conference Paper and Presentation, Session S1, 'Travel behaviour analysis, modelling and forecasting,

The expanding sphere of travel behaviour research', 11th International Conference on Travel Behaviour Research, Kyoto, 16–20 August.

TranSecon-Consortium (1996–1998), TranSecon, Modelling Results, Site Graz, European Commission under the Competitive and Growth Programme of the 5th Framework Programme.

Thaller, O. (2000), 'Impact Analysis of Urban Road-Use Pricing on Travel Behaviour, the Environment and the Economy', Dissertation, Band 102, Forschungsarbeiten aus dem Verkehrswesen, Bundesministerium für Verkehr, Innovation und Technologie, Wien, Österreich.

Chapter 3

Validation and Comparison of Choice Models

Stefano de Luca and Giulio Erberto Cantarella

1. Introduction

During the last decade the community of urban transportation modellers and planners has widely recognized that increases of travel demand can no longer be accommodated through a supply-side approach only, due to constraints on available budget as well as natural resources. Hence, rather than (or better, together with) relying on increases of capacity, modern transport policies (also) follow a demand-side approach, trying to affect the amount and pattern of demand flows.

Travel demand management (TDM) measures are receiving an ever increasing attention both by researchers and practitioners. The appraisal of such measures requires a travel demand analysis including careful segmentation of users into categories and trip purpose as well as an estimate of demand elasticity through choice models, regarding for example: number of trips, time of day, destination, mode and route, and their relationship with features of transportation supply as described by level of service attributes. Hence, issue of choice model assessment is becoming more relevant than in the past.

The basic tools to carry out travel demand analysis are commonly based on random utility theory (RUT). A systematic framework was first introduced in the well-known book by Domencich and McFadden (1975), through the application of models derived from RUT. Since then, most effort in literature has been devoted over the years to choice model formulations, as reviewed by Ben-Akiva and Lerman 1985; Cascetta 2001 and Train 2003, and results of several real-case applications have been reported. By contrast, less attention has been paid to methods for choice model validation and comparison against real data. Recently other approaches have been proposed for choice modelling, such as fuzzy utility models (for instance Cantarella and Fedele 2003) or neural networks (for instance Cantarella and de Luca 2005a and 2005b), making the issue of model assessment even more relevant.

Choice models should be assessed w.r.t. three criteria:

- *interpretation*: the parameters can be given a clear meaning, in so far as reasonable ranges can be defined for their values,
- *reproduction*: the model ably reproduces the choice context used for calibration,

- *generalization*: the model may be used to reproduce transportation scenarios different from those used for calibration.

It may well be the case that a very sophisticated choice model actually only slightly outperforms a simpler one; moreover, the larger the number of parameters is the more likely over-fitting may occur; hence the model may poorly perform when applied to different choice scenarios (bad generalization).

This chapter proposes a general assessment protocol to validate a choice model against real data and to compare its effectiveness with other models, not necessarily specified through the same approach. It is the authors' opinion that many of the indicators usually used to validate and compare discrete choice models often fail to highlight model generalization capabilities and to provide insights as to which modelling approach should be preferred (e.g. random utility models vs fuzzy utility models or neural networks models). Indeed, although in many case studies rho-square statistics (available only for random utility models) or %right (see section 3.3 for further comments on this indicator) are considered adequate to support validation/comparison procedures, it may be well the case that the differences in the indicators are small and it may not be easy to single out the model of preference. These considerations are even more relevant when models other than those of random utility ones are also considered. Hence, it is useful to search for indicators, based on different standpoints, which provide a better insight into model effectiveness. In this chapter consolidated indicators as well as new ones are presented within a general framework.

Our numerical examples refer to a real case: the mode choice behaviour of students travelling to and from the campus of the University of Salerno, located in the countryside close to the city of Salerno in the southern Italian region of Campania. The database contains 2,808 interviews concerning student journeys to the campus from outside the city of Salerno. The sample was obtained by stratified random sampling based on interviews at parking locations. Four modes may be available: car as driver (C), share 31%; car as passenger (P), 9%; car-pool (CP), 32% and bus (B), 28%. The results of two choice models are reported: (i) MultiNomial Logit (MNL) with linear utility specification, as *benchmark*; (ii) Cross-Nested Logit (CNL) to simulate general transport modes correlation. Since the aim of this chapter is to describe a comparison/validation protocol, examples are included for explanatory reasons only. Hence the aim is not to demonstrate the superiority of CNL with respect to MNL and no deep comments are provided regarding the application itself.

After a formal introduction to specification (section 2.1) and calibration of choice models against a sample of observed choices (section 2.2), a procedure for the validation and comparison of choice models will be presented (section 3). Major findings and research perspectives will be discussed in section 4.

2. Specification and Calibration of Choice Models

A discrete choice model simulates the relationship between user choices and the features of each choice alternative. To this aim, the choice made by a user in the sample may be described by choice fractions equal to 1 for the chosen alternative, to 0 otherwise. Let

$K = \{1, \ldots, n\}$ be the choice set, assumed non-empty and finite, n being the number of alternatives;

$p^{obs}_{k,i} = 0/1$ be the observed choice fraction associated to alternative k by user i (in the sample) with $\sum_k p^{obs}_{k,i} = 1$;

$p^{sim}_{k,i} \in [0,1]$ be the choice fraction associated to alternative k by the choice model, with $\sum_k p^{sim}_{k,i} = 1$.

Behavioural choice models can be derived from explicit formal assumptions about user behaviour, the most widely applied being *utility-based* according two assumptions:

> A. PERFECT RATIONALITY HYPOTHESIS: the decision-maker, i.e. each user of a transportation system facing any type of choice (trip destination, transportation mode, …),
>
> a.1 considers a set of mutually exclusive alternatives,
>
> a.2 gives each alternative a value of perceived utility,
>
> a.3 chooses the (an) alternative with the maximum perceived utility;

> B. UNCERTAINTY HYPOTHESIS: the perceived utility of each alternative is modeled taking into account uncertainty regarding information available to the user as well as the modeler.

Moreover, the *perceived utility*, U_k, for each alternative k is considered dispersed around a central value, called *systematic utility* v_k, a function of alternative attributes x_k (which may be measured in the current scenario or assumed in a design scenario), and parameters β (estimated through a sample of observations) considered stable over the choice scenarios.

If the perceived utility is modeled through a random variable, the systematic utility being its mean, $v_k = E[U_k]$, the above leads to the well-known RUT. The probability that a user chooses an alternative k is given by the probability that the perceived utility of the alternative be maximum, $p_k = Pr[U_k = \max_j U_j]$.

Recently fuzzy numbers have also been also proposed for modelling perceived utility (see Cantarella and Fedele 2003), but limited experience is available. The feasibility of behavioural non-utility-based choice models, such as those (Batley and Daly 2006) based on elimination by aspects theory (Simon 1990; Tversky 1972a/b) or based on the prospect theory (proposed by Kanheman and Tversky 1979), has been recently investigated but this issue is still at a research level.

On the other hand, any regression function between user choices and alternative attributes can be considered a *non-behavioural* or *regressive* choice model. Usually such models are non-utility based, examples being gravitational models for trip distribution or newly introduced Multi Layer Feed Forward Networks (Cantarella and de Luca 2005a). Recently utility-based MLFFN have also been also proposed, Cantarella and de Luca (2005b).

2.1 Specification of a choice model

A non-utility-based choice model is simply expressed by a function between choice probabilities and the alternative attributes: $p = p(x; \gamma)$ where γ are duly defined parameters. By contrast, any utility-based choice model may be expressed by two functions.

Utility function defines for choice alternative k the relationship between a central value of utility (systematic utility in RUT) and the alternative attributes, $v_k = v(\mathbf{x_k}; \beta)$, whose expression is often a linear combination of Level-of-Service (LoS) and Socio-Economic (SE) attributes, x_{jk}: $v_k = \sum_j \beta_j x_{jk}$. Non-linearity w.r.t. LoS attributes, such as travel time, can be easily considered, through Box-Cox transformation.

Choice function defines the relationship between choice probabilities and the central values of utility $p = p(v; \gamma)$, whose expression depends on perceived utility distribution. The simplest example of a random utility model (RUM) from RUT is the MultiNomial Logit (MNL): $p_k = \exp(v_k/\theta) / \sum_h \exp(v_h/\theta)$, with parameter $\theta = \gamma_1$, obtained assuming perceived utilities U_k i.d. according to a Gumbel variable with mean v_k and common variance $\sigma^2 = \theta^2 \pi^2 / 6$.

2.2 Calibration of a choice model: presentation of results

Parameters of the utility function, β, as well as those of the choice function, γ, can be calibrated by trying to reproduce a sample of observations of user choices (disaggregate) and/or demand flows (aggregate). Any distance function (calibration function) between observed and modeled values, such as the most widely used Euclidean one, can express how well the observations are reproduced by the set of parameters; the minimum of the distance function leads to the parameters estimates. Maximum likelihood estimators, commonly used for RUMs, may also be cast within this framework in a broad sense.

If parameters of perceived utility distribution do not depend on utility attributes, choice probabilities are generally independent of any linear transformation of perceived utility; in other words they only depend on differences of systematic utilities. Moreover, a scale parameter cannot be identified, say γ_1. Hence results of calibration are the ratios β_j/γ_1 and the values of utility parameters would be better presented as ratios w.r.t. one chosen as reference, β_1 (usually regarding monetary cost or LoS). Thus comparison of utility parameters among different models is made independent of the scale parameter value. Hence, calibration results should be presented as in the list proposed below:

1. calibration sample size, # parameters, # attributes;
2. scale parameter γ_1 definition;
3. reference utility parameter with definition and unit: β_1 / γ_1;
4. other utility parameters with definition and unit: β_j / β_1 ($j \neq 1$);
5. other utility parameters with definition, for example regarding non-linearity;
6. choice function parameters if any (apart the scale parameter, γ_1): γ_i ($i \neq 1$).

In the following the calibration results for MNL and CNL models are reported. As regards the CNL correlation structure (see Figure 3.1), three partially overlapping mode groups have been considered: G1 = {Car, Pax, C.Pool}, G2 = {Pax, C.Pool, Bus} and G3 = {Pax, C.Pool, Bus}. If g is a generic group, I_g is the generic set of alternatives belonging to group g, $\alpha_{kg} \in [0,1]$ the degree of membership of an alternative k to a group g ($\Sigma_{kg} \alpha_{kg} = 1$), θ_g is the parameter associated to an intermediate node, θ_o the parameter associated to the root (to the first choice level as in Nested Logit formulation) and δ_g the ratio θ_g / θ_o, the analytical expression of choice probability is proposed in Figure 3.1. The parameters to calibrate are the same as in the MNL model plus α_{kg} and δ_g for each group (g) and for each alternative (k).

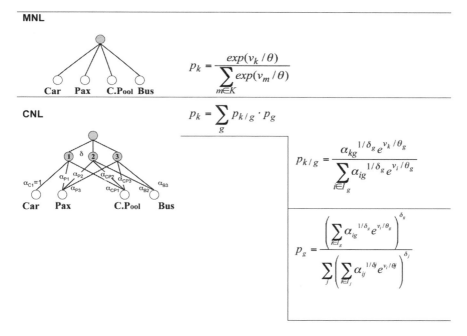

Figure 3.1   Proposed models: tree structure and mathematical formulation

Table 3.1　　Attributes used in systematic utility specification

				Type	Car	Bus	Car-pool	Pax
Level of service (LOS)	Time	Trip time	(h)	Cont.	●	●	●	●
	Cost	Trip monetary cost	(€)	Cont.	●	●	●	-
	Tacc-egr	Access-egress time revealed by the users	(h)	Cont.	-	●	-	-
	$T_{0\text{-}15}$	If trip time is lower than 15 minutes	-	Dummy	-	-	-	●
Socio-economic (SE)	CarAV	If car mode is available	-	Dummy	-	-	●	-
	Gender	If gender is female	-	Dummy	-	●	-	-
Activity related (LU)	ACT_{length}	Activity time length	(h)	Cont.	●	-	-	-
	Freq	Weekly trip frequency	-	Discr.	-	-	●	-
Others	ΔASA	Alternative specific attribute (for more details see sub-section 3.5)	-	Asa	●	-	●	●

Systematic utility is expressed as a linear combination of attributes x_{jk} w.r.t. (Table 3.1) the coefficients β_j. Level of service attributes were computed through a network model, while zoning was city based. Table 3.2 reports the calibration results.

It is worth noting that the reference utility parameter greatly increases from the MNL to the CNL model, showing that the CNL model is generally characterized by a low variance since it provides a better explanation of user behaviour.

3. Validation and Comparison of Choice Models

Even though the calibrated values of the model parameters are optimal (in the sense that they optimize the calibration function), the resulting model may yet perform poorly, since the modelling function might have been poorly specified (apart from the rather irresolvable case of the availability of poor data). The *effectiveness* of the model resulting from the specification and calibration stages must then be explicitly analysed, that is, the validation stage should be carried out before the model can effectively be used. The latter stage should allow us to analyse how a choice model addresses the following issues:

1. *description* and *interpretation* of the phenomenon through its parameters;
2. *reproduction* of observations about choice behaviour used to calibrate model parameters (calibration sample);
3. *generalization* to choice behaviour in the same transportation scenario (observations not used to calibrate model parameters – hold-out sample) and in different transportation scenarios (model sensitivity to level of service attributes).

Table 3.2   Description of the analysed models

		MNL		CNL	
Calibration sample size		2,409		2,409	
# parameters		11		18	
# attributes		11		11	
calibration parameters	scale parameter	$\theta = (\sqrt{6}/\pi)\sigma$		too complicated	
	refer. utility par $\beta_1/\theta = \beta_{cost}/\theta$	-0.657		-1.770	
	$\beta_j / \beta_1 \quad \forall j>1$				
	$\beta_{Time}/\beta_{cost}$	+1.589		+1.23	
	$\beta_{Tacc\text{-}egr}/\beta_{cost}$	+1.843		+1.13	
	$\beta_{CarAV}/\beta_{cost}$	+0.217		+0.11	
	$\beta_{Gender}/\beta_{cost}$	+1.406		+1.13	
	$\beta_{Freq}/\beta_{cost}$	-0.214		-0.12	
	$\beta_{ACTlenght}/\beta_{cost}$	-1.104		-1.47	
	$\beta_{T0\text{-}15}/\beta_{cost}$	-3.885		-4.29	
	$\beta_{\Delta ASAcar}/\beta_{cost}$	-2.981		-3.68	
	$\beta_{\Delta ASApax}/\beta_{cost}$	+4.886		+3.72	
	$\beta_{\Delta ASAcar\text{-}pool}/\beta_{cost}$	+3.982		+2.24	
other utility parameters		none		none	
choice function parameters					
			α (C1)	1.00	
			α (P1)	0.10	
			α (P2)	0.54	
			α (P3)	0.36	
			α (CP1)	0.55	
			α (CP2)	0.12	
			α (CP3)	0.33	
			α (B2)	0.20	
			α (B3)	0.80	
			δ	0.20	

Choice models parameters should allow an interpretation of the phenomenon, giving a clear meaning of the variables and of their relationships. The parameters interpretation allows a first validation of the choice model quality and gives first insights to the analyst and to the policy makers. Such a kind of analysis is meaningful for utility-based models (such as random utility models or fuzzy utility ones) or, more generally, for those models where a parameter is associated to each single variable (such as utility-based neural networks, Cantarella and de Luca

2005b). The analysis can be carried out about the values of utility parameters as described in sub-section 3.1. It is based on the foreseeable signs of the calibrated coefficients, and on the ratios between the coefficients of different variables. Wrong signs of the coefficients likely indicate errors in available data and/or model misspecification. The ratios, in particular between travel time and monetary cost coefficients (Value of Time), can be compared with the results of other calibrations and/or the expectations about the users' willingness to pay existing in literature.

A choice model at least should reproduce the users' choices (or choice fractions) that have been used to calibrate its parameters (calibration sample). Such an analysis may be carried out through some benchmarking indicators well-consolidated in practical application (most indicators in section 3.2), whilst others are being proposed in this chapter for the first time (*clearness analysis* in section 3.3). The application of these indicators to the calibration sample aims at assessing how close the choice model reproduces the observations in the calibration sample. Even though reproduction capabilities are usually used to evaluate and choose the best model or approach, it should be pointed out that the most performing model (approach) may show very poor generalization capabilities because of over-fitting phenomena (due to high value of alternative specific attributes, dummy variables, etc.). Thus, the choice model might not be able to reproduce users' behaviours even if they belong to the same transportation scenario, and it might not be able to simulate model sensitivity.

To analyse both reproduction and generalization capabilities, it should be good practice to break down the available data set into a calibration sample and a hold-out one to be used for validation and comparison (some indications about the hold-out sample size are reported in section 4 – conclusion). In particular the described indicators, when applied to the hold-out sample, allow us to assess how well the calibrated choice model is expected to perform w.r.t. other transportation scenarios (generalization). Such an analysis, apart from the benchmarking indicators used for reproduction analysis mentioned before (and described in sections 3.2 and 3.3), may also be carried out through elasticity analysis (see section 3.5) and through *Analysis of Alternative Specific Attributes' (ASA) role* (see section 3.4), being proposed in this chapter for the first time. All reported indicators, w.r.t. calibration or hold-out samples can be used for comparison with other choice models.

All the above considerations are summed up in the scheme proposed in Figure 3.2, which also addresses the issue of transferability of results to a different case study.

3.1 Analysis of utility parameters

Clearly this analysis is meaningful only for utility-based models. In an initial informal stage consistency between the meaning of the j-th attribute and the sign of the relative parameter β_j is checked. As already said in the previous sub-section, unexpected signs of parameters likely indicate errors in available data and/or model misspecification. Moreover the ratios between the parameters of

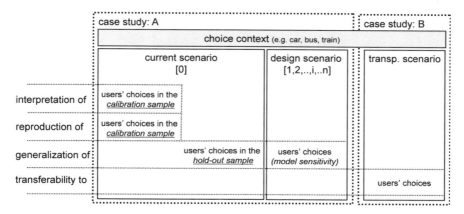

Figure 3.2   Interpretation, reproduction, generalization and tranferability

some pairs of attributes may be expected to be greater than one, such as waiting time and on-board time for transit. In addition the ratio between the parameters of monetary cost and travel time attributes can be considered an estimate of the Value-of-Time (VoT), which can also be estimated through other approaches. As it can be observed from Table 3.2, all values regarding the report example meet this requirement.

Interestingly, this stage may well result in the model being rejected, in which case there is no need to carry out the other analysis described below, but a new specification should be considered, by changing the choice and/or the utility function.

For RUMs, if utility parameters are estimated through maximum likelihood estimators, $\beta^{ML}_{;j}$ (actually results of calibration are the ratios $\beta^{ML}_{;j}/\gamma_1$, as already noted), the t-test may be applied to verify statistical significance of parameters, for large samples of available data, through statistics:

$$t_j = |\beta^{ML}_{;j}| / Var[\beta^{ML}_{;j}]^{0.5}$$

where an approximate estimate of the variances (and covariances) of parameters β_{MLj} can be easily obtained since equal (minus) the inverse of the log-likelihood function Hessian approaches their dispersion matrix as the sample size increases. Usually the size of the available sample is large enough to approximate the T random variable through a Normal r.v.; if the value of t_j is greater than 1.96, the value $\beta^{ML}_{;j}$ may be considered (statistically) different from zero at a confidence level 0.95. Examples are not reported for the sake of brevity.

3.2 Aggregate indicators

The indicators described below when applied to the calibration (hold-out) sample help us to understand how the model reproduces (generalizes) the observed choice scenario (to other choice scenarios). All the indicators are to be compared with a

Table 3.3   Observed market shares (MS$_{obs}$) vs estimated market shares (MS$_{mod}$)

Transport mode	MS$_{obs}$	MNL		CNL	
		MS$_{mod}$	Δ_{MNL}	MS$_{mod}$	Δ_{CNL}
Car	30.9%	30.9%	-	30.5%	-0.4%
Car as passenger	9.5%	9.5%	-	10.4%	+0.9%
Bus	32.0%	32.0%	-	31.4%	-0.6%
Car-pool	27.6%	27.6%	-	27.7%	+0.1%

reference value obtained from the crudest choice model, where all simulated choice fractions are equal, say equal to one over the number of choice alternatives.

*   *Simulated vs. observed shares for each choice alternative*   Differences take a null value over the calibration sample for any logit model calibrated through maximum likelihood (see for instance Train 2004), thus they are useful only when referred to the hold-out sample and/or to other choice models (Table 3.3).
*   *Log-Likelihood value*   Tests for the Log-Likelihood value are meaningful only for RUM's. This value is always less than or equal to zero, zero meaning that all choices in the calibration sample are simulated with probability equal to one. Usually, the comparisons carried out are based on the goodness of fit statistic (pseudo-ρ^2) and the likelihood ratio test; less widely used is the comparison test (it will be called 'adjusted ρ^2') based on the relation proposed by Horowitz (1983) and also reported in Ben-Akiva and Swait (1984).
*   *The goodness of fit statistic*   checks the null hypothesis that the maximum value of log-Likelihood, $\ln L(\beta^{ML})$, is equal to the value corresponding to null coefficients, $\ln L(0)$. Thus their difference is due to sampling errors. This test is based on the so-called (pseudo-)*rho-square* statistic:

$\rho^2 = (1 - \ln L(\beta^{ML}) / \ln L(0)) \in [0,1]$

This statistic can be used to check the model's ability to reproduce the observed choices. It is equal to zero if $L(\beta^{ML})$ is equal to $L(0)$, i.e. the model has no explanatory capability; it is equal to one if the model gives, for each user in the sample, a probability equal to one to the alternative actually chosen (and zero to the other alternatives), i.e. the model perfectly reproduces observed choices. Usually, the model with a better *rho-square* statistic is preferred, even if the differences are small, which is often the case (see Table 3.4), insofar this criterion does not seem very effective.

The 'adjusted ρ^2' test on the relation proposed by Horowitz (1983) is based on an enhanced value of rho-square statistic (sometimes called rho-square bar):

$\bar{\rho}^2 = (1 - (\ln L(\beta^{ML}) - N_\beta) / \ln L(0))$

Table 3.4   Indices and tests based on Log-Likelihood value (L(0)=-2,805)

		MNL	CNL
L(β*)		-1,931	-1,855
pseudo -ρ²		0.312	0.337
pseudo -ρ²bar		0.308	0.330
LR(βᴹᴸ)	*vs β = 0*	≠*	≠*
*symbol ≠ denotes that the null hypothesis is rejected
LR(βᴹᴸ)	CNL *vs* MNL	*better**
Adjusted ρ²	CNL *vs* MNL	*better**
** the word 'better' denotes that the null hypothesis is rejected

which attempts to eliminate the effect of the number of parameters included in the model to allow the comparison of models with different numbers of parameters. This test checks the null hypothesis that the statistic $\bar{\rho}_1^2$ for model 1 is not greater than the statistic $\bar{\rho}_2^2$ (assuming $\bar{\rho}_2^2 \leq \bar{\rho}_1^2$) for model 2, their actual difference being due to sampling errors. It is based on the relation: $Pr(\mid \bar{\rho}_1^2 - \bar{\rho}_2^2 \mid > z) \leq \Phi(z)$, where $\Phi(\cdot)$ is the distribution function of standard normal, $z = - [-2 \text{ z ln } L(0) + (N_1 - N_2)]^{1/2}$, and N_1 and N_2 are the number of parameters in model 1 and 2 respectively. This test can be used to ascertain whether model 2 can be considered (statistically) better than model 1 [in Table 3.4, the word 'better' denotes that the null hypothesis is rejected, otherwise the symbol • appears].

The Likelihood Ratio test, $LR(\beta^{ML})$ in Table 3.4, checks the null hypothesis that the maximum value of log-Likelihood, $\ln L(\beta^{ML})$, is equal to the maximum value corresponding to a reference model with null utility parameters or to a simpler one. Hence thus the difference is due to sampling errors. This test is based on the *Likelihood Ratio* statistic:

$$LR = -2 [ln \, L(\beta°) - ln \, L \, (\beta^{ML})]$$

which, on the null hypothesis, is asymptotically distributed according to a chi-square variable with a number of degrees of freedom equal to the number of constraints imposed (say the number of parameters). This test can be used to check whether utility parameters are (statistically) different from zero or from those of a simpler model.

As stated for the rho-squared test, the likelihood ratio and the 'adjusted ρ²' and the likelihood ratio tests might not be very significant. Indeed, small differences in the likelihood values are sufficient to verify such tests. In Table 3.4, it is shown how CNL model verify both tests, even though a little difference between *pseudo -ρ²* values.

Simulated vs. observed choice fractions for each user in the sample

$$MSE = \Sigma_i \, \Sigma_k \, (p^{sim}_{k,i} - p^{obs}_{k,i})^2 \, / \, N_{users} \geq 0$$

Mean square error between the user observed choice fractions and the simulated ones, over the number of users in the sample, N_{users}. As well as MSE indicators, the corresponding standard deviation (SD) may be computed, representing how

Table 3.5   Aggregate indicators based on users choice fractions

	MNL	CNL
MSE	0.41	0.35
SD	0.33	0.24
MAE	0.82	0.66
FF	59%	67%

the predictions are dispersed, if compared with the choices observed. If different models have similar MSE errors, the one with smaller SD value is preferable.

$$\text{MAE} = \Sigma_i \, \Sigma_k \, |p^{sim}_{k,i} - p^{obs}_{k,i}| \, / \, N_{users} \geq 0$$

Mean absolute error, analogous to MSE.

$$\text{FF} = \Sigma_i \, p^{sim}_{i} \, / \, N_{users} \in [0,1]$$

Fitting Factor (FF). It is the ratio between the sum over the users in the sample of the simulated choice probability for the mode actually chosen, $p^{sim}_{user} \in [0,1]$, and the number of users in the sample, N_{users}. FF = 1 means that the model perfectly simulates the choice actually made by each user (say with $p^{sim}_{user} = 1$). It is easy to demonstrate that: MAE = 2 × (1 − FF).

Examples are given in Table 3.5. It can be easily observed that CNL outperforms MNL w.r.t. to all reported indicators.

3.3 Analysis of clearness of predictions

It is common practice that this analysis is carried out through the *%right* indicator, that is the percentage of users in the calibration sample whose observed choices are given the maximum probability (whatever the value) by the model. This index, very often reported, is somewhat meaningless if the number of alternatives is greater than two. For example, w.r.t. a three-alternative choice scenario, two models giving fractions (34%, 33%, 33%) or (90%, 5%, 5%) are considered equivalent w.r.t. this indicator.

Really effective analysis can be carried out through the indicators proposed below:

- $\%_{clearly\ right}(t)$ percentage of users in the sample whose observed choices are given a probability greater than threshold t by the model (41% for t = 66% in Figure 3.3);
- $\%_{clearly\ wrong}(t)$ percentage of users in the sample for whom the model gives a probability greater than threshold t to a choice alternative differing from the observed one (13% for t = 66% in Figure 3.3);
- $\%_{unclear}(t) = 100 - (\%_{clearly\ right} + \%_{clearly\ wrong})$ percentage of users for whom the model does not give a probability greater than threshold t to any choice (46% for t = 66% in the Figure 3.3).

These three indicators may be defined for each alternative and/or for all the alternatives available to users in the sample. As for aggregate indicators, presented

Table 3.6   Clearness analysis

threshold	MNL			CNL		
	$\%_{\text{clearly right}}$	$\%_{\text{unclear}}$	$\%_{\text{clearly wrong}}$	$\%_{\text{clearly right}}$	$\%_{\text{unclear}}$	$\%_{\text{clearly wrong}}$
0.50	62%	-	38%	66%	-	34%
0.66	39%	41%	20%	41%	46%	13%
0.90	18%	78%	4%	25%	74%	1%

in sub-section 3.2, the indicators described above when applied to the calibration (hold-out) sample allow us to understand how the model reproduces (generalizes) the observed choice scenario (to other choice scenarios). Different models can be compared by estimating the indicators against a fixed threshold, or estimating the difference between the areas below diagrams plotted against a threshold in a fixed range. The indicators (or the corresponding diagrams) may help to understand how a model approximates choice behaviours, and they may give much more significant insights than the poor $\%_{\text{right}}$ indicator (equal to 71% for both the models proposed).

In Table 3.6, the indicators against the threshold: 0.50, 0.66, 0.90 are reported (a threshold less than 50% is rather meaningless). In Figure 3.3 they are plotted for both models against any threshold in the range 0.5–1.0. Although the results point

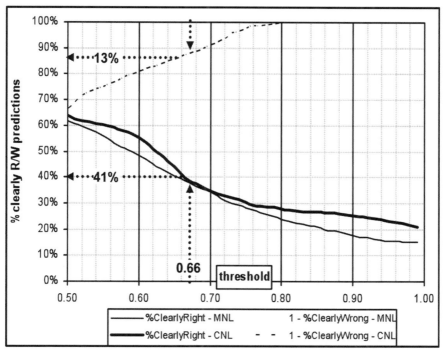

Figure 3.3   Clearness analysis

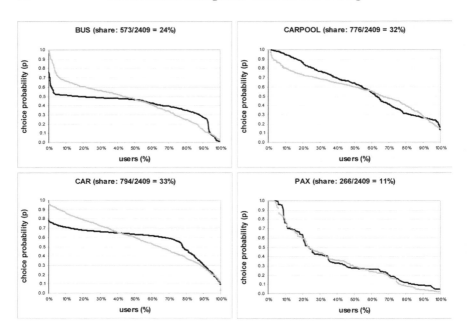

Figure 3.4   Fraction of users as choice probability threshold changes

out the better performance of CNL, it should be noted that the CNL model does not greatly outperform the MNL. Indeed, as shown in Figure 3.3, the CNL%*clearly right* diagram it is only slightly better than the MNL.

It is also worth analysing for a given probability p, the fraction of users who get a simulated choice probability greater than p. In the graphs above (Figure 3.4) different diagrams area proposed for each transport mode. It can be noted that the CNL (black line) is quite similar to the MNL model (grey line) as regards car as passenger, but quite different as regards the other transport modes. In particular, CNL gives better predictions for low values of probabilities, and as such should be preferred.

Integrating the areas under both curves, it is possible to estimate different indicators able to measure model effectiveness, and to appreciate differences between models and/or approaches.

3.4 Analysis of the ASA role

When modelling transportation mode choice behaviour a common practice is to add an alternative specific attribute, ASA_k, or modal constant for each alternative k:

$$v_k = \sum_j \beta_j x_{jk} + ASA_k \ \forall \ k \geq 1$$

or with respect to ASA_1 taken as reference:

$$v_1 = \sum_j \beta_j x_{j1} + ASA_1$$

$$v_k = \sum_j \beta_j \, x_{jk} + \Delta ASA_{k,1} + ASA_1 \quad \forall \, k > 1$$

where $\Delta ASA_{k,1} = ASA_k - ASA_1$ (clearly $\Delta ASA_{1,1} = 0$).

The use of ASA's is very rare in other choice contexts.

It should be noted that if choice probabilities are independent of any linear transformation of perceived utility (section 2.2), as in very often case, a constant may be added to the systematic utility, v_k, of each choice alternative, k, without affecting choice probabilities. In this case, the utility function takes the following simpler expression (by adding $-ASA_1$):

$$v_1 = \sum_j \beta_j \, x_{j1}$$
$$v_k = \sum_j \beta_j \, x_{jk} + \Delta ASA_{k,1} \quad \forall \, k > 1$$

The above formulation stresses that only the differences $\Delta ASA_{k,1}$ may actually be calibrated. For this purpose let m be the number of attributes but ASA's and $x_{m+h-1,k}$ be a dummy attribute, one for each alternative (but one) = 0 if $k \neq h$ or = 1 if $k = h$, it yields:

$$v_k = \sum_j \beta_j \, x_{jk} + \sum_{h=2,K} \beta_{m+h-1} \, x_{m+h-1,k}$$

After calibration the parameters β_{m+h-1} will give an estimation of $\Delta ASA_{k,1}$ (see Table 3.2). It is worth noting that the reference alternative may easily be changed since:

$$\Delta ASA_{k,h} = ASA_k - ASA_h = ASA_k - ASA_1 + ASA_1 - ASA_h = \Delta ASA_{k,1} - \Delta ASA_{h,1}$$

Table 3.7 **Example of $\Delta ASA_{k,h}$ matrix (for MNL model), values are not scaled to β_{cost}**

MNL		$\Delta ASA_{k,B}$		k/h	C	B	CP	P
Car	C	+1.96		C		+1.96	+4.57	+5.17
Bus	B	–		B	-1.96		+3.21	+2.61
Car-pool	CP	-3.21		CP	-4.57	-3.21		+0.59
Car as passenger	P	-2.61		P	-5.17	-2.61	-0.59	

The values $\Delta ASA_{k,h}$ may be arranged into a matrix with null values on principal diagonal, $\Delta ASA_{k,k}$ being null by definition, as exemplified in Table 3.7.
ASAs may play a major role in obtaining significant utility parameters, but the greater they are the poorer the model is expected to perform when applied to other choice scenarios (poor generalization).

The role of ASAs can be analysed through the ASA-impact matrix Q, with an entry q_{kh} for each pair of (different) choice alternative (k, h) with $k \neq h$, as described below. Once the calibration has been carried out, the values of parameters β_j and of $\Delta ASA_{k,1}$ (with $\Delta ASA_{1,1} = 0$) are known. For a user (not explicitly indicated below for simplicity sake), let

v_k be the value of systematic utility for choice alternative k,

$v_{0k} = v_k - ASA_k$ be the value of systematic utility without considering ASA, or basic utility.

For any two different choice alternatives (k, h), with $k \neq h$, let $\Delta v_{kh} = v_{0k} - v_{0h}$ be the difference in the values of the basic utility, easily be computed by:

$$\Delta v_{kh} = (v_k - v_h) - (ASA_k - ASA_h) = (v_k - v_h) - (ASA_k - ASA_1 + ASA_1 - ASA_h)$$

or

$$\Delta v_{kh} = (v_k - v_h) - (\Delta ASA_{k,1} - \Delta ASA_{h,1}).$$

The entries of matrix **Q** are defined as the number of users in the sample (the frequency) for which the difference in basic systematic utility values is less than the difference between the differential ASA:

$$q_{kh} = Fr[\, |\Delta v_{kh}| < |ASA_k - ASA_h| \,] = Fr[|\Delta v_{kh}| < |\Delta ASA_{k,1} - \Delta ASA_{h,1}| \,] \in [0,1]$$

the value of the principal diagonal, q_{kk}, being null by definition. Clearly, matrix **Q** does not depend on the choice of reference alternative.

According to the above definition, each entry of matrix Q gives the fraction of users (in the sample) for which the ASA weighs more than half the systematic utility, insofar as small values generally denotes better models. (However it should be noted that small values may also occur for two alternatives with similar values of systematic utilities). Matrix Q can be computed both for calibration and hold-out samples.

Table 3.8   Number of users with k and h available

k\h	Car	Bus	Car-pool	Car as passenger
Car	–	1,581	1,127	793
Bus		–	1,574	1,270
Car-pool			–	1,296
Car as passenger				–

Table 3.9   Example of matrix Q (MNL model – calibration sample)

k\h	Car	Bus	Car-pool	Car as passenger
Car	–	72%	100%	100%
Bus		–	90%	99%
Car-pool			–	35%
Car as passenger				–

Examples of matrix Q are given in Tables 3.9 and 3.10. In Table 3.8 the number of users that have (at least) both modes k and h available are reported. These values allow the relevance of each pair of modes (k,h) to be appreciated within the choice context.

Table 3.10   Example of matrix Q (CNL model – calibration sample)

k\h	Car	Bus	Car-pool	Car as passenger
Car	–	27%	100%	100%
Bus		–	37%	98%
Car-pool			–	6%
Car as passenger				–

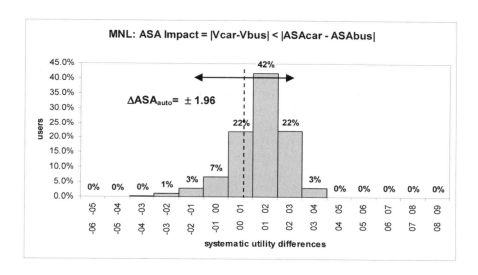

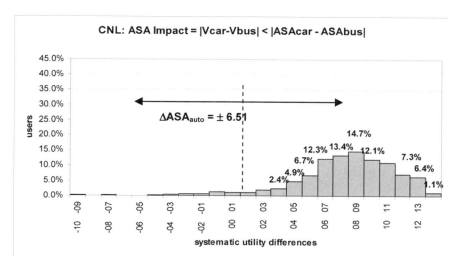

Figure 3.5   ASA versus systematic utility

Although all the previous indicators showed that CNL only slightly outperforms MNL, the above results point to a significant difference between the two models; MNL is greatly affected by ΔASA values, meaning that variations in the level of service will not greatly affect market shares. Such a condition may be a characteristic of the phenomenon, but it might also be a drawback of MNL. On the other hand, CNL generally dominates MNL, in particular Car vs. Bus, Bus vs. Car-pool and Car-pool vs. Car as passengers are much better distinguished by CNL than MNL through attributes other than ASA. Anyhow Car vs. Car-pool, Car vs. Car as pass. And Bus vs. Car as passengers still remain not effectively distinguished. Proposed indicators can be very useful for identifying the best modelling solution when all the others indicators fail to highlight great differences.

A descriptive way to analyse the role of ASA may be achieved by defining the frequency distribution of $(v_k - \Delta ASA_{k,1}) - v_1$ over the users in the sample. In Figure 3.5 above, the distributions $(v_{car} - \Delta ASA_{car,1}) - v_1$ have been plotted for both models. Interestingly, confirming what was shown in the previous tables, the CNL utility differences are less affected than the MNL utility differences.

Another ASA-impact indicator, not discussed here for brevity's sake, is given by the mean difference between the ASA value and the basic utility over all the users in the sample.

It should be stressed that the presented result must not to be confused with elasticity analysis (see next section). Elasticity analysis allows us to identify which model is more elastic than the others (more reacting to variations of attributes), without suggesting which is the best. Conversely, using ASA-impact analysis we may identify which model is least affected by ΔASA values, in other words, the model with the smallest part of systematic utility not measurable with attributes.

3.5 Elasticity analysis

A further approach, which is well-consolidated in the literature, helps understand how the model generalizes to other choice scenarios. This is called elasticity analysis and is based on indicators obtained from partial derivatives (or finite differences) of choice probabilities w.r.t. attributes as in Table 3.11.

For each attribute elasticity values may be collected in a square matrix with a row and a column for each choice alternative. Generally, larger elasticity values are

Table 3.11   Differential and/or finite difference elasticity

elasticityfor alternative k	direct probability of k w.r.t. an attribute of k	crossed k≠h probability of k w.r.t. an attribute of h
differential	$(\partial p_k / \partial x_{jk}) \cdot (x_{jk} / p_k)$	$(\partial p_k / \partial x_{jh}) \cdot (x_{jh} / p_k)$
finite difference	$(\Delta p_k / \Delta x_{jk}) \cdot (x_{jk} / p_k)$	$(\Delta p_k / \Delta x_{jh}) \cdot (x_{jh} / p_k)$

Table 3.12   Direct elasticity

	MNL	CNL
Bus time	0.06	0.08
Car time	0.05	0.06
Bus cost	0.38	0.43

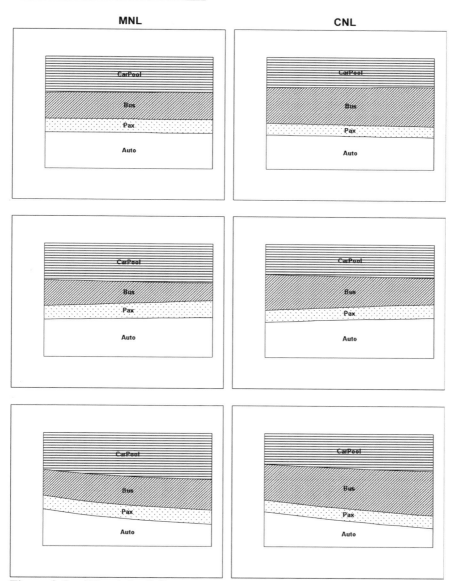

Figure 3.6   Direct elasticity

preferred, assuming a better generalization of the model, but no explanation is given of such a practice.

For the sake of example, finite difference (direct) elasticity values for some LoS attributes are shown in Table 3.12 and in Figure 3.6.

Figure 3.6 shows choice probabilities vs. variations of LoS attributes for the two models (MNL and CNL) and for the four transport modes. The graphs propose the choice probabilities as bus time decrease by 50%, and bus cost and car cost increases by 50%. The graphs are consistent with Table 3.12, and point out a small elasticity with respect to bus time and higher values with respect to bus and car cost. The two models show similar trends, but CNL is more sensitive to monetary cost effects. It should be noted that the graphs have different starting points, since MNL, unlike CNL, perfectly reproduces the calibration sample market shares (as already noted).

Table 3.13   Procedure

Description of the analysed model			
• calibration sample size and hold-out sample size • # parameters • # attributes • calibration function (usually max log-Likelihood for random utility models)			
	indicator	model	sample
calibration parameters	γ_1 (definition and unit) β_1 / γ_1 (definition and unit) β_j / β_1 (definition and unit) $\forall j>1$ other utility parameters γ_i $\forall i>1$	all utility-based utility-based utility-based all	- calibration calibration calibration calibration
utility parameter analysis	informal test formal test (T-test)	Utility-based RUM only	calibration calibration
aggregate indicators	MSE, SD MAE FF Log-Likelihood tests indicators	all all all RUM only	cal / hold-out cal / hold-out cal / hold-out cal / hold-out
clearness analysis	$\%_{clearly\ right}$ (50%, 90%) $\%_{clearly\ wrong}$ (50%, 90%) $\%_{unclear}$ (50%,90%) *values and/or diagrams*	all all all	cal / hold-out cal / hold-out cal / hold-out
ASA impact analysis	matrix **Q**	utility-based	cal / hold-out
elasticity analysis	differential finite difference *values and/or diagrams*	closed form all	

4. Conclusions

In this chapter several benchmarking indicators have been introduced to validate and compare choice models within a general protocol, proposed for adoption as common practice, and summarized below (Table 3.13).

Importantly, the final selection, among all the calibrated models, should be made by also taking account of *efficiency*, or rather, computational speed and memory requirements.

The use of multi-criteria analysis techniques based on benchmarking indicators appears worthy of further research effort and will be addressed in future work, which will also report results regarding other types of choice models, such as non-linear utility functions through Box-Cox transformations, fuzzy utility models, etc.

Others issues appear worthy of further research effort, such as the definition of the calibration vs hold-out sample. According to a very simple approach, the size of the calibration sample can be obtained by progressively increasing the number of observations, randomly sampled out of the available data, and by calibrating the choice model until the choice shares obtained are close to the observed ones (up to an error threshold). To this end a MultiNomial Logit can be used as the benchmarking choice model.

Moreover, it seems sensible to carry out a preliminary analysis, including:

- dispersion of LoS attribute values as stated by users against the mean values given by the supply model (validation of supply model);
- dispersion of SE attributes among users in the sample;
- relevance of attributes as measured by variance;
- correlation among attributes as measured by covariance.

Last, but not least, the transferability of results to a different case study is still an open issue.

Acknowledgements

The authors wish to thank Viviana Fedele for her fruitful comments and discussions on some of the topics in this chapter.

References

Ben Akiva, M. and Lerman, S. (1985), *Discrete Choice Analysis Theory and Application to Travel Demand* (Cambridge, MA: MIT Press).

Batley, R.P. and Daly, A.J. (2006), 'On the equivalence between elimination-by-aspects and generalised extreme value models of choice behaviour', *Journal of Mathematical Psychology* 50: 456–67.

Ben-Akiva, M. and Swait, J. (1984), 'The Akaike Likelihood Ratio Index', Working paper, Department of Civil Engineering, MIT, Cambridge, MA.

Cantarella, G.E. and de Luca, S. (2005a), 'Multilayer feedforward networks for transportation mode choice analysis: An analysis and a comparison with random utility models', *Transportation Research C*, 13: 121–55.

Cantarella, G.E. and de Luca, S. (2005b), 'Modelling transportation choice through utility-based multi-layer feedforward networks', in Attoh-Okine, Nii O. et al. (eds), *Applied Research in Uncertainty Modeling and Analysis*, pp. 341–68.

Cantarella, G.E. and Fedele, V. (2003), 'Fuzzy vs. random utility models: an application to mode choice behaviour analysis', Proceedings of European Transport Conference 2003.

Cascetta, E. (2001), *Transportation Systems Engineering: Theory and Methods* (The Netherlands: Kluwer Academic Publishers).

Domencich, T.A. and McFadden, D. (1975), *Urban Travel Demand: A Behavioral Analysis* (New York, NY: Elsevier).

Horowitz, J. (1983), 'Statistical comparison of non-nested probabilistic choice model', *Transportation Science* 17: 319–50.

Kahneman, D. and Tversky, A. (1979), 'Prospect Theory: An Analysis of Decision under Risk', *Econometrica* XLVII: 263–91.

Simon, H.A. (1990), 'Invariants of human behaviour', *Annual Review of Psychology* 41: 1–19.

Train, K. (2003), *Discrete Choice Methods with Simulation* (Cambridge: Cambridge University Press).

Tversky, A. (1972a), 'Choice by elimination', *Journal of Mathematical Psychology* 9: 341–67.

Tversky, A. (1972b), 'Elimination by aspects: A theory of choice', *Psychological Review*, 79: 281–99.

Chapter 4

On-Street Parking Pricing: *Ex Ante Ex Post* Profile Analysis following a 50% Increase in On-Street Parking Charges in Dublin City

Andrew Kelly and Peter Clinch

Introduction

Rising car ownership levels and increased dependence on private motor transport is a well-documented trend in many cities across the globe. Increasing levels of traffic congestion pose considerable challenges for traffic managers and there are many costs associated with failure to manage transport effectively and these range from lost time to higher concentrations of acid precursor and greenhouse gas emissions. In response, where infrastructural possibilities are limited or exhausted, a large field of research has been devoted to transport demand management (TDM) tools and policies. Within this field, road pricing and congestion pricing have often been described as the 'first-best' approach to the management of the demand for road space. Consequently the structure, effectiveness and modelling of this measure has been investigated by numerous authors including de Palma and Lindsey (2006), Sterner (2003), May et al. (2002), Goh (2002), and Verhoef (1996, 2002).

The incidence of this type of measure is growing and there are two high profile success[1] stories of road and congestion pricing respectively already implemented in London (fixed fee) and Singapore (variable fee). However, whilst road and congestion pricing can allow a transport manager to influence directly the length of trips, chosen route and the timing of trips, perhaps the greatest barrier to widespread implementation of road pricing has been the perception of it as a politically unpopular measure which should only be countenanced when sufficient provision has been made in terms of alternative transport. Disagreement over what qualifies as 'sufficient alternatives' and the scarcity of pioneering politicians with the capacity to effect change can serve to limit the pace of change with regard to the introduction of such 'new' TDM measures.

By comparison there are undoubtedly a far higher number of operational, priced parking schemes across the globe, with general public acceptance or experience (in much of Europe at least) that a parking space in a prime central area is a scarce resource which must be rationed by pricing, i.e. one would expect to pay for such a service. Thus, given so many people are already conditioned to the concept of a parking charge and the required infrastructure is often already in place, considerable

---

1 Successful in terms of reduced congestion and increased commuter mobility.

interest has developed with regard to the potential for parking pricing as a 'second best' proxy for, or companion to, congestion/road charging in cities. A timely representation of this interest from the policy side has been the Transport Policy Special Edition on Parking (Volume 13, Issue 6, November 2006).

Selected literature on parking pricing as a TDM

Parking pricing is important with regard to transport demand management and urban traffic congestion for two broad reasons. Firstly, there is the direct *demand-level* influence of the price of parking. This influence operates by the same principles as any normal pricing instrument within a market. In the context of private motor travel, the cost of parking for those who pay themselves is often the highest monetary component of an individual car trip. Thus a change in the level of parking price carries a heavier weight in the generalized cost function and can exert a strong influence on the initial decision to drive.[2] Indeed, prior research has shown that the level of parking price can be a major factor with regard to trip generation decisions and modal shift (Higgins 1992; Button and Verhoef 1998, UK Department of Transport 2002, Kelly and Clinch 2006).

It is this price influence which led Garland et al. (2002) to label parking pricing as a potential 'push' measure in the TDM 'toolkit'. The concept being that, as opposed to a 'pull' measure such as public transport subsidies which seek to encourage users from their private vehicles by making alternatives relatively more attractive, the 'push' measure influences private motorists away from driving by making it relatively less attractive to other modes via increased trip costs.

Secondly, there is the indirect influence of parking policy (or, rather, inappropriate parking policy) on congestion via associated effects. On a broader scale, Shoup (2005) has shown comprehensively how free or mispriced parking and minimum parking requirements have contributed toward urban sprawl and private car dependence in the United States. On more of a local level however, parking policy and, specifically, vacancy rates of parking areas have important implications for urban congestion levels. The reason for this is that 'cruising' for parking (search time) can be a major contributor to congestion (Arnott and Inci 2006, Shoup 2006). The issue is that relatively inexpensive parking can lead to increased demand for spaces which can lead to a longer amount of time being spent searching for parking spaces. Consequently in busy high demand areas, inappropriate tariffs for parking can be a contributor to congestion by attracting too many searching vehicles. As these vehicles cruise for an available space they must remain in the traffic system, travel at a slower speed, stack with 'through traffic' and other searching vehicles alike and thereby slow the entire system until they find a space. As noted by Arnott and Rowse (1999) this process increases

---

2   It is accepted that parking charges will have little or no direct impact upon levels of 'through-traffic' and therein lies a weakness relative to road or congestion pricing with regard to mode choice and trip decision.

traffic volume, slows it down, and generates additional costs in terms of time lost both to the individual searching and those who they delay.

Thus research has shown the importance of properly managed and price-rationed parking facilities as a component of transport demand management. This chapter endeavours to contribute to our understanding of the consequences of such pricing schemes using a case-study of a central area of Dublin city and examining the consequences of a 50% increase in on-street parking prices.

Methodology

The area chosen for the case study is one of Dublin's prime parking areas, St. Stephen's Green in the centre of Dublin. St. Stephen's Green is one of the most popular and best-known on-street parking areas in the city centre[3] and is located just south of the river Liffey, which divides Dublin city into northern and southern halves. Parking spaces are available on each side of this large square park located at the centre of one of Dublin's most popular shopping and entertainment areas. In addition to the on-street parking facilities there are two multi-story car parks in the immediate area, with a third in easy walking distance.

Aside from Stephen's Green itself as an attraction, the immediate area contains a number of office buildings, bars and restaurants, and the entrance to a large Shopping centre, which is built upon its own substantial parking facility. The area also borders a number of other prime streets in the city, including Grafton Street and Dawson Street, two extremely popular shopping and social districts of the city. The area is often described as the 'heart' of the city centre.

Stated-Preference Methodology

Stated-preference data for the purposes of this chapter were derived from two face to face parking surveys commissioned in sequential years. The scope of these surveys was quite broad and targeted a wide range of information for parking-policy related studies. The questionnaires were designed by the authors with the input of the Director of Traffic of Dublin City Council and a professional survey company who were commissioned to implement the survey. The population being sampled was those people who park their car between Monday and Friday at peak hours (08:00 hours to 17:00 hours) on-street at St. Stephen's Green. Interviewers positioned themselves along different sections of St. Stephen's Green and approached people as they returned to their cars. The interviews lasted approximately ten minutes each.

---

3   Since the conclusion of this study, the area has changed significantly with the introduction of tram lines, a one-way circular driving system and a reduction in the availability of on-street spaces.

The first such survey began on St. Stephen's Green in late July 2000 and an effective sample of 1,062 responses was achieved in two weeks (10 days). The second survey took place approximately a year later in the same location in early August of 2001. A revised but comparable questionnaire was drafted and the same market research company contracted to administer the questionnaires. The sample size for this second survey was 1,002.

The Pricing Instrument

This research was carried out in co-operation with the Director of Traffic of Dublin City Council. This facilitated a form of experiment whereby a profile of parkers could be taken before and after an on-street parking price change. At the time of the second data collection in 2001, the price of on street parking in Dublin city had been altered from the two tier system in 2000 of either IR£1 per hour (€1.27) or IR£0.80 per hour (€1.02). A new 5-tier system was brought into place with both central bands of the new pricing structure increasing by 50%. As Stephen's Green is located in the centre of the inner-most ('Very High Demand') zone, this meant that it and all neighbouring on-street parking areas within a 15-minute walking distance now had an hourly tariff 50% higher than the previous year. Thus some consistency was maintained in terms of the cost of alternative on-street parking, as the proportional increase was the same for on-street parking in the broader area.

Table 4.1   Nearby MSCP charges and OS charges for 2000 and 2001

	2000 Hourly Rate	2001 Hourly Rate
Dawson MSCP	€2.03	€2.29
Drury MSCP	€2.03	€2.29
On-Street	€1.27	€1.90

Note: Rates converted from Irish Punt to Euro at rate of 1: 1.27.

Changes in alternate sources of paid parking (Multi-Storey Car Parks [MSCPs] were as presented in Table 4.1. MSCPs change their pricing more frequently and are more often privately owned than city managed. Pricing changes within MSCPs are generally small and progress in line with inflation; a query to the MSCP parking management on St. Stephen's Green suggested that they have not noticed a change in parking events as a result of such changes. Notably over the two years, on street parking has always been the cheaper alternative, despite the narrowing margin of difference.

In addition to the price instrument, effort was invested into identifying potential confounding factors, other than price, which may have influenced changes in profile. As part of the overall parking study, consideration was given to changes in the supply of parking spaces, MSCP price changes, new road laws, growth in traffic levels and vehicle registration, the rate of inflation and real income growth. The brief outcome of these considerations was no monitored change in parking supply on-street or through MSCP facilities, inflation being largely compensated for by income growth, and a shift in a nearby road law only affecting one of the exit routes for leaving the parking area. Despite no clear factor other than price having been identified as likely to cause a pronounced change in the profile of parkers in the test area, it is important to stress that this was, of course, not a controlled experiment and, as such, everything else is unlikely to be completely equal before and after the price change. This should be borne in mind when interpreting the results below.

Results

The first question to investigate is whether or not on-street parking demand was affected by the level of change in on-street tariffs. A complementary study which monitored the actual parking meter demand data in the case study area showed a reduction in average parking events of just over 4% between 09:00 hours and 18:00 hours following the price change (Kelly and Clinch 2004). Thus, from a demand perspective, there was a change in behaviour between the two years. In this results section, the profiling data from year 1 and year 2 – *ex ante* and *ex post* of the 50% increase in on-street pricing – are presented. The objective is to evaluate any potential shift in the characteristics of those parking in the area *ex post* of the 50% on-street pricing increase.

Age and Class

The first profile changes considered are the age and social class[4] proportions from year 1 and year 2 as presented in Figure 4.1. In the brackets of social classes F (lowest class), C2 (lower middle class) and DE (upper and middle lower classes) we note there is no large change between the two years. One of the more common criticisms of pricing measures is their regressive nature. In this particular case it would seem that the concerns of serious negative impacts upon demand in the lower socio-economic groupings are not substantiated by these data for this price change. In fact the only change in class ratings is an exchange between classes AB (upper class) and C1 (upper middle class). Interestingly the change is in the direction of fewer AB class users and more C1s in 2001. As such it would seem that based on these top-level results that the lower-class spectrum has not been

---

4   The social class brackets are those originally developed by the National Readership Survey (NRS) in the United Kingdom.

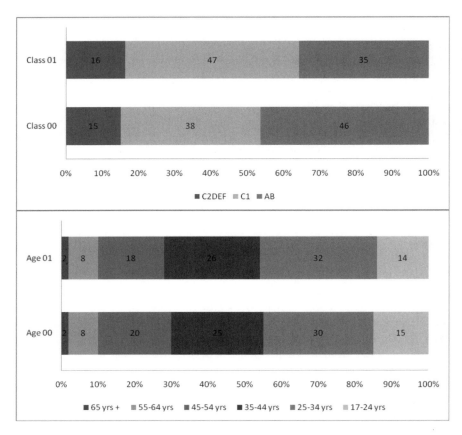

**Figure 4.1   Comparison of age and class from 2000 (n= 1062) and 2001
(n=1007)**

pushed out of the market by the price increase, and the sole change was a transfer
between the upper class and the upper middle class. However, there will, of course,
be a welfare impact in terms of the higher cost of the parking event.

With respect to age, there is an almost indistinguishable difference between the
age spread of users from 2000 to 2001 and there remains a well-distributed age
profile of parkers in the area in both years, irrespective of the price changes.

In addition to data on age and class, information was also collected directly on
income levels. However income related questions are more frequently rejected in
face-to-face surveys, and these surveys were no exception with an average of more
than 60% of the samples in both years refusing to give income data. Thus basic
comparisons of the responses to this question were far less useful due to distortion.
A proxy question for income was included in the form of a question on engine size
and the results of this are presented in Table 4.2. Whilst no attempt is made here to

Table 4.2   Income and engine sizes

Engine Size	Percentage 2000 | n	Percentage 2001 | n
1 litre	6.4% | 68	5.4% | 54
1.1/1.2 litre	10.8% | 115	8.6% | 87
1.3/1.4 litre	20.8% | 221	19.5% | 196
1.5/1.6 litre	19.6% | 208	21% | 211
1.7/1.8 litre	14.4% | 153	16.1% | 162
1.9/2 litre	13% | 138	13% | 131
2+ litre	12.3% | 131	14.5% | 146
Don't Know/Other	2.6% | 28	2% | 20

infer the household income bracket from vehicle engine size, the data do at least indicate a good consistency between the two years. Thus if engine size is serving as a (probably poor) proxy for income, there is again little evidence of a strong regressive effect from the tariff increase.

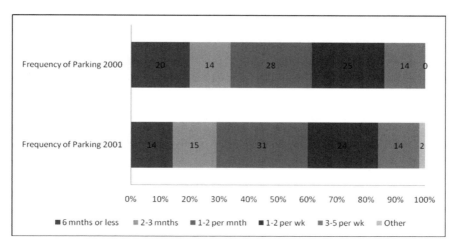

Figure 4.2   Frequency of parking to area and purpose of trip 2000 (n = 1062) and 2001 (n = 1007)

Frequency of Parking

The next results to be examined comparatively were the frequency of parking in the area, as presented in Figure 4.2. Frequency of parking is relevant as it gives an indication of the impact of the tariff on all users, from random to extremely regular. In terms of results however, there are again no large changes in the proportions between the two years. The only noticeable change is the drop in parkers who only visit the area every six months or less from 20% in 2000 to 14% in 2001. This could be indicating a slight shift away from the more sporadic visitors, although the change is small. A shift in users parking once or twice a month and once every two or three month would seem to account for the change.

Thus in terms of parking regularity of users, the evidence would suggest that the level of price change implemented had only a weak impact on this aspect of parker profile within the test area, with the mix of different frequency users parking on-street in the area remaining consistent.

User Origins

User origin identifies the starting point of the respondent's journey. Figure 4.3 presents the results from this question in both years. The response options range as follows:

- No reply given.
- Travelled from outside of the County of Dublin.
- Travelled from inside the County of Dublin but from outside the city and suburb areas.
- Travelled from inside Dublin city or suburbs.

With regard to no reply or those who travelled long distances (i.e. outside of the county) we note only a minor change. However, in 2001, 28% of the sample travelled from inside Dublin County, as opposed to 15% in the previous year. In other words, a higher share of individuals are driving from further out to park in the case-study area following the price increase. This increased share has replaced users travelling from within the city or suburbs. In 2001 there was a ten percentage-point drop from the previous year in the share of people travelling from within the city and suburbs. This is likely to be a result of users closer to the city, opting not to travel and pay the increased tariff, which would be consistent with the concept of parking charges bearing more heavily on those who travel shorter distances, for whom the charge makes up a greater proportion of total cost.

In this particular category then we notice there has been a noteworthy change in the profile of the parkers with fewer people with relatively close origins to this city-centre parking resource parking in the case study area.

Search and Walking Times

Next we consider the data from 2000 and 2001 in relation to aspects of the users' parking visits on the day they were surveyed. This includes search time for a space, duration of the visit, the walking distance to their destination, and in general terms the longest amount of time they would spend walking to their destination. These

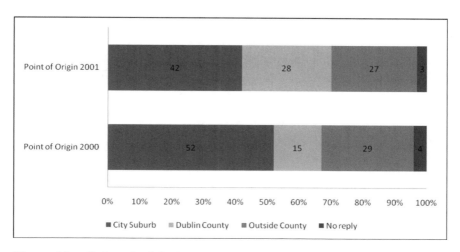

Figure 4.3 **Point of origin for those queried (2000) (n = 1062) and 2001 (n = 1007)**

Table 4.3 **Parking duration of users on the day surveyed only**

Length of time parked on day surveyed	Percentage of all users and count 2000	Percentage of all users and count 2001
Up to 30 minutes	16.9% | 120	9.2% | 93
31 to 1 hour	22.3% | 237	22.3% | 225
1 to 2 hours	30% | 319	39.6% | 399
2 hours up to 3 hours	16.6% | 177	15.9% | 160
More than 3 hours / Repark	12.2% | 130	7.5% | 75
Don't know	1.8% | 19	5.5% | 55

factors are rated as crucial factors with regard to the parking decision within the works of Arnott and Rowse (1999), Tsamboulas (2001) and Shiftan (2002).

As the results are quite close, the comparative analysis of the duration of their parking on the day they were surveyed in Table 4.3 is somewhat distorted by more (5.5% vs. 1.8%) users in 2001 claiming they 'Didn't Know'. In 2001 there are notably few people 'reparking'[5] after three hours, this would be an expected reaction to the higher parking charges with the tariffs making all-day meter feeding a very expensive habit. There are also fewer extremely short duration parkers (less

---

5   On-street parking in the city is limited to a three hour maximum stay. In some case a small proportion of people may 'meter-feed' and simply pay for another three hours every three hours to allow them to park all day.

than 30 minutes). The biggest differential before and after the price change is in those parking one to two hours with almost 10% more of the sample in 2001 parking for this length of time. Other than these results, the proportions parking for 31 minutes to an hour or two to three hours are remarkably consistent over the two years. It is important to reiterate, however, that these results are based solely on the responses of users parking in the area on the day they were parking, thus these results are based on just over 1000 individual parking events as opposed to total parking levels in the area in the time under study.

However, the corresponding revealed preference data from the parking meters for the area following the change indicated that the biggest change in the area subsequent to the 50% increase in pricing was a considerable 16.5% reduction in average parking duration (Kelly and Clinch 2004). These data cover all of the full six weeks and all parking events that took place during the empirical data-gathering period.

Table 4.4   Time spent searching for a parking space for all users 2000 (n=1062) and 2001 (n=1007)

Time	2000	2001	Difference
Up to 5 minutes	63.8%	67.8%	+ 4
5 to 10 minutes	20.9%	19.3%	-1.6
11 + minutes	12.7%	9.1%	- 3.6
Don't know	2.5%	3.8%	+1.3

In Table 4.4 we are presented with data on the length of time users spent searching for a parking space. The principal policy goal of the 50% increase in the parking tariff was to increase turnover of spaces, while endeavouring to maintain a 10% aggregate vacancy rate to ensure it was easier to find a space and, thus, reduce search time and 'cruising congestion'. Whilst the differences noted are modest, the results do suggest that the 'direction' of change in search times was in line with policy objectives given that there had been some moderation of search times to the 'lower than five minutes' bracket.

Table 4.5   Time spent walking to destination from parking for all users 2000 (n=1062) and 2001 (n=1007)

Time	2000	2001	Difference
Up to 5 minutes	62.6%	67.2%	+ 4.6
5 to 10 minutes	22.8%	25.1%	+ 2.3
11 + minutes	6.9%	7.1%	+ 0.2
Don't Know	7.7%	0.6%	- 7.1

Table 4.5 examines the amount of time users spend walking to their destination from their parking spot. Although in 2001 the results for all time categories have increased, this is likely due to the significant shift in users who claimed they 'didn't know'. In 2000, 7.7% gave this response versus only 0.6% in 2001. This significant level of non-responses (for users who obviously had some walk time ahead of them) makes it difficult to draw significant conclusions from the other results, as their combined differences might be the same if the 'Don't Know' respondents had answered.

Table 4.6   Maximum amount of time all users would spend walking to destination from parking 2000 (n=1062) and 2001 (n=1007)

Time	2000	2001	Difference
Up to 5 minutes	19.7%	14.7%	- 5
5 to 10 minutes	35.8%	25.6%	- 10.2
11 + minutes	39.4%	59%	+ 19.6
Don't know	5.2%	0.7%	- 4.5

Table 4.6 is related to walking distance, and does provide some notable results. This table shows us the maximum amount of time users claim they would spend walking to their destination. The difference between 2000 and 2001 is quite pronounced, even disregarding the 4.5% difference in the 'don't know' category.

The main change is a very clear drop in the proportions of people who would only walk for up to 5 or 5 to 10 minutes in 2000. These levels have fallen by 5% and 10.2% respectively. The biggest alteration is noted however in the category of 11 minutes of more, where we see almost 20% more of the sample in 2001 state they would spend this amount of time walking to their destination. As such their walking time threshold would appear to have altered significantly following the citywide price increase in on-street charges. However, Table 4.5 showed that the actual lengths of time spent walking to their destination from their parked vehicle vary significantly from their stated maximum threshold for amount of time they would be willing to walk to their destination. Thus whilst users claim they would walk for longer in 2001, there is no evidence to suggest they actually have actually had to start doing so.

Conclusions

This chapter has considered the changes in profile and behaviour in a central on-street parking area of Dublin, following a general 50% increase in on-street city parking costs. The motivation for the tariff shift was principally to adjust the price of parking in line with those of MSCPs who adjust their tariffs far more regularly to account for inflation and respond to demand levels. In addition this was an ideal opportunity to introduce the new five-tiered parking tariffs system to the broader Dublin area. However, a criticism of pricing measures is that, because they influence parking demand and behaviour and consequently influence the 'profile' of those parking in the area, they may have a greater impact on the demand levels of certain consumers. Therefore, this study set out to monitor the change and to assess any potential shift as a result of this pricing change.

In terms of parking-demand change, related work from Kelly and Clinch (2004) has shown a drop in both parking events (4.18% drop) and average parking duration (16.5% drop) following the price change. Thus a clear change in behaviour occurred *ex post* of the pricing change. However, in terms of the profile of parkers, this chapter has shown that despite the influence of the price increase on parking demand, there were few demand changes observed at this price change level. Further related research by Kelly and Clinch (2006) indicates that there are price thresholds at which far more pronounced impacts on the profile of parkers are likely to occur. In addition, there may, of course, be significant welfare effects as a result of the rise in the cost of a parking event.

The results have shown a generally quite consistent level of profile in terms of age, social class and frequency of visit, with no indication of a more than proportional reduction in parking demand from lower class brackets. A noticeable change was remarked in relation to the reduction in the number of shorter journey trips in favour of those travelling from further out in the county. This has positive implications in terms of the potential to influence road users and conforms to how the literature would expect distance traveled to vary in relation to an end-point charge such as parking pricing. Overall, the above result combined with the drop in total parking events (and the subsequent reduction in associated parking congestion) and a net gain in terms of management revenue, was considered to be a successful TDM implementation by the city management team.

Acknowledgements

Financial support from the Irish Council for the Humanities and Social Sciences and Dublin City Council is greatly appreciated. We are most grateful to Owen Keegan, Director of Traffic Dublin City Council, for his advice and support. However, the views expressed are those of the authors.

Bibliography

Arnott, R. (2006), 'Spatial competition between parking garages and downtown parking policy', *Transport Policy* 13(6): 458–69.

Arnott, R. and de Palma, A. (1991), 'Does providing information to drivers reduce traffic congestion?', *Transportation Research Part A: General* 25(5): 309–18.

Arnott, R., de Palma, A. and Lindsey, R. (1991), 'A temporal and spatial equilibrium analysis of commuter parking', *Journal of Public Economics* 45(3): 301–35.

Arnott, R. and Inci, E. (2006), 'An integrated model of downtown parking and traffic congestion', *Journal of Urban Economics* 60(3): 418–42.

Arnott, R. and Rowse, J. (1999), 'Modeling Parking', *Journal of Urban Economics* 45(1): 97–124.

Button, K.J. (1993), *Transport Economics* (Cheltenham: Edward Elgar).

Button K.J. and Verhoef E.T. (1998), *Road Pricing, Traffic Congestion and the Environment* (Cheltenham and Northampton: Edward Elgar).

Bonsall, P. (2000), 'Legislating for modal shift: background to the UK's new transport act', *Transport Policy* 7(3): 179–84.

Bonsall, P., Shires, J., Maule, J., Matthews, B. and Beale, J. (2007), 'Responses to complex pricing signals: Theory, evidence and implications for road pricing', *Transportation Research Part A: Policy and Practice* 41(7): 672–83.

Clinch, J.P., Convery, F.J. and Walsh, B.M. (2002), *After the Celtic Tiger: Challenges Ahead* (Dublin: O'Brien Press).

de Palma, A. and Lindsey, R. (2006), 'Modelling and evaluation of road pricing in Paris', *Transport Policy* 13(2): 115–126.

de Palma, A., Lindsey, R. and Niskanen, E. (2006), 'Policy insights from the urban road pricing case studies', *Transport Policy* 13(2): 149–61.

de Palma, A., R. Lindsey, and Proost, S. (2006), 'Research challenges in modelling urban road pricing: An overview', *Transport Policy* 13(2): 97–105.

de Palma, A. and Proost, S. (2006), 'Imperfect competition and congestion in the City', *Journal of Urban Economics* 60(2): 185–209.

Garling, T.D., Eek, D., Loukopoulos, P., Fujii, S., Johansson-Stenman, O., Kitamura R., Pendyala, R. and Vilhelmson, B. (2002), 'A conceptual analysis of the impact of travel demand management on private car use', *Transport Policy* 9(1): 59–70.

Goh, M. (2002), 'Congestion management and electronic road pricing in Singapore', *Journal of Transport Geography* 10(1): 29–38.

Higgins, D. (1992) Parking taxes: effectiveness, legality and implementation, some general considerations, *Transportation* 19(3): 221–30

Kelly, J.A and Clinch, J.P (2004), 'Temporal Variance of Revealed Preference On-Street Parking Price Elasticity', Planning and Environmental Policy Working Paper Series, 04/02 (Dublin: University College Dublin).

Kelly, J.A. and Clinch, J.P. (2006), 'Influence of varied parking tariffs on parking occupancy levels by trip purpose', *Transport Policy* 13(6): 487–95.

May, A.D., Liu R., Shepherd S.P. and Sumalee A. (2002), 'The impact of cordon design on the performance of road pricing schemes', *Transport Policy* 9(3): 209–20.

May, A.D. and D.S. Milne (2000), 'Effects of alternative road pricing systems on network performance', *Transportation Research Part A: Policy and Practice* 34(6): 407–36.

Shiftan, Y. (2002), 'The effects of parking pricing and supply on travel patterns to a major business district', in Stern, E., Salomon, I. and Bovy, P.H.L., *Travel Behaviour* (Cheltenham: Edward Elgar).

Shoup, D. (2005), *The High Cost of Free Parking* (Chicago: APA Planners Press).

Shoup, D. (2006), 'Cruising for Parking', *Transport Policy* 13(6): 479–86.

Small, K.A. and Yan, J. (2001), 'The Value of 'Value Pricing' of Roads: Second-Best Pricing and Product Differentiation', *Journal of Urban Economics* 49(2): 310–36.

Sterner, T. (2003), *Policy Instruments for Environmental and Natural Resource Management* (Washington: Resources for the Future).

Stradling, S.G., Meadows, M.L. and Beaty, S. (2000), 'Helping drivers out of their cars: Integrating transport policy and social psychology for sustainable change', *Transport Policy* 7(3): 207–15.

Thorpe, N., Hills P., and Jaensirisak S. (2000), 'Public attitudes to TDM measures: a comparative study', *Transport Policy* 7(4): 243–57.

Tsamboulas, D.A. (2001), 'Parking fare thresholds: a policy tool', *Transport Policy* 8(2): 115–24.

UK Department of Transport (2002), Attitudes to Local Bus Services. Available online at http://www.transtat.dft.gov.uk/tables/2002/fperson/busloc/busloc02.htm.

Verhoef, E.T. (1996), *The Economics of Regulating Road Transport* (Cheltenham: Edward Elgar).

Verhoef, E.T. (2007), 'Second-best road pricing through highway franchising', *Journal of Urban Economics*, 62(2): 337–61.

Verhoef, E.T. (2002), 'Second-best congestion pricing in general networks. Heuristic algorithms for finding second-best optimal toll levels and toll points', *Transportation Research Part B: Methodological* 36(8): 707–29.

Verhoef, E.T. (2002), 'Second-best congestion pricing in general static transportation networks with elastic demands', *Regional Science and Urban Economics* 32(3): 281–310.

Chapter 5

Modelling Impacts of Tolling Systems with Multiple User Classes

Kathryn Stewart

1. Introduction

The classical road tolling problem is to toll network links such that, under the principles of Wardropian User Equilibrium (UE) assignment, a System Optimizing (SO) flow pattern is obtained. Such toll sets are however non-unique and further optimization is possible: for example, minimal revenue tolls create the desired SO flow pattern at minimal additional cost to the users. In the case of deterministic assignment, the minimal revenue toll problem is capable of solution by various methods, such as linear programming (Bergendorff et al. 1997) and heuristically by reduction to a multi-commodity max-flow problem (Dial 2000). However, it is generally accepted that deterministic models are less realistic than stochastic, and thus it is of interest to investigate the principles of tolling under the stochastic modelling conditions. Recent work has defined a Stochastic System Optimum (SSO) (Maher et al. 2005) and has developed methodologies to examine the minimal revenue toll problem in the case of Stochastic User Equilibrium (SUE) (Stewart and Maher 2006). This work has however been based on the assumption of a fixed demand stochastic equilibrium model with a single user class.

It is of interest to consider the case for tolling to achieve optimal traffic flows through a network when potentially a different set of link tolls may be applied to different sections of the driving population. It may well be of interest to have different charging rates for different classes of vehicles, such as standard cars and HGVs and additionally it may be politically desirable to exempt certain classes of vehicles from paying any toll, such as PSVs, Taxis etc. Such differences in vehicle classification may be modelled as Multiple User Classes (MUC), where the different groups of drivers are assigned different generalized cost functions to account for the difference in travel time and route constraint between groups. In stochastic modelling this may be achieved by assigning different values to the dispersion parameter (Maher and Hughes 1996a), and objective functions for MUCSUE have been defined as extensions of the SUE objective function. (Maher and Hughes 1996, Maher 1998). In an MUCSUE assignment model no driver could reduce their perceived travel cost by changing route in each class, whilst all classes are assigned in the network allowing for interaction.

This chapter will extend the formulation for SSO to include MUC, such that total perceived network travel costs for all classes are minimized and will present an objective function for MUCSSO. To achieve such a flow pattern under an MUCSUE assignment, link tolls will be applied, which may differ for each user class. Marginal Social Cost Price (MSCP) tolling will be examined for differing user classes, and then the possibility of reduced (or minimal) revenue tolling strategies to produce the same effect will be illustrated. It may be politically desirable to allow that one or more MUCs should be exempt from tolls, and the possibility of producing toll sets that apply to less than the total number of user groups, but still result in the MUCSSO flow pattern being achieved will be considered. The methods used to derive toll sets will be equally applicable to any stochastic assignment method, however logit-based assignment will be used to present illustrative results on small toy networks.

Under deterministic assignment the System Optimal (SO) solution where the Total Network Travel Cost (TNTC) is minimized is well established as being the 'desired' flow pattern, i.e. which would give the most beneficial flow pattern throughout the network. In the case of economic benefit maximization, marginal social cost price tolls (MSCP) may be applied to network links so that the SO is achieved. Under stochastic assignment though, the desired flow pattern is not immediately obvious. Previous work (Stewart and Maher 2006) has suggested two possible desired flow patterns in the stochastic case: the SSO (Maher et al. 2005), where economic benefit is maximized and the Total Perceived Network Travel Cost (TPNTC) is minimized, and the 'True SO' where TNTC is minimized, i.e. the same SO flow pattern as in the deterministic case. This chapter will also consider tolling to achieve the deterministic SO flow pattern under MUCSUE and will compare toll levels derived.

Section 2 summarises the MUCSUE model, section 3 defines a suitable objective function for MUCSSO and discusses how the MUCSSO flow pattern may be easily determined from standard techniques, section 4 discusses possible tolling methodologies under MUCSUE to produce desired flow patterns and section 5 summarises the chapter and comments on future work.

2. Stochastic User Equilibrium with Multiple User Classes (MUCSUE)

Standard SUE models assume that all drivers perceive network costs according to the same distribution and thus form a single user class. It can however be useful to separate drivers into distinct Multiple User Classes, by assuming that they have either different cost functions, or different perceptions of cost variability.

Models with Multiple User Classes (MUCs) may for instance be used to assess the utilization of route guidance systems whereby some drivers have more accurate information than others (assuming that only a certain percentage of vehicles are fitted with such systems). In stochastic assignment this would be represented by the user having a different value of the relevant variability parameter; in the logit model the value of θ would be higher (as $\theta \to \infty$ the stochastic model tends to the deterministic where all users would be assumed to have perfect network knowledge), and in the probit model the parameter β would be lower to represent greater network knowledge. Both Van Vuren and Watling (1991) and Maher and Hughes (1996) assume that the MUCSUE applies to the situation of route guidance.

Multiple user classes may also be used to model different groups of drivers who may have differing generalized cost (GC) functions: such as HGV drivers, where generalized cost functions would be higher to represent, for example, the increased time taken for journeys (including the increased link delay due to higher pcu level) and potentially (if both time and money terms were included in the GC) the higher value of time associated with commercial trips. Whilst it is possible to model MUCSUE quite generally (with users having completely different forms of generalized cost function (Daganzo 1982)), it is a convenient and widely used assumption that the cost functions should be multiples of each other (e.g. Conners et al. 2005). The model of MUCs where cost functions are multiples of each other can be easily seen to be equivalent to those where the variability parameter differs by user class. This may be readily illustrated using the logit model, where the probability of assigning flow to each path i is:

$$p_i = \frac{\exp - \theta(C_i)}{\sum_j \exp - \theta(C_j)} \tag{1}$$

The flow on link a of user class m is;

$$c_a^m = \alpha^m c_a(x_a) \tag{2}$$

with corresponding link cost (for user class m), where the parameter is a scalar multiplying factor for the value of time for user class m, and is the common cost on link a (a function of the total flow on that link where $x_a = \sum_m x_a^m$).

It can be seen that the probability of a driver in class m being assigned to route i is:

$$p_i^m = \frac{\exp - \theta(C_i^m)}{\sum_{j,m} \exp - \theta(C_j^m)} \tag{3}$$

which is equivalent to:

$$p_i^m = \frac{\exp - \theta\alpha^m(C_i)}{\sum_{j,m} \exp - \theta\alpha^m(C_j)} \tag{4}$$

where each user class has a different value of the variability parameter.

In MUC models which include two or more user classes, each group is separately in equilibrium and at MUCSUE no user in any class can improve on their perceived travel cost by unilaterally changing routes.

This chapter is concerned with tolling different user classes at different rates, so will be considering the form of the model where cost functions are multiples of one another related to the value of time (i.e. cars, HGVs, Buses, exemptions) rather than considering the case for multiple users with or without route guidance.

3. Formulation of Stochastic Social Optimum with Multiple User Classes (MUCSSO)

Maher et al. (2005), defined the Stochastic Social Optimum as being that flow pattern where the Total Perceived Network Travel Cost would be minimized and demonstrated that this flow pattern could be produced under standard stochastic assignment techniques by applying Marginal Social Cost Price (MSCP) link tolls. Thus SUE + MSCP tolls produced the SSO. Whilst MSCP tolls also produced the solution where economic benefit was maximized, it was shown that other sets of tolls could produce the SSO flow pattern under SUE. In particular it is possible to find minimal revenue tolls that produce this effect (usually by mathematical programming methods). It might be desirable in the Multiple User Class case to assign different tolls to each user group so that the overall system has a combined desirable flow pattern.

Maher et al. (2005), derived an objective function for the SSO based on replacing unit-link costs with marginal link costs, which was seen to be analogous to the objective function for the SO in the deterministic case.

$$Z_{SUE}(\mathbf{x}) = -\sum_a \int_0^{x_a} c_a(u)\,du + \sum_a x_a c_a(x_a) - \sum_{rs} q_{rs} S_{rs}[\mathbf{c}(\mathbf{x})] \tag{5}$$

$$Z_{SSO}(\mathbf{x}) = -\sum_a \int_0^{x_a} m_a(u)\,du + \sum_a x_a m_a(x_a) - \sum_{rs} q_{rs} S_{rs}[\mathbf{m}(\mathbf{x})] \tag{6}$$

where at the SSO solution it is therefore the case that:

$$y_a(\mathbf{m}(\mathbf{x})) = x_a \ \forall \ a$$

where y_a are the auxiliary flows in a stochastic loading.

Maher and Hughes (1996) showed that the Sheffi and Powell (1982) objective function for SUE (5), could be easily extended to include MUCs as below;

$$Z_{MUCSUE}(\mathbf{x}) = -\sum_a \int_0^{x_a} c_a(u)du + \sum_a x_a c_a(x_a) - \sum_{rsm} q_{rsm} S_{rsm}[\mathbf{c}(\mathbf{x})] \qquad (7)$$

where the third term is summed over every user class m, so that q_{rsm} is the demand from origin r to destination s for user class m, and S_{rsm} is the expected minimum perceived cost (satisfaction) summed over the same. Thus the results of Maher et al. (2005) and Maher and Hughes (1996) may be combined to formulate an objective function for Stochastic Social Optimum with Multiple User Classes:

$$Z_{MUCSSO}(\mathbf{x}) = -\sum_a \int_0^{x_a} m_a(u)du + \sum_a x_a m_a(x_a) - \sum_{rsm} q_{rsm} S_{rsm}[\mathbf{m}(\mathbf{x})] \qquad (8)$$

where arguments regarding convexity are in direct analogy to those given in Maher et al. (2005) and where at the MUCSSO solution it is again the case that:
$$y_a(\mathbf{m}(\mathbf{x})) = x_a \qquad \forall\, a$$
where y_a are the auxiliary flows in a stochastic loading.
Thus the desired flow pattern at SSO may be determined by conducting a stochastic assignment where unit-link cost functions are replaced by marginal cost functions. Thus if the target solution is known it can then be replicated by tolling under SUE.

4. Tolling to Achieve Desired Flow Patterns under MUCSUE

It would be desirable to induce or approach 'System Optimizing' flow patterns under stochastic user equilibrium assignment with multiple user classes. Under deterministic assignment the System Optimal (SO) Solution where the Total Network Travel Cost (TNTC) is minimized is well established as being the 'desired' flow pattern, i.e. that which would give the most beneficial distribution of network flows. In the case of economic benefit maximization , marginal social cost price tolls (MSCP) may be applied to network links so that this SO is achieved. Under stochastic assignment though, the desired flow pattern is not immediately obvious. Two possible desired flow patterns have been suggested in the stochastic case: the SSO (Maher et al. 2005), where economic benefit is maximized and the Total Perceived Network Travel Cost (TPNTC) is minimized, and the 'True SO' where Total Network Travel Cost is minimized, i.e. the same SO flow pattern as in the deterministic case. Such a decision as to what flow pattern is desired would be made by the relevant planning team; in reality it is likely that a sub-optimal objective may be considered due to additional considerations, e.g. acceptability issues associated with 'high-cost' system optimizing tolls.

The toll level is also of interest; as in the single user class cases for either deterministic or stochastic modelling environments, it will be possible in the multiple user class case that other tolls than marginal social cost price tolls could be used to create certain desired flow patterns. It is of particular interest to investigate minimal revenue (or low revenue) toll sets as these may be derived to maintain zero-toll paths through the network which is beneficial from an equity perspective (Stewart 2007). MSCP tolls are also often rather high and there is some doubt that they would be implementable politically despite their theoretical economic benefit of forcing the user to pay the full cost of their externalities (Dial 1999; Newberry and Santos 2003; Wong et al. 2003). (Although there is also some evidence that MSCP-based pricing could be more acceptable if presented as part of a package of measures (Sikow-Magney 2003).)

In addition to the possible choice of toll level, there is the possibility in the MUC case to apply different tolling methodologies to different user groups. For instance it might be felt that it is politically unacceptable to charge ordinary motorists for the full cost of their externalities in the form of a toll and that it would be politically beneficial to extract only the smallest amount of revenue possible whilst still achieving an optimal re-routing through the network (i.e. minimal revenue tolling). However if a political objective was to encourage modal shift of freight from road to rail or waterways, then it might well be seen as beneficial to charge HGVs the full MSCP toll rate. Under MUCSUE because any individual modal class is independently in SUE it would be possible to charge one user group minimal revenue tolls and another marginal social cost price tolls and still maintain both the overall system and the individual user class flow patterns at the Stochastic Social Optimum flows. In addition it might be feasible to maintain the overall flow pattern as a System Optimal flow pattern, but to 'overcharge' one user group to 'subsidise' another user group to achieve this. This is discussed further in section 4.1.

It is also important in terms of tolling networks to consider that it will usually be deemed socially necessary to exempt certain user classes from paying any toll at all. It is likely that some 'ordinary' vehicles which would be assumed to form a single user class in terms of having the same generalized cost function, might nonetheless form separate user classes if some of those vehicles (for example, taxis, blue badge holders or certain residents) were required to be toll exempt. It could be possible to still achieve a desired optimizing (either SO or SSO) flow pattern, by charging the users who were not toll exempt a requisite amount more to compensate for the exemptions. This would essentially result in more tolled users having to deviate from their desired path while allowing the exempt drivers to essentially distribute themselves in Wardropian manner. These issues are illustrated in section 4.2.

It would also generally be considered desirable to exempt public service vehicles (buses etc.) from any network tolling scheme; these users would form a separate user group irrespective of any charge levied and would be expected to have a higher cost function than for a general motorist (to account for the higher occupancy levels). Buses however would be assumed to have fixed routes and not to be possible candidates for rerouting, so whilst their presence on their designated route will contribute to the cost on that link and affect the routing of other vehicles and consequently the toll levels required to provide the incentive for rerouting, they would not themselves be distributed according to flows on links. This issue is not explicitly examined in this chapter as the presence of fixed bus routes could be included in the free flow cost part of the generalized cost function, and consequently it would be unnecessary to model for such services in the same manner as for the other possible user classes mentioned.

For both the cases of HGV tolling and tolling with exempt vehicles (taxis/blue badges), tolling to achieve both the SO and the SSO is considered, as is the difference between MSCP-tolls and Minimal Revenue tolls.

4.1. Tolling HGVs and Cars

In considering the issue of charging using different tolling methodologies for charging ordinary vehicles (cars) and HGVs a simple two-link example (given in Figure 5.1 below) will be used for clarity and illustrative purposes. (In the UK context the M6-toll vs M6 could be represented by a simplified two-link network).

The following notation will be used; $(c_i, x_i, t_i$: link/path-costs, link/path-flows, link/path-tolls). There is a total demand of 1000 vehicles between origin 1 and destination 2.

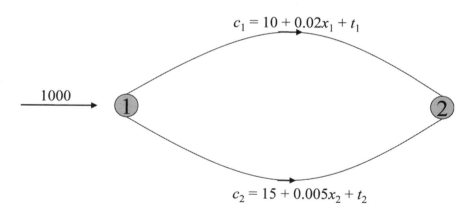

Figure 5.1   Two-link network

The demand of 1000 (which includes both user classes) must be split between the two paths, so

$$x_1 + x_2 = 1000$$

The flow on link a of user class m is x_a^m with corresponding link cost (for user class m):

$$c_a^m = \alpha^m c_a(x_a) \tag{2}$$

where the parameter α^m is a scalar multiplying factor for the value of time for user class m, and $c_a(x_a)$ is the common cost on link a (a function of the total flow on that link where $x_a = \sum_m x_a^m$).

For illustrative purposes it will be assumed that there are only two user classes, HGVs (h) and cars (c), logit-based SUE will be used with $\theta = 0.1$, $\alpha^c = 1$ and $\alpha^h = 2$ (HGVs are assumed to have double the generalized cost associated with them as that for the average car). A proportion P of all vehicles are HGVs, the rest are cars.

The probability of assigning flow to path 1 under logit SUE is:

$$p_1^c = \frac{1}{1 + \exp\theta(c_1^c - c_2^c)} \qquad p_1^h = \frac{1}{1 + \exp\theta(c_1^h - c_2^h)} \tag{9}$$

$$c_1^c - c_2^c = 0.025x_1 - 10 + T^c \qquad c_1^h - c_2^h = 2(0.025x_1 - 10) + T^h \tag{10}$$

Where for simplicity the single toll difference $T = t_1 - t_2$ may be determined for each user class.

After n iterations (when convergence is assumed to have occurred), the flow on path 1 may be expressed as;

$$x_1 = \frac{1000(1 - P)}{1 + \exp\theta(0.025x_1 - 10 + T^c)} + \frac{1000P}{1 + \exp\theta(2(0.025x_1 - 10) + T^h)} \tag{11}$$

At either of the desired flow patterns (SSO or SO) the link flows are easily determined for both the aggregate link flow and the individual user class flows. Thus assuming x_1 is known, T^c and T^h may be determined in relation to each other.

To achieve the SSO, MSCP tolls for each user class will produce the required toll differences, and in this two-link example minimal revenue tolls may be readily obtained by setting the lowest path toll for each user class to zero. MSCP tolls and Min Rev tolls to achieve the SSO are given in Table 5.1 below.

It can be seen that for both the MSCP and Min-Rev tolls the link tolls for the HGV user class will be twice the link tolls for cars as the generalized cost for HGVs was double that of cars. Whilst this gives the user class split on the two links as shown in the table, and will minimize the total network cost, there might

Table 5.1   SSO flows and associated MSCP and Min-Rev link tolls: TNTC = 19728

SSO	x_i^c	x_i^h	x_i	t_{mscp}^c	t_{mscp}^h	$t_{min-rev}^c$	$t_{min-rev}^h$
1	355.4	29.9	385.3	7.71	15.41	4.63	9.27
2	544.5	70.1	614.7	3.07	6.14	0	0
Revenue				4412	892	1646	277
Total Rev				5304		1923	

be a case for maintaining the flow split at the SSO on aggregate but relaxing the individual flow components of the split. For instance instead of charging HGVs twice the toll that is levied upon a car, there might be political justification to charge a higher multiple, or to fix the toll level for a car and produce an SSO flow pattern by re-routing the HGVs.

Table 5.2 shows the effect of minimal revenue tolling for both user classes, but redistributing the toll cost, so that the car toll is varying in fixed increments and the HGV toll is adjusted to ensure that the SSO aggregate flow pattern in Table 5.1 is maintained.

Table 5.2   MUC link tolls for HGV and cars to maintain SSO aggregate flow pattern

$t_{1\ fixed}^c$	$t_{1\ min-rev}^h$	x_i^c	x_i^h	x_i	Rev	TNTC
4.63	9.27	355.4	29.9	385.3	1923	19728
4.5	10.8	358.4	26.8	385.3	1902	19729
4	17.1	369.1	16.4	385.3	1756	19734
3.5	29.6	379.9	5.43	385.3	1491	19738
3.3	48.9	384.3	1.0	385.3	1317	19739

As may be seen from Table 5.2, the main justification for pursuing a toll strategy that heavily penalized HGVs with respect to cars would be to price them off a certain link. In the two-link example, by the time the car toll had been reduced to 3.3, an excessively high toll would be required to essentially remove all HGV traffic from link 1 if the desired SSO flow pattern was still to be replicated by the tolls.

Table 5.3   SO flows and associated Min-Rev link tolls: TNTC = 19557

SO	x_i^c	x_i^h	x_i	$t_{min-rev}^c$	$t_{min-rev}^h$
1	283	17	300	10.27	20.85
2	617	83	700	0	0
Revenue				2913	355
Total Rev				3268	

While the SSO flow pattern minimized perceived total network travel cost (PTNTC), it does not minimize 'actual' TNTC, which occurs at the flow pattern created at the deterministic SO solution. Table 5.3 above shows data for the 2-link network where minimal-revenue tolls have been placed on link 1 only for both HGV and cars to replicate the 'true' SO under MUCSUE.

It can be seen from Table 5.3 that the true SO does indeed give a lower value of TNTC, but at the expense of a required revenue to achieve that flow pattern which is about 2.5 times the revenue required to produce the stochastic system optimal flow pattern. Using Min-Rev tolls though to achieve the SO will give optimal re-routing benefit and is still less expensive to the users than marginal social cost pricing.

4.1. Tolling Exempt and Non-Exempt Vehicles

In the case where a certain proportion of vehicles are exempt from paying a toll, then the user class (or classes) which are being charged must bear the deficit and pay 'more than their fair share' of the toll costs if network optimality (either SO or SSO) is to be achieved.

In this case the link cost functions will be the same for each user class, the only difference in the second user class is that it is to be toll exempt (exempt = (e)). If equations 9–11 are revisited then we find:

The probability of assigning flow to path 1 under logit SUE is:

$$p_1^c = \frac{1}{1 + \exp\theta(c_1^c - c_2^c)} \qquad p_1^e = \frac{1}{1 + \exp\theta(c_1^e - c_2^e)} \tag{12}$$

$$c_1^c - c_2^c = 0.025x_1 - 10 + T^c \qquad c_1^e - c_2^e = 0.025x_1 - 10 \tag{13}$$

Where for simplicity the single toll difference $T = t_1 - t_2$ may be determined for the tolled user class (P = the proportion of exempt vehicles). After n iterations (when convergence is assumed to have occurred), the flow on path 1 may be expressed as:

$$x_1 = \frac{1000(1 - P)}{1 + \exp\theta(0.025x_1 - 10 + T^c)} + \frac{1000P}{1 + \exp\theta(0.025x_1 - 10)} \tag{14}$$

Again, for either of the desired flow patterns (SSO or SO) the link flows are easily determined for both the aggregate link flow and the individual user class flows. Thus assuming x_1 is known, a unique toll difference T^c may be determined.

Table 5.4 below shows some comparative data when $\theta = 0.1$ and $P = 0.1$, and Figures 5.2 and 5.3 show comparative graphs of the toll that would be required to be placed on link one to create SSO or SO flow patterns as θ and P both vary.

It can be seen from Table 5.4 that, as in the case of cars and HGVs a larger total toll revenue is required to be extracted to produce the SO flow pattern (TNTC minimized). The SSO flow pattern doesn't give the best network optimality, but comes at a greatly reduced cost which must be imposed upon the users.

Table 5.4   SSO and SO flows and associated Min-Rev link tolls

	$t^c_{1\ min-rev}$	x^c_1	x^e_1	x_1	Rev	TNTC
SSO	5.29	339.1	50.6	389.7	1794	17951
SO	12.4	244.0	56.0	300	3025	17750

It may be observed from the graphs that the tolls required to produce an SO flow pattern are roughly about twice as large as those required to produce an SSO flow pattern, from Table 5.4 for $\theta = 0.1$ and $P = 0.1$ the reduction in TNTC in attempting to achieve the SO rather than the SSO is only about 1% and probably not worth it. If in any situation it is desired to attempt to produce the maximum network benefit from re-routing, care must be taken when tolling to attempt to replicate the SO as whilst on some occasions with some networks it can be worthwhile, in others, such as the above example it is demonstrably not.

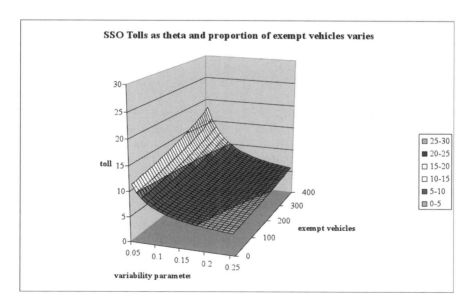

Figure 5.2   SSO: Min-Rev link tolls on link 1

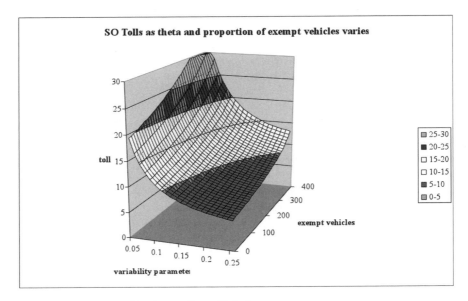

Figure 5.3   SO: Min-Rev tolls on link 1

It has been shown however that whatever the desired flow pattern it seems feasible to still obtain an optimized network with respect to re-routing, without needing to impose tolls on 100% of the traffic. If the minority were to be tolled and bear all the cost and the majority to be exempt, then as in the HGV and car example previously, it would not generally be possible to achieve this. Whilst the tolled traffic is the strong majority, it is feasible to still create optimal re-routings.

This chapter has used a two-link network rather than a more general network for ease of illustration. It is possible to extend the algebraic formulation to calculate sets of path-tolls differences in a similar manner, but owing to issues discussed more generally in Stewart and Maher (2006) it would be more sensible to calculate suitable link-tolls heuristically by extending the heuristic derived to do this in the single user class case (ibid.).

5. Summary

This chapter has discussed and illustrated some issues surrounding tolling when not every user class is to be tolled separately. The theoretical economics solution of applying MSCP tolls which forces users to pay for their full external costs are easy to calculate under MUCSUE when MUCSSO is the desired flow pattern. An objective function for MUCSSO, which follows naturally from previous work, has been presented.

It is possible in the MUC case (as in the single user class case) to find other tolls than the MSCP-tolls which still produce the MUCSSO. In the illustrative two-link example it was easy to derive minimal-revenue toll sets from MSCP-toll sets, but this is less trivial to do for a general network and will generally require either path-enumeration, mathematical programming or a heuristic method (such as presented in Stewart 2007). The feasibility of deriving toll sets to replicate the SO under MUCSUE was also established in the two-link case. It could be observed that whilst min-rev tolls to replicate the SO were more expensive to the users than those to replicate the SSO, they were still less expensive than the MSCP-tolls.

The case of one user class being toll exempt rather than having a different generalized cost function was then considered. Again it was feasible to create valid optimizing toll sets (for both SO and SSO) in this small example, but further work will need to be completed on more general networks.

Lastly it is clear that imposing tolls on a network will directly affect demand as well as being able to influence route choice. Elastic Demand (ED) may be readily included in stochastic equilibrium models (Maher and Hughes 1997), and in the SSO case, MSCP tolls may be derived by using marginal cost functions in an SUEED algorithm. Recent work (Stewart 2006) has extended the objective function for SSO to SSOED where elastic demand is included. It has also been shown that in the deterministic case with elastic demand, that all tolls (that would produce SOED under UEED) generate the same toll revenue, where SOED represents economic benefit maximization (Hearn and Yildirim 2002), and this result extends to tolling to achieve SSOED under SUEED. It is however possible to reduce the toll revenue required if the condition for economic maximization is relaxed, and a sub-optimal value of network demand may be permitted. Stewart and Maher (2005) present the case for seeking particular optimal flow solutions (for certain demand values) under SUEED with reduced revenue toll sets being applied.

It is of interest to allow for both MUCs and ED, and future work will combine the above results to present an objective function for MUCSSOED as an extension to that for MUCSUEED (Maher and Zhang 2000), and will further discuss the options for reduced revenue tolls to create MUCSSO solutions under MUCSUEED for particular values of demand. The possibility of allowing for zero tolled user classes will again be discussed.

References

Bergendorff, P., Hearn, D.W., Ramana, M.V. (1997), 'Congestion Toll Pricing of Traffic Networks, Network Optimization', in Pardalos, P., Hearn, D.W., Hager, W.W. (eds), *Lecture Notes in Economics and Mathematical Systems* Vol. 450, (Springer-Verlag), pp. 51–71.

Conners, R., Sumalee, A. and Watling, D. (2005), 'Equitable Network Design', *Journal of the Eastern Asia Society for Transport Studies* 6:1382–97.

Daganzo, C.F. (1982), 'Unconstrained extremal formulation of some transportation equilibrium problems', *Transportation Science*, 16(3): 332–60.

Dial, R.B. (1999). 'Minimal-revenue congestion pricing part I: A fast algorithm for the single origin case', *Transportation Research B*, 33(3): 189–202.

Dial, R.B. (2000), 'Minimal-revenue congestion pricing part II: An efficient algorithm for the general case', *Transportation Research Part B* 34(8): 645–65.

Hearn, D.W. and Yildirim, M.B. (2002). 'A Toll Pricing Framework for Traffic Assignment Problems with Elastic Demand', in M. Gendreau and P. Marcotte (eds), *Current Trends in Transportation and Network Analysis: Papers in Honor of Michael Florian*, (Kluwer Academic Publishers), 135–45.

Maher, M.J. and Hughes, P.C. (1996), 'Estimation of the potential benefit from an ATT system using a multiple user class stochastic user equilibrium assignment model', in Stephanedes, Y.J. and Filippi F. (eds), *Applications of Advanced Technologies in Transportation Engineering* (American Society of Civil Engineers), 700–704.

Maher, M.J. and Hughes P.C. (1997), 'An algorithm for SUEED stochastic user equilibrium with elastic demand', Presented at the 8th IFAC Symposium on Transportation Systems, Chania, Crete.

Maher, M.J. (1998), 'Algorithms for logit-based stochastic user equilibrium assignment', *Transportation Research B* 32(8): 539–50.

Maher, M.J. and Zhang, X. (2000), 'Formulation and algorithms for the problem of stochastic user equilibrium assignment with elastic demand', in Proceedings of the 8th Euro Working Group Meeting on Transportation, Rome, September 2000.

Maher, M.J., Stewart, K. and Rosa, A. (2005), 'Stochastic Social Optimum Traffic Assignment', *Transportation Research B* 32(8), 753–67.

Newbery, D. and Santos, G. (2003), 'Cordon tolls in eight English towns: theory simulations and impacts', in Proceedings of The Theory and Practice of Congestion Charging: An International Symposium, Imperial College London.

Sikow-Magny, C. (2003), 'Efficient Pricing in Transport-overview of European Commissions's Transport Research Programme', in Schade, J. and Schlag, B. (eds), *Acceptability of Transport Pricing Strategies* (Oxford: Elsevier), pp. 13–26.

Stewart, K. and Maher, M.J. (2005), 'Minimal Revenue Network Tolling: System Optimisation under Stochastic Assignment with Elastic Demand', 4th IMA International Conference on Mathematics in Transport, 7–9 September 2005, University College London.

Stewart, K. (2006), 'Minimal Revenue Network Tolling: stochastic social optimisation under stochastic assignment with elastic demand', 38th Annual Conference of the University Transport Study Group, Trinity College, Dublin, 4–6 January 2006.

Stewart, K. and Maher, M.J. (2006), 'Minimal revenue network tolling: system optimisation under stochastic assignment', in Hearn D.W., Lawphongpanich S., and Smith, M. (eds), *Mathematical and Computational Models for Congestion Charging, Applied Optimization*, Vol 101 (New York, Springer).

Stewart, K. (2007), 'Tolling traffic links under stochastic assignment: modelling the relationship between the number and price level of tolled links and optimal traffic flows', *Transportation Research A: Policy and Practice* 41(7): 644–54.

Van Vuren, T. and Watling, D. (1991), 'Multiple user class assignment model for route guidance', *Transportation Research Record* 1306, 22–32.

Wong, S.C., Ho, H.W., Yang, H. and Loo, B. (2003), 'The first-best and cordon-based second-best congestion pricing in a continuum traffic equilibrium system', Proc. The Theory and Practice of Congestion Charging: An International Symposium, Imperial College London.

Chapter 6

The Network Society and the Networked Traveller

Kay W. Axhausen, John Urry and Jonas Larsen

1. 'Networked' Everything

Since the late 1990s the word 'network' has become a buzzword, which is being used to add interest, even when the context is divorced from the technical meaning of the term: a set of entities linked by identifiable bonds, e.g. intersections by roads, airports by scheduled flights, telephone exchanges by cables, persons by common descent, joint activity or a common history. Still, this usage reflects that many commentators need a shorthand to characterise a now clearly noticeable shift in the economic and social structure of their societies (see for example Castells 1996; 1997; 1998; Friedman 2005 or Barabasi 2002). The ongoing reduction in the costs of travel (see below) and the even steeper reduction of telecommunication costs (see below) have allowed the individual to decouple itself in many aspects of daily life from its immediate local environment. The individual was formerly not so aware of the networked nature of its social and commercial life, as it shared many, maybe most partners with those around it. The individual has now become aware that its network – more likely, than not – is rather different from the one of its physical neighbours. These individualised networks of contacts justify the description of today's travellers as *networked travellers*, even more so as they rely heavily on technological networks and the services on them to build, maintain or restructure their private and commercial social networks. They own networking tools including cars and bicycles (for road travel), season tickets and discount/ loyalty cards for reduced price public transport travel (land and air), land line and mobile phones, computers and internet access facilities and rights (cable and wireless). They are likely to build and maintain private home pages, profiles on social networking web sites, address books and link collections. They may publish web logs and share photographs through publicly-accessible websites.

The networked travellers, as a rule, do not form communities with their neighbours any more. They share the same public and semi-public spaces[1] around their front door, but it is unlikely that their networks of friends, acquaintances, work colleagues, fellow parishioners etc. will overlap. They might not even know

---

1   Hallways, atriums, gardens, parking lots and other facilities operated for the benefit of a group of owners and their tenants.

their neighbours.[2] The literature on neighbourhood assumes that spatial vicinity is matched by social vicinity, as it would be produced if the memberships of the residents' social networks would substantially overlap (see Day 2006 for a comprehensive literature review). Lloyd challenges this myth already in 1984, when he writes:

> as the late Philip Abrams (1980) so cogently argued, we still carry an image of the traditional community – a 'densely woven world of kind neighbours, friends and co-workers, highly localized and strongly caring within the confines of quite tightly defined relationships'. But such communities were the response to poverty and insecurity now hopefully abolished in western urban industrial society ..... .

Still, this view of the social world still seems to be prevalent in many policy discussions, especially in transport and urban planning. This chapter will reinforce this old message in its empirical part and then discuss the policy implications of the associated spatially-distributed social capital of the networked traveller in the network society. Drawing on a new survey undertaken at ETH the following section will show how large the distances between our respondents and their important contacts are. This will be supplemented by information about the spatial distribution of the membership of Swiss service clubs. The main section will then discuss the interactions between policies to increase the generalised costs of contact and the spatial distribution of social contacts and what policy implications derive from these interactions.

Before this discussion, the chapter will offer an argument why industrializing countries have for the last 200 years pursued investment strategies, which as an unintended side effect have dissolved the once spatially dense and socially tight neighbourhoods and villages (see Figure 6.1). The link between the economies of scale and scope and welfare, as measured in market prices of goods, had been highlighted by A. Smith in 1776, a time when the positive effects of road and canal construction had already been amply demonstrated in the Netherlands, France and the UK (see for example Vries and Van der Woude 1997). These facilities enabled the larger market areas, which are a necessary precondition for those larger or more specialised firms especially if society wants to avoid detrimental spatial monopolies, or does not want to rely on population growth alone. They enable these larger market areas by lowering the generalised costs of travel and transport. The virtuous cycle between increased scale and higher gross domestic product and therefore larger investment capital for transport facilities and the associated lower generalised costs of travel and transport has been maintained since. The investment takes two forms: the industrialised societies have invested

---

2   In the UK General Household Survey 2000/01 47% claimed to know most or many of the neighbours of their street or block (See www.esds.ac.uk for access to the data and simple tabulations from it). The questions did not specify the meaning of 'know'.

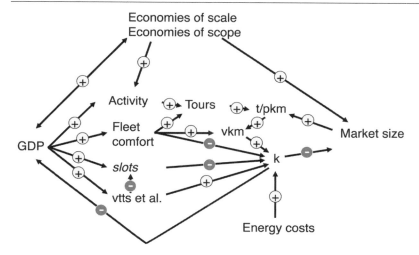

k: Generalised costs of travel; slot: Time-space window allocated to a movement on the available infrastructure or the services operated on them; vtts: Value of travel time savings

Figure 6.1   Qualitative model of market size for goods and services

in more slots[3] to move persons and goods, more direct and with more reserve capacities by building infrastructures. Prime examples are the various national freeway systems built since the 1950s, the Japanese and European national high speed rail systems and, finally, expanded regional commuter rail networks. The extensive empirical literature on the productivity effects cannot be reviewed here, but see Graham 2007; Axhausen and Tschopp 2007 or Shirley and Winston 2004 for recent examples. Societies collectively, in the case of public transport, and individuals personally have invested in larger, faster and more comfortable vehicle fleets. Mass motorization is the prime example of this transformation.

   This positive feedback loop is dampened by a lag between the growth in demand and the growth in the supply of slots. The increase in market size and area produces increases in ton and person kilometres and, in conjunction with the increase in fleet size, more than proportional increases in vehicle kilometres. Without rationing or pricing the resulting competition for the existing slots results in congestion and higher generalised costs of travel. This congestion is perceived more acutely as time goes by, as the travellers' willingness to pay for travel time savings grows (vtts) with their average real incomes.

---

   3   The transport infrastructure provides slots for moving persons and vehicles. For air traffic, rail roads and canal ships these slots are explicit and familiar, but they occur also in road traffic through traffic lights, and they are self organised whenever pedestrians, cyclists and car drivers interact and compete for road space.

1950	2000

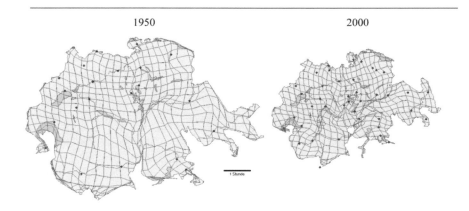

Figure 6.2   Road travel time – scaled maps of Switzerland (same scale for both year)

Maps: Axhausen, Dolci, Fröhlich, Scherer and Carosio (2006); the highway investment has halved the size of the country in terms of travel time.

This ever growing market size has not been confined to the traded goods. The residents of this shrinking world (See Figure 6.2 for the example of Switzerland since 1950) have adjusted their residential location to obtain better and more housing on larger lots outside the urban cores. They have used their ever cheaper cars (See Figure 6.3 for the quality adjusted prices of Swiss cars) to travel and to migrate, for example for a better education or for a better employer. The even more dramatic fall in telecommunication costs (See Figure 6.4 for the US long distance market) has been the basis for maintaining contact with those left behind after one of those moves. The next section will show what is currently known about the spatial distribution of persons known and important to the average person today.

2. Current Knowledge about the Social Network Geographies

The networked travellers have to maintain their social networks by remaining in contact with those persons who are important to them, or with whom they want to spend time (see below for a detailed discussion of social capital). One of the best known sociologists of social networks, Barry Wellman, has recently admitted that there is very little literature on the spatial distribution of the members of social networks (Mok and Wellman 2007):

> To the best of our knowledge, this is the first study that systematically examines the role of distance in social networks in an era after the advent of cars, phones and planes but before the coming of the Internet (and other new media, such as mobile phones).

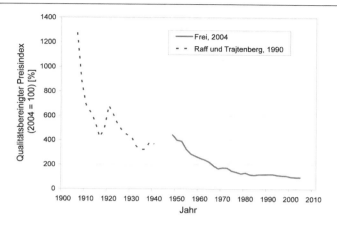

**Figure 6.3   Quality adjusted 2004 purchase prices for private cars
1906–2004**

Data: Frei (2005) for Switzerland 1950–2004; Raff and Trajtenberg (1985) for the USA
1906–1940. The Swiss time is very likely underestimating the drop in the quality adjusted
prices since 1985, as appropriate time series data on vehicle electronics were not available
for analysis.

In this paper he and his co-author analyse a small sample of 29 egocentric social
networks, which had been geocoded in the 1979 data which had sat idle since
then. The work since then has focused on convenience samples based on prior
data sets collected for other purposes (See Mok and Wellman 2007 for examples
from the literature) or employs very rough categorizations of distance, such as
'same neighbourhood, same city, same country, abroad'. Another example, also
based on an administrative sample, is the membership of the Swiss affiliates of an
international service club. Such clubs have the mission to recruit locally and one
would expect their members to live close to the location of their weekly meeting.
The analysis shows that the mean distances involved can be substantial and that
even these archetypically parochial clubs are quasi-regional institutions today.
In many clubs members have to travel on average about 10 km to their weekly
meetings.

In a 2006 survey, Frei and Axhausen have collected information about nearly
300 ego-centric social networks from a representative sample of Kanton Zürich
residents (See Larsen, Urry and Axhausen 2006 for qualitatively similar results
based on a much smaller sample of interviews) Axhausen, Frei and Ohnmacht
2006 describe the survey method and provide some initial modelling results. The
respondents were asked to report both the persons, who are socially and emotionally
important for them, also those with whom they spend leisure time. The survey
mixed a face-to-face interview (about 60 minutes) and with a self-completion

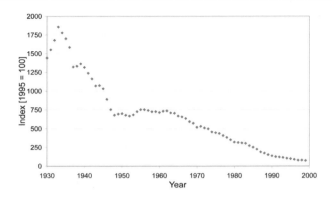

Adapted from FCC, 2001

**Figure 6.4   Real costs of US interstate and international telephone calls
             1930–2000**

Note: Adapted from FCC, 2001.

questionnaire, which the respondents returned after the interview. They reported
twelve contacts on average, whose home addresses were geocoded at the level of
municipality or postal code, which is rather detailed in the Swiss context, where
the average population of a municipality is only 2,500 residents.

The distribution of the great-circle-distances (Figure 6.5) between the
respondents and their contacts has two parts: a 'local' mass, i.e. inside the
municipality or postal code of about ⅓ of the contacts: and an approximately
lognormal part with a discontinuity due to intercontinental contacts. The scale
and reach is impressive. The respondents generally combine local with non-local
contacts (Figure 6.6), which reflects the need and desire for sociability in the
vicinity of the home. The share of respondents, who have only local contacts,
is small, 8%; even with a wider definition (up to 20% non-local contacts) the
share grows only to 15%. Slightly less rare are respondents who have only non-
local contacts (5% or 12% for the wider definition of 80% and more non-local
contacts). When one considers that the postal code covers areas larger then the
'neighbourhood' of urban planning, then one can see, that the imagined community
of the neighbourhood is unlikely today (See Campell and Lee 1992 for a 1988 US
survey with documents about 15 known neighbours; or Campell 1990 for a 1939
US survey, in which the respondents could still identify 32 neighbours on their
residential block; see Crow, Allan and Summers (2002) for a qualitative study of
today's rather non-involved neighbouring style; for neighbouring in the context of
a 'netville' see Hampton and Wellman (2001 and 2003).

The number of face-to-face visits drops exponentially with the distance to the
contacts (Figure 6.7), which reflects both the time and monetary costs of long-

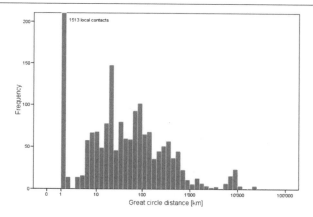

Figure 6.5   Distribution of great circle distances between the respondents and their contacts

Note: The great circle distance accounts for the spherical shape of earth. Distances between local contacts were coded as 1 km.

distance travel, especially for intercontinental travel. Nevertheless, even these intercontinental journeys occur regularly and one can assume that they are of relatively long duration. The phone and asynchronous contacts (email and short text messages (SMS) show a much slower distance decay due their lower costs, but also due to the reduced needs to co-ordinate and to debrief fewer joint meetings. (See Axhausen and Frei 2008 for an initial formal model of these processes).

Given the number and spatial distribution of personal contacts it is not surprising, that about 40% of travel and of kilometres travelled are classified as leisure in official statistics (See the tables in Larsen, Urry and Axhausen 2006). But leisure travel is dominated by being with and meeting other people, as can be easily seen in Figure 6.8, which shows how many persons travel with the respondents on their way to various types of leisure activities.

3. Hypotheses about Travel and Social Capital

The evidence presented so far has clearly shown that the public is generally not living local lives, but lives which involve contacts across a wide range of spatial scales. They construct these networks over the course of their lives from the friendships, 'colleagueships' and contacts they are able to form and to maintain. Ascribed contacts such as family and work clearly play a role, but they do not dominate. Local contacts are sought, but they are not central to the networks. The networks are generally not strongly overlapping, but distinct, especially those not involving contacts from school or work (see also Hogan, Carrasco and Wellman,

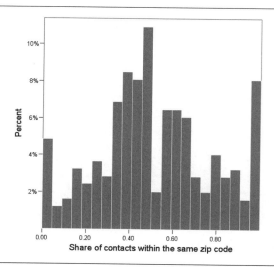

Figure 6.6   Share of respondents with a given share of contacts among all contacts within their residential postal code or municipality

2007). These networks, these contacts are valuable to and are esteemed by the persons involved.

One short hand term for this value is *social capital*. The view of social capital taken here is different from much of the literature. It is close to the conceptualization of Völker, Flap and Lindenberg (2006). The literature as reviewed by Lin (1999), Burt (2000) or Sobel (2002) emphasise the benefits, but not the joint action required to produce these benefits. Sobel (2002) begins his paper with:

> Social capital describes circumstances in which individuals can use membership in groups and networks to secure benefits.

Lin (1999) contrasts two views. The structural view, also endorsed by Burt (2000) or Granovetter (1973), locates social capital in the brokerage available to persons occupying 'structural holes' in a network, i.e. those who provide the links between otherwise distinct subgroups. The alternative view, attributed by Lin to Coleman and Bourdieu, emphasizes mutual recognition, trust and solidarity in a group. Taking Grieco (1987, 1996) as a starting point, social capital is defined here as the

> Stock of joint abilities, shared histories, understandings and commitments enabling the skilled performance of joint activity, even at a distance

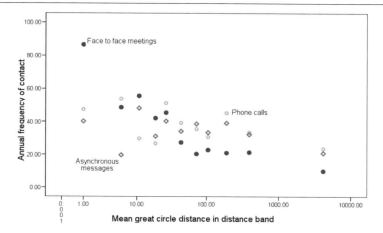

Asynchronous messages comprise here SMS or "texting" (short message service) and email

Figure 6.7　**Average number of annual contacts by distance and mode of contact**

Note: Asynchronous messages comprise here SMS or 'texting' (short message service) and mail.

of a pair or larger number of persons. In contrast to discussions of human capital or team work, the range of activity is not limited here to gainful employment, but explicitly includes activity which is purely social, enjoyable and hedonic. The return on this social capital is the above average enjoyment, monetary gain, speed of the joint performance in comparison to the conduct of the activity with a randomly selected person, even a randomly-selected person trained for the specific activity. In this sense, it is a true capital, i.e. a stock of past achievement and work, stored and put to use in future activity.

This definition sees social capital in the first instance as a private good. Other members of the social networks to which a particular pair or group of persons belong might not be aware of the social capital available to a particular member. Even if they are aware of it, the type and strength of their link with the person concerned might not be strong enough to claim access to that social capital or connection. The management of such claims rests with the persons who have built their social capital through joint action and thinking. On the other hand, the joint awareness of the social capital available and accessible within a group committed to certain goals enables effective joint action of the group as a whole. The trade in favours, support and information, to which social capital is reduced in the colloquial use of the term, has to be seen as a by-product of the maintenance of the social capital as defined above. It is the oil which smoothes the joint performance

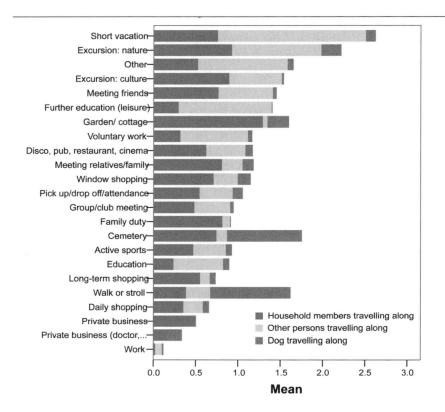

Figure 6.8   Mean number of persons travelling with the respondents of the 2003 Thurgau six-week travel diary survey by type of leisure

Note: See Löchl, Schönfelder, Schlich, Buhl, Widmer and Axhausen (2005) for the data

needed to maintain the social capital.[4] It has to be stressed that this view of social capital implies on-going engagement of the persons involved as one has to assume that the skills atrophy when not exercised regularly (see below).

This private good perspective of social capital sits uneasily with the term 'social'. It can become social only to the extent that an ascribed group, such as for example family, church, party,[5] neighbourhood, local government, can claim access to its members› social capital through appeals to their loyalty to the group or idea.

---

4   Networks of patronage, actually hierarchies of patronage are different, because they are based on trading favours (money, employment, permits, etc.) against political support (inside the firm or for public office), but do not imply joint action.

5   To the extent that children grow into the religious and ideological affiliations of their parents.

It can become social also through the voluntary pooling in voluntary organizations. Employers are normally strictly limited to the commercially-relevant parts of their employees' social capital. Trust in the intentions and reciprocity of the others is crucial for the pooling of social capital, as otherwise free riding will undermine the willingness of the group members to participate in medium term.

It is clear that social capital as defined above does not require the spatial proximity of the actors involved. It requires regular joint activity, but not co-presence. Still, many activities require co-presence (as discussed in Larsen, Urry, Axhausen 2006) It is reasonable to assume, that social capital has 'economies of scope', through which an initial endowment provides the basis for a larger range of joint activities and therefore skills, making the inclusion of activities requiring co-presence more likely. Nevertheless, social capital does not require trust between the parties, i.e. confidence that the other party will keep the first party's interests in mind and will act selflessly on it (see Seligman 2000). This is especially true, when the range of joint activity is limited in scope and overall importance.

The social capital structures are predicated on the current structures of the generalized costs of travel and contact and the associated distribution of population, employment and activity opportunities. See Axhausen 2007 and 2006 for an argument about the underlying dynamics between social networks and the generalized cost of travel and contact. The key results for the policy discussion here are the following hypotheses:

H1: The size and spread of the social network geographies is inversely proportional to the generalised cost of travel and contact

and the associated subhypothesis:

H1.1: The duration of a face-to-face contact will be proportional to the generalized costs involved, but with marginal decreases in the increased duration.

H2: Given the current levels of social capital any increase in the generalized costs of travel will be generally ignored in the short run and will only become visible in the observed sizes of the social network geographies after some time, i.e. a hysterisis pattern of initially slow change followed by fast decrease later will be observed

and the associated subhypothesis:

H2.1 the selectivity of the contacts will become higher, i.e. the persons will focus on those with whom they are linked with high levels of social capital. These contacts could be anywhere.

Given the level of technological development of the electronic means of communication, one can safely assume that it will be impossible to increase the user costs of electronic communications, short of a massive destruction of existing capacities, especially of fibre optic cables and antennae towers. In all likelihood, in the medium term all charging systems for private use will adopt a fixed-fee approach for the provision of the requested capacity (number of slots) and pay-per-use will disappear.

4. Policy Implications

Against the background of global warming (see for example the recent Stern Report to the British government[6]), the concerns about social exclusion (see for example Raje et al. 2004 or Begg et al. 2001), but also economic development (see the recent Eddington report,[7] also to the British government), professional opinion expects that government policy will aim to stop the virtuous cycle sketched above selectively by trying to decouple economic and travel demand growth in general, while helping population groups and regions which are at a disadvantage (for a literature review of this idea, see for example Schneider et al. 2006 or McKinnon 2007). This vision is complemented by sectoral politics aiming at the reduction of the specific energy consumption and CO_2 emissions of transport. While the policy mix will vary from country to country and from location to location, it is likely that it will involve direct rationing or pricing of CO_2 emissions, regulatory approaches to fleet consumption, efforts to reduce the spatial reach of economic activity, investment in public transport, cycling and walking, densification of housing and higher specifications for housing with regards to energy consumption. While it is unclear if this policy mix is the most efficient, or even if decoupling is a reasonable goal as such, current public opinion seems to favour such an approach. The alternative approach of providing capacity where visibly needed, and lowering the generalized costs of travel further through investment in speed and accessibility, while enforcing CO_2 reduction and energy savings goals through dedicated and offset taxes, seems less likely to be adopted.

Before analysing how the structures of the network geographies discussed above would interact with these policies it is worth highlighting some of their implications under current conditions. The possibility to maintain contacts over long distances should increase the selectivity of them, while increasing their payoffs. It will also reduce the willingness to engage new contacts locally or elsewhere. New contacts are investments of time, money and social capital opportunity costs with an uncertain payoff. In the past the costs of long distance travel and communication forced people to adjust their circle of contacts. As

---

    6   www.hm-treasury.gov.uk/independent_reviews/stern_review_economics_climate_change/stern_review_report.cfm.

    7   www.hm-treasury.gov.uk/media/39A/41/eddington_execsum11206.pdf.

everybody was subject to these constraints, new opportunities arose for everyone, especially in the more fluid social environment of the city. Today the archetypal, but limited opportunities for such enforced new contact formation are change of school, military service, start of university, change of work, the parents of the class mates one's children.[8]

In an environment where most residents have the bulk of their social contacts beyond the municipal boundary of their place of residence, it will become more difficult to recruit competent persons for local office. The attachment of the residents is likely to be less to the place of residence, but to the region, which generally captures most of their contacts and of their daily life. In this environment it will be difficult to initiate and sustain local political or civic action, unless there is a clear and present localized danger, such as a new road, rail line or other nuisance.

To the extent that such a national and international contact network becomes the accepted desirable social norm it defines high levels of skill in terms of foreign language acquisition, confidence and ability to negotiate the transport system and initially unfamiliar environments, in addition to the time and money required for travel and subsistence. For those unable or excluded from the acquisition of these resources the non-local orientation of their physical neighbours excludes them from their daily life and reduces their possibility of interaction and therefore of social capital creation.

For the bulk of the residents the immediate environment around their residence is populated by strangers. While in countries with strong residential sorting by income and ethnicity the residents can assume that their neighbours should be very likely very similar in attitudes and socio-demographic circumstance, they do remain mostly strangers. (See for example Blakely and Snyders 1997 and Low 2003 for the ambivalence of 'community' in gated developments). Many residents respond to this situation with feelings of insecurity and fear. One could label this condition *localised anomie*, as the persons are well integrated on the regional and larger scale, but disoriented and without many local links in the residential environment. The response to this feeling is investment in personal safety, e.g. reinforcement of doors, alarms and intruder detection systems, private security forces in gated developments or co-operative buildings, avoidance of walking and cycling. Given the lack of local support from their networks, the residents will have to rely on commercial and government-sponsored services in case of need: from the trivial watering of flowers to home care during an illness or after an accident. The freedom from the social control of the neighbours comes at a cost in times of crisis.

The policy mix chosen to implement the goals mentioned above will involve different types of measures, which will be discussed in turn. The focus will not be on their likely success or the size of their contribution to the problem to be

---

8   The linkages and information flows between urban dog owners created by the affinities of their dogs would be an interesting issue, as these are independent of the social standing of the owners.

solved, but how they will interact with current social network structures and what additional policies might have to be developed to balance the negative effects of these interactions.

The extensive literature on the interaction between spatial form and travel behaviour shows, in simplifying summary, that density in conjunction with local services encourages walking and cycling, but will not change total vehicle mileage much (e.g. Cao, Mokhtarian and Handy 2007; Simma and Axhausen 2004 or Boarnet and Crane 2001). In none of this work, nor in the extensive writing of the New Urbanists (e.g. Congress for New Urbanism 2000) is the scale of the residents' social network geographies discussed or in the modelling work controlled for. While the feeling of local trust and safety is discussed, it is not operationalized for an analysis of its effects. In the first instance one would not expect that densification policies, such as infill development, easier permissions for mixed housing and commercial developments or additional floors on existing structures, have an impact on the social network geographies, as they would not change the overall cost structure of travel and communication. The resistance against such policies should provide a short-term focus for the joint action of the residents. It is unclear how much new local social capital such an effort would build and how long it would be maintained by the residents. The increased walking and cycling will improve local exposure, but the current style of managing retailing and entertainment venues is not conducive to building local social capital, as the managers are generally not local residents, nor are they owners and therefore less likely to engage with the local customers through credit or social interaction beyond the store (See Rae 2003 for an absorbing and detailed description of the opposite conditions in New Haven before 1930).

The accelerated adoption of energy saving and CO_2 reducing technologies through regulation, tax write offs or direct subsidy will interact with the social network geographies only to the extent that they change the budget constraints of the residents or the marginal costs of travel. It is hard to envision that the transition to natural gas and later fuel cell vehicles will not be buffered by subsidies, as it already happened during the much cheaper adoption of catalytic converters (See Frick, Carle, Wokaun and Axhausen 2007 for the related issue of funding the refuelling infrastructures required for the new fuels). The additional degrees of freedom of the vehicle owners (reduction in the power, weight and size of the vehicles owned; car sharing) will allow them to maintain the same level of transport services without increases in expenditure. If the shift will not be buffered by subsidies, then it will be worth considering measures to encourage formal or informal shared car ownership through a selective subsidy in the form of reduced cost parking provisions.

An increase in fuel taxation via a CO_2 tax will be part of either style of policy package. While it will have less of an impact in Europe, where the increase will be on top of an already high base, it will be rather noticeable in the US or other low fuel tax countries. It is reasonable to assume that the increase will be balanced through tax reductions elsewhere, especially car ownership taxation or income tax. As all consumption taxes, it will be regressive, as lower income residents tend to buy cheaper cars and pay little or no income taxes. The higher marginal costs will affect them more than higher-income residents, but even those will change their behaviour as their expenditures are now more tightly tied to car use. The rebalancing of the tax load reduces the sunk cost effect of the upfront payments associated with car use (ownership taxation, insurance, leasing rates, one-off purchase costs). A general shift to pay-as-you-drive insurance will reinforce the effect.[9] The same holds for any taxation policy which recovers the currently untaxed benefits of company cars more fully.

One would expect *ceteris paribus* both a reduction in total mileage driven and a more than proportional reduction in longer journeys with cars and planes, as the fuel costs become more prominent for these journeys. This response requires an adjustment in the social capital renewal strategies. Initially, one would expect that contacts further away will be visited less frequently but for longer. The persons might also make increasing use of side trips associated with professional travel. If the railways are able to absorb their higher energy costs better, or if they are exempted from the CO_2 taxation, they should be able to encourage visits along their corridors, especially high speed corridors. In the long run, one would expect that the travellers adjust their social network geographies by reducing their size.

Public policy could reduce the costs in the first phase by providing more long weekends, which are already extensively used today for visiting friends and relatives. If they already exist but are concentrated in certain times of the year, it would be worth redistributing them around the year to provide more flexibility and steadiness. The UK 'bank holidays' are a good example in comparison with bunching of holidays before and after Easter in many other European countries.

In the longer run, public policy should increase the support of the formation of local and regional social capital in areas of legitimate public interest, such as politics, sport, arts, traditional festivities and customs through the support of the organizations behind these activities. Beyond these domains, it could support meeting points through appropriate land use regulation and use regimes, which rebalance the needs of the neighbours of such meeting places with the needs of their visitors and users. Putnam, Feldstein and Cohen (2003), describe a range of successful initiatives of building local social capital trough organizing, sometimes sponsored by local government, sometimes by foundations or religious institutions. See Venkatesh (2006) though for the difficulties of successful organizing in poor neighbourhoods with insufficient internal resources.

The final policy, which is likely to be introduced in both approaches, is revenue-neutral traffic demand management. This policy reflects the inherent difficulties of adding slots and capacity in an urban environment, in which the residents affected by the additional externalities of such new infrastructures tend to have strong levers in the planning systems to stop, delay or redesign such a project

---

9   See for example www.norwichunion.com/pay-as-you-drive for the UK market, but similar schemes are offered in Italy and elsewhere.

(See Flyvberg et al. 2003, for the typical cost inflation in large scale infrastructure projects, which are partially due to such politically necessary, but initially unacknowledged adjustments of the projects). One would expect similar effects as with carbon taxation, but less pronounced, as the travellers can additionally adjust the timing of their activities. On the other hand, the time-space regime of societies is rather rigid in the short term, so that not all adjustment will be easily possible. Public policy could support the adjustment process by the liberalization of opening hours, the extension of opening hours of public institutions, appropriate regulatory frameworks and infrastructures for delivery services and by providing as much flexibility in employment regulations as is compatible with the productivity of the firms (encouragement of job sharing, telework, part-time work etc.).

5. Conclusions

This discussion has shown that the current spatial distribution of social capital limits the speed with which citizens can adjust their behaviour to policy initiatives currently contemplated to achieve the policy goals of the reduced social exclusion, fewer greenhouse gas emissions and improved welfare. The expected impact on these structures may very well make the citizens unwilling to see these policies adopted in the first place. In the referendum-driven politics of Switzerland, for example, this concern would limit the willingness of the national government to put such ideas forward. The policies needed to address or reduce these concerns are all outside transport policy proper. Transport policy makers will have to enlarge the scope of their policy making and find new partners if they want to be successful in their core mission: the provision of a transport system which provides the services needed for everyone at minimum social cost.

6. Acknowledgements

This chapter benefited from the hospitality of the Technion, Haifa and its staff during the first author's stay as a Lady Day Visiting professor during the spring of 2007. Some of the ideas were discussed during a Department of Geography seminar at the Hebrew University, Jerusalem. The support and input of Professors Yoram Shiftan (Technion), Eran Feitelson and Ilan Saloman (Hebrew Universtiy) is gratefully acknowledged, as are the comments of the anonymous referee.

References

Abrams, P. (1980), 'Social change, social networks and neighbourhood care', *Social Work Service*, 22(1): 12–20.

Axhausen, K.W. (2006), 'Social factors in future travel: A qualitative assessment', *IEE Proceedings Intelligent Transport Systems*, 153(2) 156–66.

Axhausen, K.W. (2007), 'Activity spaces, biographies, social networks and their welfare gains and externalities: Some hypotheses and empirical results', *Mobilities*, 2(1): 15–36.

Axhausen, K.W. and Frei, A. (2008), 'Contacts in a shrunken world', paper presented at the 87th Annual Meeting of the Transportation Research Board, Washington D.C., January 2008.

Axhausen, K.W., Frei, A. and Ohnmacht, T. (2006), 'Networks, biographies and travel: First empirical and methodological results', paper presented at the *11th International Conference on Travel Behaviour Research*, Kyoto, August 2006.

Axhausen, K.W., Dolci, C., Fröhlich, Ph., Scherer, M. and Carosio, A. (2006), 'Constructing time-scaled maps: Switzerland 1950 to 2000, *Arbeitsberichte Verkehr und Raumplanung*, 342 (Zürich: IVT, ETH Zürich).

Barabasi, A.L. (2002) *Linked: How Everything Is Connected to Everything Else and What It Means* (New York: Plume).

Begg, I., Berghman, J., Chassard, Y., Kosonen, P., Kongshåj-Madsen, P., Matsaganis, M., Mayes, D., Muffels, R., Salais, R. and Tsakloglou, P. (2001), 'Social exclusion and social protection in the European Union: Policy issues and proposals for the future role of the EU', (London: South Bank University).

Blakely, E. and Snyders, M.G. (1997), *Fortress America* (Washington D.C.: Brookings Institution).

Boarnet, M.G. and Crane, R. (2001), *Travel by Design: The Influence of Urban Form on Travel* (Oxford: Oxford University Press).

Burt, R. (2000), 'The network structure of social capital', in Staw, B. and Sutton, R. (eds), *Research in Organizational Behaviour* Vol. 22 (New York: JAI Press), pp. 345–423.

Campell, K.E. (1990), 'Networks past: A 1939 Bloomington neighbourhood', *Social Forces*, 69(1): 139–55.

Campell, K.E. and. Lee, B.A. (1992), 'Sources of personal neighbor networks: Social integration, need or time', *Social Forces*, 70(4): 1077–1100.

Cao, X., Mokhtarian, P.L. and Handy, S.L. (2007), 'Do Changes in Neighborhood Characteristics Lead to Changes in Travel Behavior? A Structural Equations Modeling Approach', *Transportation*, 34(5), 535–56.

Castells, M. (1996), *The Rise of the Network Society: I The Information Age – Economy, Society and Culture* (Oxford: Blackwells).

Castells, M. (1997), *The Power of Identity: The Information Age – II Economy, Society and Culture* (Oxford: Blackwells).

Castells, M. (1998), *End of Millennium: The Information Age – III Economy, Society and Culture* (Oxford: Blackwells).

Congress for New Urbanism (2000), *Charter of the New Urbanism: Region; Neighborhood, District and Corridor; Block, Street and Building* (New York: McGraw Hill).

Day, G. (2006), *Community and Everyday Life* (London: Routledge).

FCC (2001), *Long distance Telecommunication Industry* (Washington, D.C., FCC).

Flyvbjerg, B., Bruzelius, N. and Rothengatter, W. (2003), *Megaprojects and Risk: An Anatomy of Ambition* (Cambridge: Cambridge University Press).

Frei, A. (2005). 'Was hätte man 1960 für einen Sharan bezahlt?', MSc Thesis, Department Bau, Umwelt und Geomatik, ETH Zürich, Zürich.

Frick, M., Carle, G., Wokaun, A. and Axhausen, K.W. (2007), 'Optimization of the compressed natural gas (CNG) refueling station distribution: Swiss case studies', *Transportation Research D*, 12(1): 10–22.

Friedman, T.L. (2005), *The World Is Flat: A Brief History of the Twenty-First Century* (New York: Farrar, Straus and Giroux).

Graham, D.J. (2007), 'Agglomeration, Productivity and Transport Investment', *Journal of Transport Economics and Policy*, 41(3): 317–43.

Granovetter, M. (1973), 'The strength of weak ties', *American Journal of Sociology*, 78(6): 1360–80.

Grieco, M.S. (1987), *Keeping it in the Family: Social Networks and Employment Chance* (London: Tavistock Publications).

Grieco, M.S. (1996), *Worker's Dilemmas: Recruitment, Reliability and Repeated Exchange* (London: Routledge).

Hampton, K.N. and Wellman, B. (2001), 'Long distance community in the network society: Contact and support beyond Netville', *American Behavioral Scientist* 45(3): 477–96.

Hampton, K.N. and Wellman, B. (2003), 'Neighbouring in Netville', *City & Community* 2(4): 277–311.

Hogan, B., Carrasco, J.A. and Wellman, B. (2007), 'Visualizing Personal Networks: Working with Participant-Aided Sociograms', *Field Methods* (19)2: 116–44.

Larsen, J., Urry, J. and Axhausen, K.W. (2006) *Mobilities, Networks, Geographies* (Aldershot: Ashgate).

Lin, N. (1999), 'Building a network theory of social capital', *Connections*, 22(1): 28–51.

Lloyd, P. (1984), 'Community Action: Panacea or Placebo', *RAIN*, 63(8): 13–15.

Löchl, M., Schönfelder, S., Schlich, R., Buhl, T., Widmer, P. and Axhausen, K.W. (2005), 'Untersuchung der Stabilität des Verkehrsverhaltens', final report for SVI 2001/514, *Schriftenreihe*, 1120 (Bern: Bundesamt für Strassen, UVEK).

Low, S.M. (2003), *Behind the Gates: The New American Dream* (London: Routledge).

McKinnon, A.C. (2007), 'Decoupling of road freight transport and economic growth trends in the UK: An exploratory analysis', *Transport Reviews*, 27(1): 37–64.

Mok, D. and Wellman, B. (2007), 'Did distance matter before the Internet?, Social Networks', DOI 10.1016/j.socnet.2007.01.009 (accessed April 2007).

Putnam, R.D. (1999), *Bowling Alone: The Collapse and Revival of American Community* (New York: Simon & Schuster).

Putnam, R.D., Feldstein, L.M. and Cohen, D. (2003), *Better Together: Restoring the American Community* (New York: Simon & Schuster).

Rae, D.W. (2003), *City: Urbanism and Its End* (New Haven: Yale University Press).

Raff, D.M.G. and M. Trajtenberg (1995) Quality-adjusted prices for the American automobile industry: 1906–1940, *Working Paper*, **5032**, National Bureau of Economic Research, Cambridge.

Raje, F., Grieco, M.S., Hine, J. and Preston, J. (2004), *Transport Demand Management and Social Inclusion: The Need for Ethnic Perspectives* (Aldershot: Ashgate).

Schneider, C., Maibach, M., Trageser, J., Peter, M. and Rudel, R. (2006), 'Entkopplung zwischen Verkehrs und Wirtschaftswachstum, SVI 2001/524', Final report to the UVEK (Zürich: Infras and Lugano: IRE).

Seligman, A.B. (2000), *The Problem of Trust* (Princeton: Princeton University Press).

Shirley, C. and Winston, C. (2004), 'Firm inventory behavior and the returns from highway infrastructure investments', *Journal of Urban Economics*, 55(2): 398–415.

Simma, A. and Axhausen, K.W. (2004), 'Interactions between travel behaviour, accessibility and personal characteristics: The case of the Upper Austria', *European Journal of Transport and Infrastructure Research*, 3(2): 179–98.

Smith, A. (1999 [1776]), *An Inquiry into the Nature and Causes of the Wealth of Nations* (London: Penguin).

Sobel, J. (2002) 'Can We Trust Social Capital?', *Journal of Economic Literature*, 40(1): 139–54.

Tschopp, M. and Axhausen, K.W. (2007), 'Transport infrastructure and spatial development in Switzerland between 1950 and 2000', paper presented at the *86th Annual Meeting of the Transportation Research Board*, Washington, D.C., January 2007.

Venkatesh, S.A. (2006), *Off the Books: The Underground Economy of the Urban Poor* (Cambridge: Harvard University Press).

Völker, B., Flap, H. and Lindenberg, S. (2006), 'When are neighbourhoods communities? Community in Dutch neighbourhoods', *European Sociological Review*, DOI:10.1093/esr/jcl022 (accessed April 2007).

Vries, J. de and Van der Woude, A. (1997), *The First Modern Economy: Success, Failure, and Perseverance of the Dutch Economy, 1500–1815* (Cambridge: Cambridge University Press).

Chapter 7

An Evaluation of Future Traveller Information System and its Effectiveness in Demand Management Schemes

Amy Weihong Guo, Phil Blythe, Patrick Olivier,
Pushpendra Singh, Hai Nam Ha

Background

Traveller information, which provides users with the relevant available travel options, is generally acknowledged as having the potential to change traveller behaviour through informed choice. Providing timely and reliable information which is appropriate to travellers' needs could potentially benefit the whole transport system (Kenyon and Lyons 2003; Khattak et al. 1993; Schofer et al. 1993; Polydoropoulou and Ben-Akiva 1999; Lyons et al. 2001; Lyons 2003a; Eastman 1998; Edwards et al. 2006; Guo and Blythe 2005; Guo et al. 2006c). Thus, it is often believed that traveller information should be a core element of travel demand management schemes, particularly those attempting to affect a modal split away from the private car and onto more environmentally friendly forms of transport.

Current traveller information, ranging from paper-based timetables and road atlases, to web-based dynamic journey/route planners and in-vehicle navigation systems is widely available and accessible. However, constant and personalized travel assistance to on-trip public transport passengers is unseen. This in turn may have inhibited the current use of public transport services. An underlying information infrastructure is yet to be established that will allow real-time integration across all transport services and options. Although the provision of a timely personalized integrated multimodal information service supporting people on the move remains an aspiration, the goal of this study is to develop a methodology that permits the evaluation of such systems and their impacts on changing traveller behaviour and consequentially supporting demand management objectives.

A Vision of Future

Technological developments in computing and telecommunications are ushering in the era of ubiquitous connectivity whereby everything and everyone will be connected through a pervasive computing infrastructure (Miles and Walker 2006). Computers will in essence disappear into the fabric of everyday life (Weiser 1991,

ERCIM 2006). Artificial (or ambient) intelligence (AmI), may, in the future, be employed in transport systems to gather process and disseminate information of the state and performance of transport networks. AmI requires ubiquitous, or pervasive, computing, a concept first articulated by Mark Weiser at the XEROX Parc laboratory in 1988. In essence it means that technology recedes into the background, implying a need for ubiquitous communications in the form of ad-hoc networks between numerous, perhaps portable, very low cost computing devices. In Ducatel et al.'s article 'Scenarios for Ambient Intelligence in 2010' (Ducatel et al. 2001), a dynamic transport infrastructure is described where individuals are made aware of traffic conditions, guided to unfamiliar destinations, speed limits are altered to mitigate environmental pollution and car sharing is facilitated by automatic systems.

As a result, environments will be sensitive, adaptive and responsive to user capabilities, needs, habits, gestures and even emotions (Gates 2002; Stanford 2003, Streitz et al. 2005). Pervasive computing has the potential to change the transport infrastructure and information delivery radically, allowing real-time monitoring of networks and services, and the delivery of tailored (bespoke) information and context-specific travel assistance. The user will no longer need to search disparate sources of information for the most appropriate travel option, but instead will receive context-aware and personalized travel information and support.

This vision of a fully connected pervasive information service is a component of the future transport system envisaged by the recently published report by the Foresight Directorate of the UK government's Office of Science and Technology, 'Intelligent Infrastructure System' study (Blythe 2006a, Foresight 2006), which explored in detail the implications and impacts of new and emerging science and technology over the next 50 years. To understand the potential impact of such systems, a series of scenarios was developed (Blythe 2006b) which, as a discussion catalyst, helped to identify a number of key issues and unknowns that need to be addressed and researched to better understand the effectiveness of future information delivery. These included: user perception, user acceptance, human-machine interaction and the impact on traveller behaviour. Such issues are core elements of an ongoing debate between policy makers, system developers and transport service providers in relation to the benefits of investing in future traveller information services.

Evaluation Through User Participation

Evaluations of information systems can be conducted for a number of purposes: to formally establish the functionality of a system, to explore the usability of a system and its interface, or as in this case, to assess the impact of a system on user behaviour. Rossi et al. (2004) describe an effective evaluation method as requiring an accurate description of the system performance and user participation as a means of assessing the value of the system. Though tests can be conducted with respect to formally defined specifications of system behaviour, evaluation through user participation permits the use of the system to be observed and user perceptions to be explored, based on their actual experience of the system. Here, the term *user experience* is used to capture the specific notions of knowledge, experience and satisfaction gained through the use of traveller information systems (TIS).

Choice of evaluation method

As the *SmartTravel* system that we wish to evaluate does not yet physically exist, the evaluation of the notion of user experience requires the consideration of a number of factors:

- Current use of TIS.
- Current mode choices with respect to journey types.
- The utility of FTIS and in particular personal travel assistance.
- The likely use of FTIS.
- The likely impact of FTIS on travel choices.

Evaluation can be performed either in the relatively controlled environment of a development laboratory or in the field (Dix et al. 2004). In a field study, a minimally functioning prototype of the system is deployed in the target environment (or one very similar) (Gartner and Reiss 1987; Jeffery 1988; Smith and Russam 1989; Boyce et al. 1991; Rillings and Lewis 1991; Khattak et al. 1993; Peirce and Lappin 2003; Chatterjee and McDonald 2004). The principal advantage of field studies is that they allow the use of the real transport networks and the direct observation of users within genuine travel scenarios. In contrast to laboratory-based studies, field studies have the advantage of ecological validity, both in the fact that users are less conscious of their participation in the study (and the impact this has on their behaviour) and in the spatial and temporal constraints to which they are subject. The term *ecological validity* indicates the degree of the closeness of the test environment to the actual environment in which the system is used. Hence field studies emphasise the importance of a high-fidelity of user experience (Schofer et al. 1993; Dix et al. 2004) and encompass the study of actual information needs, reactions to information provided, and genuine journey choices. The term *high-fidelity of user experience* refers to a realistic representation of the proposed user experience. By comparing behaviour before and after use, the impact of a proposed system can be isolated.

However, a consequence of ecological validity is that rigorous field studies are problematic to conduct. From a methodological perspective, due to the lack of control over certain elements of the study, significant effort is required to distinguish the root causes of journey-making choices. In addition to characteristics of the subjects and the journeys themselves, field studies incorporate many additional environmental and contextual factors (e.g. the weather, unexpected variations in transport provision, and incidental occurrences such as receiving a phone call).

Furthermore, the physical design of the information provided and a subject's past experience of travel information (and travel information systems) also influences the decision making process. Whilst these factors have the potential to influence traveller behaviour, resource constraints mean that experimenters must use their experience in judging which need to be considered in detail (Dix et al. 2004; Schofer et al. 1993) and are core in answering the overarching hypothesis of the study. In previous studies of TIS, even detailed studies take little account of environmental and contextual factors in their data collection and analysis (Chatterjee and McDonald 2004).

Field studies usually employ travel diaries in which participants self-report their travel choices and TIS usage. This can give rise to factors that interfere with the ecological validity of a field study, in that participants feel somewhat burdened by the reporting requirements which in turn lead to depressed TIS usage as participants attempt to reduce the lengths of entries in their diaries (Peirce and Lappin 2003).

An alternative technique used in a field study, named Wizard of Oz (WOZ), has been considered here. WOZ does not require a full scale deployment of information infrastructure in place but a limited functionality prototype, and enhances the functionality in evaluation by providing the missing functionalities through human intervention (Dix et al. 2004). Such system demonstration allows the evaluation to be concentrated on the users' reactions to the system rather than the performance of the system. Though this technique requires less effort and resource commitment than establishing a full scale deployment of the system, it could enhance the difficulty of the operating process of the study significantly. As a summary, field studies enable high-fidelity of user experience and reliable and valid data to be collected, but tend to be time consuming, complex and costly.

In laboratory-based studies, participants are taken out of their usual environment to take part in controlled tests, often in a laboratory or simply a quiet room (Dix et al. 2004). By standardizing and controlling the environment and all events, laboratory studies are deliberately designed to ensure that subjects are exposed to exactly the same environment as their usual environment (De Vaus 2001). This makes laboratory studies more easily controlled than field studies. In some situations, a laboratory study can be the only option. For example, when real-world implementations of new generation TIS technologies do not exist and available resources are insufficient for a physical implementation of these technologies in the actual environment, it would be impossible to observe the actual use of such technologies in everyday life.

The performance of systems is normally demonstrated by either paper-based scenarios or computer-based simulations in laboratory studies. These methods provide low-cost, high-portability to investigate and test specific issues of behavioural concerns that are difficult to capture with survey techniques, or that cannot be adequately observed in the real world (Adler and McNally 1994). However, paper-based scenarios provide little context within which the system is intended to be used and few opportunities for subjects to interact with the system. Therefore, this method is useful to explore concepts or impacts of pre-trip information on travel choices (Kenyon and Lyons 2003), but not suitable for studies in which environmental context and interactions are highly important for the investigation, such as investigating the impacts of en-route dynamic information delivery on travel choices.

In recent years, computer-based simulations have been developed to provide viable alternatives to create the intended contexts and demonstrate the improved system performance in laboratories (Dix et al. 2004). This method provides a highly portable and easily reproduced platform to explore user experiences within scenarios (Adler and McNally 1994). A visit to the physical environment space is no longer necessary for users. However, the main disadvantage of this method is that it requires high-level programming support for the simulation to be efficient and robust.

Comparative to field studies, laboratory studies are generally easier to control, quicker and less expensive to establish. However, they are artificial and are perceived as such by subjects (Eachus 2000). This may influence the way users behave (and respond), compared to their real world interactions.

On balance, there is a need to weight the costs and the difficulty of a field study, with the costs of taking a number of users to a fully equipped and established laboratory. In this study, it is impossible to test a FTIS in the real world due to the lack of the physical and underlying information infrastructure. Undertaking a field study with a fully-implemented or even just a partially-implemented system would be extremely difficult, costly and time-consuming. The challenge therefore is to find a way in which the reality of the testing environment can be enhanced within the laboratory environment.

Immersive video

A new methodology, termed *Immersive Video,* is applied to explore user reactions towards FTIS by creating a more realistic testing environment. This methodology has been invented by the Transport Operation Research Group (TORG) and Informatics Research Institute (IRI) at Newcastle University. This study is, to our knowledge, the first-ever application of this technique transport research.

Immersive video is a functional 3D digital video system. It uses a series of shots with natural ambient sounds and various movements captured in the actual environments to re-produce a dynamic and realistic scene in a laboratory. The immersive video system consists of 4 major components:

- Real scene reconstruction.
- Traveller information simulation.
- Location definition.
- Location control.

**Figure 7.1   Reconstructed scene from a first person perspective using
video streams captured by three cameras at a metro station**

Source: This study

Real scene reconstruction   Real scene reconstruction is at the heart of immersive
video architecture. Using video streams captured by multiple cameras at different
locations from a first person perspective, and replaying the footage on the same
number of screens which are closely set next to each other in the same arrangement
as the camera setup, a spatiotemporally realistic, three-dimensional environment
model of an event is generated (see Figure 7.1). Immersive video has been proposed
on numerous occasions as an alternative form of presentation to traditional paper-
based scenarios and computer-based simulations. It provides users with a sense
that they are truly immersed in an environment (Singh et al. 2006; Moezzi et al.
1996).

To enable this 'walk-through', a scenario is developed that creates the context of
using the system and demonstrates the main features of the FTIS. For the purpose
of the scenario the hypothetical FITS system has been branded *SmartTravel* (see
The Scenario). According to the scenario, real-time traveller information and
personal travel assistance are provided at 16 decision-making points (i.e. key
locations) along the journey.

The Scenario

*Mike received a reminder from his personal device – he needs to meet Bob at
the Discovery Museum at 10:00am. Upon his confirmation of this plan, the
SmartTravel automatically planned a public transport journey for Mike. Up-to-
date information about journey times, costs, itinerary, maps, waiting areas and
public transport vehicles were provided in great detail.*

At 9:30am, Mike was alerted to depart. A map was displayed on the screen of his personal device to direct him to the metro station. His position on the map was updated in real time.

The transport system greeted Mike when he arrived at the metro station and asked him to choose a ticketing option. Mike decided to buy the return ticket. Meanwhile, he authorized the system to charge him to his SmartTravel account. Then he was guided to platform 1 and his train was just arriving.

When Mike was sitting on the train heading towards Newcastle Central, Bob sent him a text message and asked to meet at Baltic Centre, a different location. SmartTravel recognized Mike's real-time location, situation, task, and the name and location of the place Bob mentioned in the message. Upon Mike's confirmation of changing his destination, SmartTravel immediately re-planned the journey from Mike's current location to his new destination with all the details he might need. SmartTravel asked Mike to leave the train when it approached Monument station, guided him to the Royal Theatre bus stop and directed him to the QuayLink bus.

When Mike was sitting on the bus, SmartTravel presented some information on the exhibitions. Mike was told him to leave the bus when it arrived at Baltic Square bus stop.

To develop the visualization of these scenario decision-making points, which will be displayed on the three screens within the immersive video 'cave', three video cameras are lined up on a metal board, which was made especially for this task to film the actual environment and capture the ambient sounds at each of the key locations from a first-person perspective (see Figure 7.2). The purpose of using three cameras is to provide a wider field-of-view, whist the purpose of filming from a first-person perspective is to create the sense of being there at the location.

A key part of the experimental procedure is to set the focal length of the three lenses (a determinant of magnification), which must be adjusted manually using a test object placed a few metres away. This is to maintain exactly the same level of zoom of the three cameras so that the same magnification of the objects in the real environment is adopted. The facing direction of each camera needs to be coordinated so that the frames captured by the three cameras can match each other to produce a seamless picture of the actual scene. The white balance (a determinant of scene colour) is reset at each location to maintain a consistent colour of the picture. Professional editing software, Final Cut Pro, is used to match and synchronize the three video streams taken at the same location (see Figure 7.3).

The streams taken at each location are replayed on the three screens of the immersive video 'cave', standing next to each other at the same angles as the camera lenses to form a walled cave-based display in the laboratory to present the reconstructed scene with accompanying ambient sounds. The user stands in

Figure 7.2   Use of three video cameras to capture the actual scenes

Photo by L. Shi.

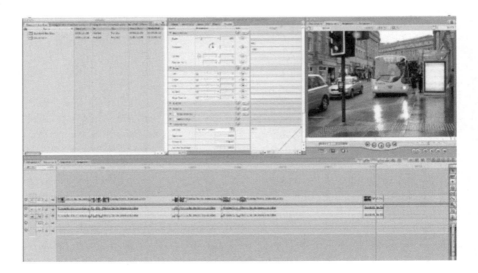

Figure 7.3   Final Cut Pro

Source: This study

Figure 7.4   A subject stands in the middle of the three screens
Source: Singh et al. (2006).

the middle of the cave-based display (see Figure 7.4). The displays on the screen determine and react to the user's location along the journey. The video streams and the ambient sounds provide the user with a rich impression and tangible experience of being at the site of an actual deployment.

Traveller information simulation   Graphical User Interfaces (GUIs) are designed for each location to represent traveller information services and personal travel assistance provided by the FTIS at that location (see Figure 7.5). Both two-dimensional maps (obtained from Google Maps™) and three-dimensional maps (obtained from Google Earth™) are adopted for personal navigation, i.e. showing the location of the user and the direction of the planned route.

Two personal devices, a Wearable Peripheral Display (WPD) and a Personal Digital Assistant (PDA), are adopted for subjects to receive traveller information services and personal travel assistance whilst interacting with the *SmartTravel* system within the immersive video environment. The WPD is used to provide peripheral information which is not central to a person's current task, but provides the person with an opportunity to know more about their travelling environment and situations. The WPD used in the trials is a pair of glasses, where information is projected onto a 'mini-screen' on the lens of the right-hand eye-piece of the glasses, analogous to a low-tech version of a fighter-pilots helmet-mounted display.

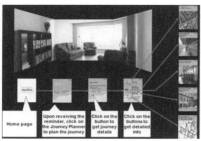

Location 1

Location 2

Location 3

Location4

Location 5

Location 6

Location 7

Location 8

Figure 7.5   Key locations and information display

Source: This study.

It provides information whilst having little impact on the user's performance on the main task (Maglio and Campbell 2000), thus the test subject can choose to glance at this information, as and when necessary, whilst concentrating on the more important information regarding the overall travel scenario, generated by the immersive video system.

In both cases, the subject stands in the middle of the cave-based displays, and determines where they are and the context of their journey scenario. The personal device is consulted to find out what information has been provided at this location. The WPD is configured to supply the user with appropriate traveller information that is generated within the scenario, as this is a 'glasses-based' technology it is purely for information dissemination and thus, the user is unable to interact with it. However, the second information device incorporated in the cave is a PDA. The PDA is configured as not only an information source but a fully interactive planning device which allows the user interact and interrogate it to gain more information by using the on-screen prompts and buttons (as one uses a PDA in the real world).

In the experimental plan, each subject will make the journey twice – one with the PDA, receiving and obtaining interactive information, and another journey scenario using the wearable device where traveller information services and personal travel assistance are received and displayed.

Location definition   In order to maintain and control the users' location in the right order, positional information of each location is needed. Positional information is collected using sensors such as GPS and Bluetooth tags. These values are used to define locations. Each location is defined by a unique value or a set of unique values. Bluetooth values are used for indoor locations (home and on-board). GPS values are used for outdoor locations. One XML (eXtensible Markup Language) file is created for each location by specifying its unique sensor value(s) and also the reachable locations from this current state. Figure 7.6 presents a fraction of an XML file, with GPS values and the state name of other locations that can be reached. The function of an XML file is to determine that, from a user perspective, the cave-based display and the corresponding information display will behave exactly as if they were in the actual location in a real-world deployment. The user's location is controlled by a wizard to ease the evaluation and prototyping of the FTIS and meanwhile, enable the discovery of context-related issues (Singh et al. 2006).

XML documents are made up of storage units called entities, which contain either parsed or unparsed data. XML provides a mechanism to impose constraints on the storage layout and logical structure (W3C 2004).

Location control   Video streams are arranged into the correct sequence, which is defined by the state-based design (see Figure 7.7), and are fed into a wizard system via the XML files.

The wizard controls the user's location by a control panel that can change the location of the user depending on the reachable locations from current state (see Figure 7.8). Due to the limited function of current immersive video, this scenario

```
<?xml version="1.0" standalone="no" ?>
<ivideo>
<sensor stype="gps" value="" irid=""
    longitude="54.977750833333333"
    latitude="1.61345555555556"
    startframe="0" endframe="3000" />
<state name="station2_4" astartframe="0"
    aendframe="3000"
    centersrcfile="../AVI/c24z1.avi"
    leftsrcfile="../AVI/l24z1.avi"
    rightsrcfile="../AVI/r24z1.avi"
    xmlfile="../XML/s24.xml"
    istartframe="" iendframe="" />
<state name="station1_1" astartframe="0"
    ...
    ...
</ivideo>
```

Figure 7.6　　An xml file

Source: Singh et al. (2006)

is deliberately designed to generate user experiences with the system rather than directly observing real choices. The subject will not be able to make their own travel choices. The determining of the location, and hence which video streams are played, is controlled by the researcher through the wizard.

In practice, the use of immersive video has considerably reduced the effort to deploy a full scale of information infrastructure in a testing environment. It also reduces the need to physically visit the place where the system will be. Both tasks would be time-consuming and require significant resources commitment. In the meantime, the reconstructed environment with real people's movement and ambient sounds has the potential to provide the user with a rich impression of being at the site of the actual deployment and real and tangible experience of using the information system.

The Evaluation

According to the scenario, one needs to travel from home to the Discovery Museum to meet a friend at 10:00am, but is requested to divert the journey to Baltic Centre when he/she is en-route. This is a local entertainment journey. To design a diversion of the journey is to create the demands for en route information and enable participants to learn one of the outstanding features of FTIS – meeting en route information needs timely and dynamically. To ensure that participants possess similar familiarity of the travelling environment, the journey starts from

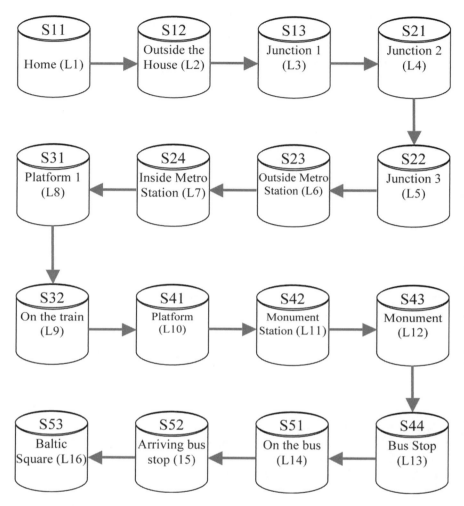

Figure 7.7   State base design

Source: This study

the same home location. This implies that all participants in the trial should live in the same neighbourhood or nearby areas and be familiar with the 'starting point'. Additionally, public transport choices throughout the selected area should be competitive with the car choice so that people's attitudes towards information about public transport are not affected by the lack of choices. Hence, the considered neighbourhood should meet two criteria, i.e. good and adequate public transport services and high car ownership, to allow the majority of the residents to have equal opportunity to participate in the study.

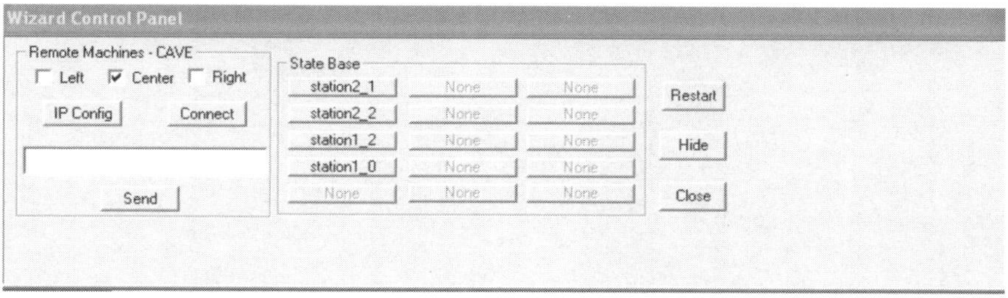

Figure 7.8   The Wizard control panel

Source: This study

Figure 7.9   Map from Google Earth™

Source: Google Earth™

in a well-prepared laboratory. A brief description of the scenario is presented to each participant at the beginning of the trial, however the details of the available services remained unexposed. Participants are made aware that all the information and personal travel assistance provided by *SmartTravel* should be presumed to be up-to-date and accurate. The explanation of what would be displayed on the cave-based screens, what would be displayed on the personal devices, and the

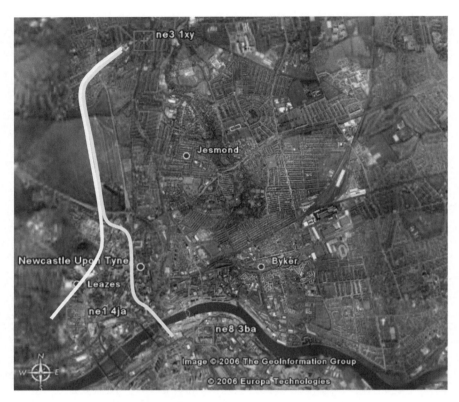

Figure 7.10   The designed journey

Source: Google Earth™

relationship between the display on the cave-based screens and the display on the personal devices are also given at this stage. To begin the immersive journey, the participant is seated in front of the cave-based screens and the first location (scenario point) on the journey displayed on the video screens, the journey then starts. During the process, the researcher sits next to the participant to provide help if needed and to make observations on how the participants interact and react to the system and information at the various stages of the journey. Upon completing the journey, a face-to-face interview is conducted with the participant, to explore issues, such as the participant's opinions on the *SmartTravel* FITS and on the use of the immersive video system as opposed to the use of more conventional ways of presenting information and scenarios.

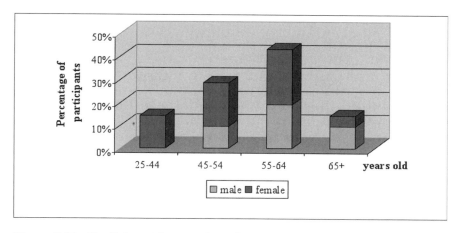

Figure 7.11   Participants' age and gender

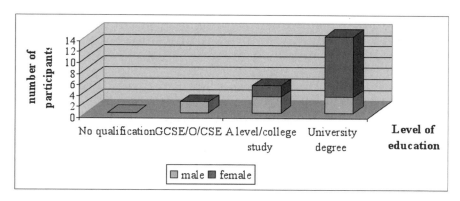

Figure 7.12   Participants' level of education

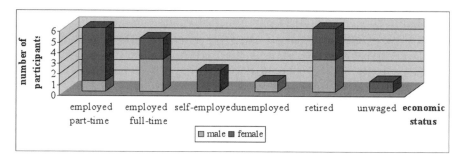

Figure 7.13   Participants' economic status

The Results

The experimental study deploying immersive video as a means of evaluating FITS commenced in Feburary 2007. Twenty local people were recruited as participants, seven male and thirteen female. The participants included a representative mixture of ages and economic status (see Figures 7.11–7.13), with some qualifications: (1) there were more female participants than male in the study; (2) female participants were relative younger than male; (3) female participants had higher level of education than male participants.

The likely utility of FTIS services

Participants were presented with a list of services provided by FTIS. In the immersive video trials, participants used most of these services whilst making a virtual journey. Through a face-to-face interview, participants expressed their perceived usefulness of the information and services immediately after their use of the system. All participants emphasized that the usefulness of the services mainly depended on their familiarity with the journey. In general, female participants believed that more services were 'useful' or 'very useful' than male participants. It seems that female participants expressed the need for more assistance in travelling or were more open to the use of additional information than male participants.

Examples of services that are delivered in response to a user's context include 'automatic re-planning of journeys when changes occurs', information on 'delays and alternative departure times/mode choices/route choices', 'personal navigation information based upon current location' and 'travel alerts'. Such services require a system to collect detailed contextual information about a user, and as a result there is a debate over the significance of privacy concerns. In fact, a lively discussion with participants arose in relation to the trade-off between privacy and the level of bespoke services available to them. Participants broadly accepted that a system should be aware where they were, where they were heading, what the purpose of the journey was, and what the constraints were in order to receive such timely and unprompted travel assistance.

Participants were positive about the automatic journey re-planning capabilities, which simply requested the user to confirm his/her new destination. Information on 'delays and alternative departure times' was generally considered to allow better time management of the user; indeed, both services were considered 'useful' or 'very useful' by all participants regardless their familiarity with the journey. Information on 'delays and alternative mode/route choices' was perceived as 'useful' or 'very useful' by all but one male participant, who claimed that he did not need any information for travelling within this country. However, further discussions revealed that participants, particularly those who travelled by car most of the time, would be keen to know both alternative mode and route choices only if they were travelling by public transport. Most stressed that if they had started a journey with the car, they would prefer to stay with their car. For car journeys, mode alternatives would only considered acceptable in the event of severe delays and the alternative mode choice was 'extremely' convenient.

Personal navigation was regarded by all participants as 'useful' or 'very useful' for travelling in unfamiliar areas, but not for familiar areas. Its utility was clearly observed during the participants' use of the system. For example, one travel option, which the majority of participants had never used in reality, was the QuayLink bus. As a result there was general uncertainty about where to take the bus upon leaving one of the metro stations (Monument metro station). The route from the Monument metro station to the Theatre Royal bus stop and the locations of the metro station and the bus stop, were clearly marked on the map and were used by all participants.

Participants were surprised by the timely and situation-based 'travel alerts'. All but two female participants considered it a useful service even for travelling in familiar areas, particularly for public transport journeys. Further discussions raised the possibility that timely and targeted travel alerts could allow participants to concentrate on non-travel activities without the anxiety that they sometimes suffer at present (with regard to missing buses and trains). Participants clearly recognized and welcomed these advantages. Information on 'journey duration', 'walking time', 'in-vehicle time', 'travel costs' and 'real-time traffic conditions' have already been assessed for web-based TIS. However, in this scenario, such information was delivered to a mobile personal device and updated in real-time. Most participants thought such information would be useful when unexpected changes occur; though others questioned its basic utility since once a journey was embarked upon it had to be completed regardless of the delay.

Over half the participants stated that they were not interested in receiving 'information on comfort', 'images of the route/vehicle', 'information on events and points of interest' and 'precise weather conditions' when deciding how to travel. They were more concerned about 'information on convenience'. Once again, this demonstrates that the ease and efficiency of making the journey is a more important factor in travel choice than issues such as comfort, the weather and type of vehicle used.

The likely use of FTIS

The participants reported that their use of FTIS, in general, would depend on two factors: journey familiarity, and journey constraints. They believed that they would be more likely to use the services for undertaking an untypical journey in a familiar area, a familiar journey with time-constraint, or when travelling in an unfamiliar area. However, some information and services were regarded as useful regardless of the familiarity and the constraints of the journey. Three of fourteen participants claimed they would use the system for commuting to work, one of seven for going to school/college, seven of eighteen for personal business trips, seven of twenty for visiting friends and family and eight of twenty for travelling to a leisure or entertainment event.

Of those participants who were in employment, all stated that they would use the system for work-related business trips. One female participant believed that she would use the system for every journey and the use of such a system whilst travelling could become a habit. However, one male participant thought that he would not use the system for journeys at a national scale (due to his personal familiarity with the national transport networks). Another male participant claimed that he would only use the system for work-related business trips. The majority of participants believed that they would use the system for going on holiday and going on a day trip because very likely they would not be familiar with the area. Most participants also believed that they would use the system for travelling to public transport terminals due to the time-constraints or a better time management.

The likely impact on travel choices

About half of participants believed that the services provided by FTIS could encourage them to make more use of public transport. Most of the other half of participants stated that they did use public transport regularly. However, the majority of participants considered that FITS would certainly encourage them to make more use of public transport when travelling in unfamiliar areas. Participants also stated that the FTIS could enhance their confidence in using public transport, make public transport journeys easier and less stressful, and always allow them to be aware of the relevant public transport options. However, participants pointed out that if they had started their journey with their car, they would prefer to finish the journey with the car, particularly for a chained journey. They would switch to public transport choices only when information on delays or congestion could be received before they got into the traffic jam and the alternative options were extremely convenient. Only proactive and sophisticated FTIS services could meet such types of user requests.

Conclusion

The use of immersive video as a means of evaluation created realistic contexts for participants to judge the services provided by FTIS precisely and specifically based on their first hand experience. Participants expressed strong interests in the services provided by the *SmartTravel* system. The initial results of this study suggest that the demand for better personalized and context-aware traveller information services and travel assistance could be high in the future. The demand would be particularly high for making unfamiliar journeys. However, the demand for public transport in the future was positively correlated to their current travel patterns. For people who barely used public transport in their everyday life, future traveller information services would have little impacts on their mode choices. The analysis implies that, to achieve modal shift away from the car to public transport efficiently, better provision of traveller information services cannot be a stand-alone solution. Other demand management techniques, such as road user charge and/or more restrictive parking standards should be introduced to restrain unnecessary car use.

Acknowledgements

The authors wish to thank the School of Civil Engineering and Geosciences in Newcastle University who funded this research, and gratefully acknowledge the support and contribution from colleagues in Transport Research Group (TORG), Informatics Research Institute (IRI), Culture Lab and Geomatics: Phil Heslop, Alasdair Sherit, Liangliang Shi, Richard Fairchild, Paulus, Adijtjandra, John Shearer, David Green, Paul Dunphy, Daniel Jackson, Phil James, Hannah Bryan, and Simon Edwards.

References

Adler, J.L. and McNally, M.G. (1994), 'In-laboratory experiments to investigate driver behaviour under advanced traveller information systems', *Transportation Research Part C: Emerging Technologies* (2): 149–64.

Blythe, P.T. (2006a), 'Intelligent Infrastructure: A Smart Future with Smart Dust and Smart Markets', *IFAC Conference on Transport Automation and Control*, Delft, The Netherlands.

Blythe, P.T. (2006b), 'Intelligent infrastructure and SmartMarkets', *Proc. Conference on EU Road User Charging*. London.

Boyce, D., Kirson, A. and Schofer, J. (1991), 'Design and implementation of ADVANCDE: The Illinois dynamic navigation and route guidance demonstration program', *2nd Annual Vehicle Navigation and Information Systems Conference*. Dearborn, MI, IEEE and SAE.

Chatterjee, K. and McDonald, M. (2004), 'Effectiveness of Using Variable Message Signs to Disseminate Dynamic Traffic Information: Evidence from Field Trails in European Cities', *Transport Reviews* (24): 559–85.

De Vaus, D. (2001), *Research Design in Social Science* (London: Sage Publications).

Dix, A., Finlay, J., Abowd, G.D.A. and Beale, R. (2004), *Human-Computer Interaction* (London: Pearson Education Ltd).

Ducatel, K., Bogdanowicz, M., Scapolo, F., Leijten, J. and Burgelman, J.-C. (2001), *Scenarios for Ambient Intelligence in 2010*. Available at <ftp://ftp. cordis.europa.eu/pub/ist/docs/istagscenarios2010.pdf>.

ERCIM (2006), Beyond the Horizon: Anticipating Future and Emerging Information Society Technologies.

Foresight (2006), 'Project Overview: Intelligent Infrastructure Futures', *Intelligent Infrastructure Systems (ISS)* Office of Science and Technology.

Gartner, N.H. and Reiss, R.A. (1987), 'Congestion control in freeway corridors: The IMIS system', in Odoni, A. (ed.), *Flow Control of Congested Networks* (Springer-Verlag).

Gates, B. (2002), 'The Disappearing Computer', *The Economist*.

Jeffery, D.J. (1988), 'Driver Route Guidance Systems: State of the Art', *Telematics-Transportation and Spatial Development International Symposium*. Hague.

Kenyon, S. and Lyons, G. (2003), 'The value of integrated multimodal traveller information and its potential contribution to modal change', *Transportation Research Part F: Traffic Psychology and Behaviour* (6): 1–21.

Khattak, A.J., Schofer, J.L. and Koppelman, F.S. (1993), 'Commuters' en-route diversion and return decisions: Analysis and implications for advanced traveler information systems', *Transportation Research Part A: Policy and Practice,* (27): 101–111.

Maglio, P.P. and Campbell, C.S. (2000), 'Tradeoffs in displaying peripheral information', *SIGCHI Conference on Human factors in computing systems*. The Hague, the Netherlands.

Miles, J. and Walker, J. (2006), 'Science Review: The potential application of artificial intelligence in transport', in Post (ed.) *Foresight Intelligent Infrastructure Systems Project* <www.foresight.gov.uk>.

Moezzi, S., Katkere, A., Kuramura, D.Y. and Jain, R. (1996), 'Immersive Video', *VRAIS '96*. IEEE.

Peirce, S. and Lappin, J.E. (2003), 'Acquisition of traveller information and its effects on travel choices: evidence from a Seattle-area travel diary survey', Volpe National Transportation.

Rillings, J.H. and Lewis, J.W. (1991), 'TravTek', *Proceedings of the 2nd Annual Vehicle Navigations and Information Systems Conference*. Dearborn, MI, IEEE and SAE.

Rossi, P.H., Lipsey, M.W. and Freeman, H.E. (2004), *Evaluation: A Systematic Approach* (London: Sage Publications).

Schofer, J.L., Khattak, A. and Koppelman, F.S. (1993), 'Behavioural issues in the design and evaluation of advanced traveller information systems', *Transportation Research Part C: Emerging Technologies* (1): 107–17.

Singh, P., Ha, H.N., Olivier, P., Kray, C., Kuang, Z., Guo, W., Blythe, P. and James, P. (2006), 'Rapid Prototyping and Evaluation of Intelligent Environment Using Immersive Video', *8th Conference on Human-computer Interaction with Mobile Devices and Services*. Espoo, Finland, ACM.

Smith, J.C. and Russam, K. (1989), 'Some Possible Effects of AUTOGUIDE on traffic in London', *IEEE international conference on Vehicle Navigation and Information Systems*. Toronto, Canada.

Stanford, V. (2003), 'Pervasive computing goes the last hundred feet with RFID systems', *Pervasive Computing*, IEEE (2): 9–14.

Streitz, N.A., Rocker, C., Prante, T., Van Alphen, D., Stenzel, R. and Magerkurth, C. (2005), 'Designing smart artifacts for smart environments', *Computer* (38): 41–9.

W3C (2004), World Wide Web Consortium, Extensible Markup Language (XML) 1.0.

Weiser, M. (1991), 'The computer of the 21st century', *Scientific American* (265): 66–75.

PART II
International Experiences with TDM Measures

Chapter 8

Variable Message Signs: Are they Effective TDM Measures?

Wafaa Saleh, Craig Walker and Chih Wei Pai

1. Introduction

Variable Message Signs (VMS) that inform drivers of adverse weather conditions (e.g., snow event, slippery roadway surfaces, etc.) have recently been attracting the attention of researchers. VMS systems that provide drivers with information regarding fog or slippery road surfaces were generally found to be beneficial in reducing speeds (Karlberg 2002; Cooper and Sawyer 2005; Al-Ghamdi 2004; Rämä and Kulmala). However Boyle and Mannering (2004) argued that the net safety effects of such message systems were not conclusive. They found that while messages for severe weather and heavy snowfall were significant in reducing speeds in the area of adverse conditions, drivers tended to compensate for this speed reduction by increasing their speeds downstream where such adverse conditions did not exist.

Signs that show speed reduction information (i.e., signs that are activated by speeding vehicles) and unexpected events (e.g., an event of an accident ahead; a closed road section) have also been routinely researched (e.g., Barnard and Cutler 2005; Barnard and Cutler 2005; Chatterjee et al. 2002; Erke et al. 2007). Barnard and Cutler (2005) reported that there was a 30%-48% reduction in accident rates through the deployment of VMS that display an advisory message urging a reduction in speed to speeding drivers. Messages displaying the information of unexpected events were found to be important in influencing the probability of diversion (Chatterijee et al. 2002; Erke et al. 2007).

Erke et al. further investigated the speeds and braking behaviours of the vehicles approaching the VMS measures that were either displayed messages or left blank without any information. Large proportions of vehicles were observed to brake while approaching the VMS. They attributed the speed reductions and braking manoeuvres to attention overload or distraction due to the information on the VMS. They suggested that safety problems may result directly from distraction, or indirectly from the reactions of the drivers to that distraction.

A review of the relevant literature suggests that comparatively consistent conclusions have been drawn among these studies – there seems to be a modification of drivers' behaviours (e.g., diversion of route due to the accident or road closure ahead) in the immediate vicinity of the measures. While a reduction of speed was observed as a result of a sign that urges a reduced speed, there was a concern for an increase in speed downstream. The net safety effects of such message systems are rather inconclusive in the literature.

There also appears to be a dearth of studies that attempt to examine the effect of VMS on accident injury severity, when an accident has occurred. The only exception is the work by Carson and Mannering (2001) that has sought to examine the effect of ice warning signs on ice-accident frequencies and severities in Washington State. They argue that signing of non-permanent road surface conditions, such as ice, is difficult because hazard formation, location, and duration are unpredictable. They found that the presence of ice warning signs was not a significant factor in reducing ice-accident frequency or ice-accident severity. They suggest that current ice-warning sign placement practices are ineffective and there is an urgent need for standardized sign-placement procedures that will reduce the frequency and severity of ice-related accidents.

This chapter investigates impacts of VMS on accidents rates and severities on Scottish trunk roads. A before and after analysis of accidents at 14 selected VMS sites in central and north-east Scotland is presented.

2. Description of the Data

The number and location of accidents at the 14 selected VMS sites on Scottish trunk roads which have been identified for analysis in this chapter have been obtained from the NADICS website (www.trafficscotland). Precise quantity and location data was then obtained via the Glasgow ITS department of the Faber Maunsell Engineering Consultancy (who had carried out the most recent installations on behalf of Transport Scotland and as such had detailed VMS records (Walker 2007)). Seven years of Stats19 accident data (2000 to 2006) at these sites was used. That is for each site (including controls), the number of accidents and the AADT (Annual Average Daily Traffic), for each of 7 years is available. The study focuses on VMS signs across four major trunk roads in Scotland that were installed after 2000 plus four control sites. The roads included are the M8 (Edinburgh – West Coast via central Glasgow), M9 (Edinburgh – Stirling), A90 (Dundee – Aberdeen) and the A720 (Edinburgh Southern Bypass). Figure 8.1 shows the location of the VMS sites in Scotland. The traffic and accidents data as well as the codes assigned to each of the 14 VMS site are presented in Table 8.1. The data obtained for each site include VMS installation data, flow information, accident information and road information. The four control sites are located on similar stretches of road (in terms of flow and accidents numbers) but have no VMS either at the site or on the prolonged approach to the site. Two control sites were taken from the A90 and two from the M8 on sections of road that were straight, either north-south or east-west, so that using GPS coordinates a section of 2km could be confidently isolated as a control site. The flows for these areas were then taken from the traffic Scotland database and the accident data from Stats19 using the GPS coordinates as a filter.

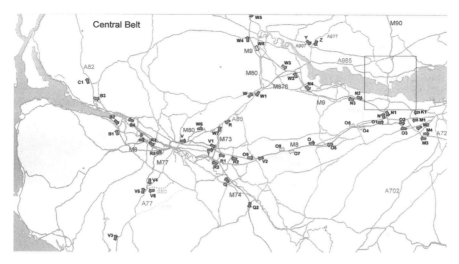

Figure 8.1   Locations of VMS in Scotland

Eastbound and westbound control sites were taken from the M8 and northbound and southbound sites were taken from the A90.

Data for accidents that occurred up to one kilometre before the VMS and one kilometre after was collected for each site. Accidents in this two kilometre qualifying zone were then disqualified if they were found to have occurred on the opposite carriageway to that which the VMS was located.

3. Investigation of Accidents Rates and Severities on Scotland's Roads

The analysis of accident rates and severities and the impacts of installing VMS signs on Scottish trunk roads have been investigated utilising a number of statistics. Firstly, accidents rates have been investigated; secondly, a comparison of before and after accidents rates at each site has then been undertaken. An estimate of the *effectiveness* of the VMS installation has been also made. A chi-squared test has been performed to investigate the before and after (installation of VMS), difference variations in accidents data. Finally, two sets of models have been calibrated to investigate the impacts of various independent variables as well as the presence of VMS signs on accidents severities.

3.1 Accident rates statistics

Accident rates and severities, and the impacts of installing VMS signs on Scottish trunk roads have been investigated utilising a number of statistics. Firstly, accident rates, represented by $\hat{k}$, or risk, in terms of accidents per 100 million veh-kilometres, where X = number of accidents, T = time (in years in this case), L = length (km) of the road in question and Q = flow on the road over the entire year (thus is typically calculated by multiplying the AADT by 365 (days in a year)), are calculated for each of the 14 VMS sites under investigation. Accidents rates (accidents per veh-km) for the control sites have also been calculated.

$$\hat{k} = \frac{X}{TLQ} \quad \text{st.error}(\hat{k}) = \sqrt{\frac{\hat{k}}{TLQ}} = \frac{\sqrt{X}}{TLQ}$$

Before and after accidents rates analysis for the grouped sites was carried out. Then similar analysis for each site have been compared in order to investigate impacts of installing VMS at these sites. The results are presented and discussed in section 4 below.

By comparing the before and after accidents data, one can estimate the *effectiveness* of the VMS installation usually denoted by a parameter θ, a factor by which the accident frequency (or rate) to be multiplied. Therefore if $\theta = 0.7$, then the accident rate has been reduced by 30% and so on. In this analysis, the effectiveness or impact of the installation of VMS is measured by θ using the following formula:

$$\theta = \frac{Y_A T_B Q_B}{Y_B T_A Q_A}$$

Where YB = Accidents Before   YA = Accidents After
      TB = Time Before (years)   TA = Time After (years)
      QB = Flow Before   QA = Flow After

The results for the estimates of impact of each VMS and the possible range of effectiveness are presented in Table 8.3. As previously discussed, four control zones were chosen that had very similar road characteristics (i.e. flows and accident numbers) to the selected sites. A comparison between each of the 14 VMS with the control zone that matched it most closely in terms of flow, geometry and time has been carried out. For each site (including controls), the number of accidents and the AADT, for each of seven years have been analysed matching the before and after periods for the VMS and the control sites. That is if the VMS site has four years of before and three of after the data for the control site is then split accordingly.

This analysis used the same formula and analysis approach as above. Table 8.4 summarizes the results of this analysis including the control zone information.

In order to assess the impact of VMS on the true underlying mean μ accident rate, a chi-squared test in which a hypothesis (H_o: that is no change in true mean acc rate per veh-km as a result of installing VMS) is constructed to see if the before and after difference is due to random variation or not for every site. The test has been carried out using a 5% significance level (critical value of $\chi^2 = 3.84$) and the results are reported in Table 8.5 for each of the 14 VMS.

3.2 Modelling accident severities

Finally, two sets of models have been calibrated; the firstly two linear regression models and then two binary logit models. The before and after information for each of the 14 VMS, which include the average accident number for the previous four years for each site and the traffic flow were tested using linear regression analysis. Two linear regression models have been calibrated: firstly a model with flow (x_1); four year average accidents (x_2) as two continuous variables and a constant and secondly a model with these variables plus a variable representing the presence of VMS as a dummy variable. The results are summarized in Table 8.6.

In the course of the investigation of the factors that affect accident severity (KSI vs. slight) two binary logit models have been calibrated. The binary logit models are estimated to evaluate the likelihood of accidents being severe or fatal against being slight, taking account of human, vehicle, weather/temporal, and environmental factors. Such models are widely used if the dependent variable is dichotomous (KSI vs. Non KSI) in the regression equation. Logistic regression allows one to predict a binary outcome from a set of explanatory variables that may be continuous, categorical, or a mixture of the two. All explanatory variables are treated as categorical variables in this current research. In the logit model, a latent variable is formulated by the following expression:

$$g(x) = \beta_0 + \beta_1 \chi_1 + \beta_2 \chi_2 + \dots + \beta_j \chi_j + \dots \beta_p \chi_p$$

where χ_j is the value of the independent variable; and β_j is the corresponding coefficient, for $j = 1, 2, 3 \dots p$, where p is the number of independent variables.

With this latent variable, the conditional probability of a positive outcome is determined by:

$$\tau(\chi) = \frac{\exp(g(\chi))}{1 + \exp(g(x))}$$

The maximum likelihood (ML) method is used to assess the model. The estimation results of the model are reported in Tables 8.7 and 8.8 below.

4. Discussion of the Results

4.1 Accident rates statistics

The results of the analysis of accidents rates and severities and impacts of installing VMS signs on Scottish trunk roads are presented in Table 8.1 while Figure 8.2 shows the AADT with the number of accidents for all the locations. From the Table it is clear that the VMS sign O3, located on the M8 to the west of Edinburgh

Table 8.1   Overall accident rate (k) 2000–2006

Road	VMS Code	X Accidents	Q (Av.)	L (km)	T (year)	K (accs/ 10^8 veh-km)	SE (accs/ 10^8 veh-km)
M9	N3	6	17515	2	7	6.70	2.74
	W2	5	18006	2	7	5.43	2.43
	W3	2	18857	2	7	2.08	1.47
	W4	2	18088	2	7	2.16	1.53
A720	M7	9	30401	2	7	5.79	1.93
M8	O3	69	31066	2	7	43.47	5.23
	O6	10	26476	2	7	7.39	2.34
	O	7	25442	2	7	5.38	2.04
	V2	10	26377	2	7	7.42	2.35
	O9	18	25036	2	7	14.07	3.32
	V1	13	36582	2	7	6.95	1.93
A90	G1	11	12285	2	7	17.52	5.28
	G2	4	10871	2	7	7.20	3.60
	D6	14	12756	2	7	21.48	5.74

shows that 69 accidents occurred over a period of seven years. Although the average flow at this site is the second largest in the study (AADT = 31066) the accident figures are by far the largest recorded. O3 is not located at a particularly strategic junction but rather on a straight section of road in the midst of a number of strategic junctions with the interchange with the Edinburgh City Bypass A720 downstream and the M9 (to the Forth Road Bridge interchange) slip road upstream. This anomaly may be due to the volume of traffic attempting to change lanes and preparing to leave the M8 at this point rather than flowing smoothly like at other locations with similar AADT. Figure 8.2 shows the number of accidents with the AADT for all the locations.

From the figure it is clear immediately that any apparent linear relationship between accidents and AADT is be almost determined by this isolated point. For the rest of the locations, accidents rates ranges from 21.48 accs/108 veh-kms on the A90 northbound, north of Dundee to 2.08 accs/108 veh-kms at VMS W3 on the M9 north of Falkirk.

Since the number of accidents at each site is low, it would be useful to first carry out the before and after analysis for the sum of the total number of accidents in the before period, and the total after, and then use the total before TLQ value

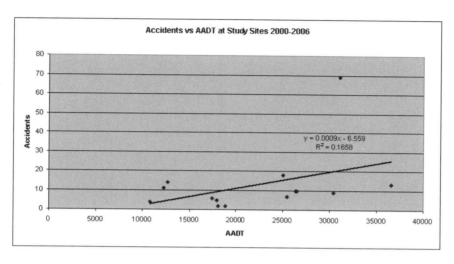

Figure 8.2   AADT and accidents

(i.e. the exposure) and the total after TLQ value. This analysis presented in Table 2, results in an overall de*crease* of the total accident rate (i.e. per veh-km) of 16.9% after installing the VMS (taking into account the 14 sites) and about 15% for the 12 sites (excluding the two sites with zero accidents in the after case.

The results of the before and after accidents rates at each site have then been compared in order to investigate impacts of installing VMS at these sites. The results are presented in Table 8.2. From the table, it is clear that there are a low number of accidents in the after data observed on parts of the M9. In particular the after data for W3 and W4 are zeros and therefore the percentage difference displayed in the table is a decrease of 100% at these sites. The data for the 12 remaining VMS sites show little uniformity in the impacts of VMS on accident rates and they certainly do not confirm the significant accident reductions that have been reported elsewhere in the literature. Indeed the split is 50/50 between sites that have experienced an increase in their accident rates and those that have experienced a safer driving environment.

However, with closer investigation of the accidents rates at each set of these sites, it appears that the % increase in accidents rates (79.88% and a SD 0.948391) is higher than the percentage decrease (-43.92% and a SD 0.186833).

Effectiveness of the VMS installation is assessed by comparing the before and after accidents data, taking into account the control sites as presented in Tables 8.3 and 8.4 below. As discussed earlier, each study site was compared with the control site that most closely matched it in terms of accident figures. It is also noted from Tables 8.2 and 8.3 that G2 on the A90 appears to have an increase of 263% which can be explained by the fact that the before and after accident numbers were one and three respectively. Nevertheless, for VMS with larger accident numbers, three

Table 8.2   Accidents data before and after installing VMS

Road	VMS Code	Accident data (Before)					Accident data (After)					k Before VMS (accs/100m veh-kms)	k After VMS (accs/100m veh-kms)	Before and After % Difference
		X Accidents	Q Average	L (km)	T (yr)		X Accidents	Q Average	L (km)	T (yr)				
M9	N3	4	17139	2	5		2	18455	2	2		6.39	7.42	16.09%
	W2	4	16571	2	5		1	21592	2	2		6.61	3.17	-52.03%
	W3	2	17764	2	5		0	21590	2	2		3.08	0.00	*-100.00%*
	W4	2	17206	2	4		0	19263	2	3		*3.98*	*0.00*	*-100.00%*
A720	M7	4	30042	2	4		5	30881	2	3		4.56	7.39	62.14%
M8	O3	46	30436	2	4		23	31905	2	3		51.76	32.92	-36.40%
	O6	6	25606	2	5		4	28653	2	2		6.42	9.56	48.94%
	O	3	24542	2	4		4	26641	2	3		4.19	6.86	63.77%
	V2	7	25563	2	3		3	26987	2	4		12.50	3.81	-69.55%
	O9	10	24377	2	5		8	26682	2	2		11.24	20.54	82.73%
	V1	7	34372	2	3		6	38240	2	4		9.30	5.37	-42.22%
A90	G1	8	12000	2	5		3	13000	2	2		18.27	15.81	-13.46%
	G2	1	10428	2	4		3	11461	2	3		*3.28*	*11.95*	*263.96%*
	D6	10	12417	2	4		4	13209	2	3		27.58	13.83	-49.87%
Total		114	298463	28	60		66	328559	28	38		**6.22**	**5.17**	**-16.96**

Control Sites

	X Accidents	Q Average	L (km)	T (yr)	k (accs/100m veh-kms)
A90 southbound control	7	11533	2	7	11.88
M 8 eastbound control	20	25647	2	7	15.26
A 90 northbound control	10	10116	2	7	19.35
M 8 westbound control	126	66462	2	7	37.10

Table 8.3   Percentage effectiveness of VMS

VMS	θ	Estimate % VMS Effect	95% CI θ		Effect range	
N3	1.160896	16.09%	0.213	6.338	-78.74%	533.82%
W2	0.479663	-52.03%	0.054	4.292	-94.64%	329.17%
W3	0	-100.00%	0.000	0.000	0.000	0.000
W4	0	-100.00%	0.000	0.000	0.000	0.000
M7	1.037703	3.77%	0.279	3.864	-72.13%	286.44%
O3	0.635975	-36.40%	0.386	1.049	-61.45%	4.91%
O6	1.489406	48.94%	0.420	5.278	-57.97%	427.80%
O	1.637746	63.77%	0.367	7.318	-63.35%	631.77%
V2	0.304464	-69.55%	0.079	1.177	-92.13%	17.74%
O9	1.827277	82.73%	0.721	4.630	-27.88%	362.99%
V1	0.577838	-42.22%	0.194	1.719	-80.58%	71.94%
G1	0.865384	-13.46%	0.230	3.262	-77.04%	226.20%
G2	3.639633	263.96%	0.379	34.991	-62.14%	3399.12%
D6	0.501324	-49.87%	0.157	1.598	-84.28%	59.85%

signs on the extremely busy M8 showed increases in accident rates, two by over 50% (83% and 64%) as did the VMS on the A720 Edinburgh Bypass (62%). A small increase was also calculated on the far quieter M9 at VMS N3 although a substantial reduction of 52% was experienced on the M9 at VMS W2.

Improved accident rates were also found at three sites on the M8 (36%, 42%, and 70% respectively) and on the remaining A90 VMS (13% and 50%) however it must be noted that the calculated reductions on the whole were less substantial than the calculated increases. This can be illustrated rather crudely, by simply summing the increases and decreases on the M8 as an example. For the six VMS studied along the M8 the net impact upon accident rates is found to be an increase of 47.2% between 2000 and 2006, mostly more significant at higher AADT (M8, A720) rather than the quieter roads (A90, M9).

From Table 8.3 it appears that the results for W3, W4 and G2 are poor for the reasons mentioned above. The VMS that are estimated to have had a reducing impact upon accident rates have a possible range of effectiveness that does not rule out an actual increase in accident rates. For two of the VMS (W2, G1) the ranges stretch to a considerable increase of 329% and 226% respectively. Indeed, of all the VMS only O3 and V2 on the M8 have upper ranges that reach into minor percentage increases in accidents. The VMS that are estimated to increase accidents all have possible ranges that include theoretical accident reduction but stretch into extremely large accident increases.

The immediate indication from Table 8.4 is that VMS have led to an increase in accidents at 10 of the 12 sites with before and after accident data. From these results it is concluded that the installation of VMS signs might have resulted in an

Table 8.4   Percentage effectiveness of VMS including the control zone information

VMS	Y_b Accs before	Y_a Accs after	X_b Accs before	X_a Accs after	VMS % Effect	Effect Range	
N3	4	2	5	2	25.00%	-88.20%	1224.07%
W2	4	1	5	2	-37.50%	-95.95%	865.03%
W3	2	0	5	2	-100.00%	0.00%	0.00%
W4	2	0	4	3	-100.00%	0.00%	0.00%
M7	5	4	4	3	6.67%	-85.45%	682.20%
O3	46	23	76	50	-24.00%	-84.32%	268.40%
O6	6	4	5	2	66.67%	-78.99%	1222.36%
O	3	4	4	3	77.78%	-78.60%	1376.72%
V2	7	3	7	3	0.00%	-86.70%	651.94%
O9	10	8	9	1	620.00%	9.31%	4642.50%
V1	7	6	7	3	100.00%	-68.62%	1174.54%
G1	8	3	9	1	237.50%	-59.06%	2682.30%
G2	1	3	4	3	300.00%	-73.48%	5932.77%
D6	10	4	15	5	20.00%	-81.94%	697.14%

Table 8.5   Chi-squared results for the 14 VMS

VMS	Observed		Accidents per year	Expected		X^2 $=\sum(O-E)^2/E$
	Accs before	Accs after		Accs before	Accs after	
N3	4	2	0.857	4.286	1.714	0.07
W2	4	1	0.714	3.571	1.429	0.18
W3	2	0	0.286	1.429	0.571	0.80
W4	2	0	0.286	1.143	0.857	1.50
M7	5	4	1.286	5.143	3.857	0.01
O3	46	23	9.857	39.429	29.571	2.56
O6	6	4	1.429	7.143	2.857	0.64
O	3	4	1.000	4.000	3.000	0.58
V2	7	3	1.429	4.286	5.714	3.01
O9	10	8	2.571	12.857	5.143	2.22
V1	7	6	1.857	5.571	7.429	0.64
G1	8	3	1.571	7.857	3.143	0.01
G2	1	3	0.571	2.286	1.714	1.69
D6	10	4	2.000	8.000	6.000	1.17

Table 8.6   Regression analysis models

Variable	Model_1	Model_2
Constant	-0.713 (-1.32)	-0.607 (-1.114)
Traffic flow	0.247 (1.018)	0.287 (1.171)
4 years average accidents	1.272 (11.623)	1.266 (11.581)
Availability of VMS	–	-0.369 (1.066)
R^2	0.868	0.874

increase in the accident rates on the roads upon which they are placed. At this point the analysis hints at a possibility of this but no more. The next step is to assess each site in terms of accident trends in order to look for evidence of something more than trend occurring at any of the sites.

The results from the chi-squared test are presented in Table 8.5. The Table strongly suggests that the VMS under investigation have not contributed to an increase in the true underlying mean μ accident rate at any of the 14 sites due to no statistically significant results being returned. None of the values are greater than the 3.84 required to reject the null hypothesis (*Ho*) that the mean rate of accidents in the before and after periods are sufficiently different. The largest results of 2.22, 2.56 and 3.01 were found for VMS O9, O3 and V2 respectively. These three VMS are all located upon the M8 and experience very high AADT. However, other signs upon the M8 return extremely low values of 0.64, 0.58 and 0.64. These signs also experience large AADT figures.

4.2 Modelling accidents severities

In this part of the analysis, two sets of models have been calibrated; firstly two linear regression models and secondly two binary logit models. The results are presented in Tables 8.6, 8.7 and 8.8.

Of the 45 principal variables which exist in the accident, vehicle and casualty datasets available in Stats19, driver age and gender as well as time of day, weather conditions and severity of accident are included in the analysis..

Table 8.6 shows the coefficient estimates, the *R2* and statistical significance of the coefficients (t-values) of the two linear regression models using OLS. From the table, it seems that the independent variables, in particular the 'four years average accidents' are statistically significant at the 5% level. The R2 values of the models of 0.868 and 0.874 are good, especially when the small numbers comprising the dataset is taken into consideration. However, the R2 values might only be high because of the single outlying, influential point as discussed above. With regards to VMS, the coefficient is negative signalling a decrease in accident numbers if VMS is present, although this is not statistically significant.

Table 8.7   Statistics summary and estimation results of the binary logistic model of accident severity (KSI v.s. slight)

Variable	Categories of each variable	Frequency	Coefficient (p-value)	O.R.
Intercept: -1.876 (0.217)				
Gender of rider	1. male	136 (76%)	0.044 (0.943)	1.045
	2. female	43 (24%)	R	R
Age of rider	1. up to 20	19 (10.6%)	-0.456 (0.661)	0.634
	2. 21~59	143 (79.9%)	-1.017 (0.206)	0.362
	3. 60 or above	17 (9.5%)	R	R
Vehicle type	1. car (private car/taxi)	143 (79.9%)	-0.835 (0.150)	0.434
	2. heavier veh (bus/HGV)	36 (20.1%)	R	R
Accident month	1. spring/summer (Mar–Aug)	84 (46.9%)	0.533 (0.025)	3.237
	2. autumn/winter (Sep–Feb)	95 (53.1%)	0.325 (0.006)	1.384
VMS measure	1. no VMS	113 (63.1%)	0.749 (0.186)	2.116
	2. automatic signal	66 (36.9%)	R	R
Weather condition	1. fine	118 (65.9%)	-0.319 (0.720)	0.727
	2. wet	44 (24.6%)	-0.602 (0.544)	0.548
	3. extreme	17 (9.5%)	R	R
Accident time	1. rush hours (1600–1859; 0700–0959)	69 (38.5%)	0.533 (0.359)	1.705
	2. late night/morning (0000–0659)	10 (5.6%)	1.446 (0.105)	4.246
	3. evening (1900–2359)	21 (11.7%)	0.176 (0.849)	1.185
	4. late morning/afternoon (1000–1559)	79 (44.1%)	R	R
Traffic flow	1. 10000–19999	42 (23.5%)	0.261 (0.688)	1.298
	2. 2000–29999	65 (36.3%)	0.079 (0.245)	1.317
	3. 30000–39999	72 (40.2%)	R	R
Dependent variable	1. KSI	22 (12.3%)		
	2. slight injury	157 (87.7%)		
Classification accuracy	1. the number of KSI that was correctly predicted: 1 (0.6%)			
	2. the number of Slight injury that was correctly predicted: 156 (99.4%)			

Observations: 179
McFadden Pseudo R-Square: 0.103
Likelihood ratio: 139.761 (with 115 D.F., p=0.058)

R: reference case; O.R.: Odds Ratio

Table 8.8 Statistics summary and estimation results of the binary logistic model of accident severity (KSI v.s. slight), conditioned on the absence of vms

Variable	Categories of each variable	Frequency	Coefficient (p-value)	O.R.
Intercept: -0.573 (0.784)				
Gender of driver	1. male	85 (75.26%)	-00814 (0.913)	0.923
	2. female	28 (24.8%)	R	R
Age of driver	1. up to 20	11 (9.7%)	-0.752 (0.628)	0.472
	2. 21~59	93 (82.3%)	-0.986 (0.339)	0.373
	3. 60 or above	9 (8.0%)	R	R
Vehicle type	1. car (private car/taxi)	92 (81.4%)	-1.616 (0.029)	0.199
	2. heavier veh (bus/HGV)	21 (18.6%)	R	R
Accident month	1. spring/summer (Mar-Aug)	54 (47.8%)	1.607 (0.019)	4.987
	2. autumn/winter (Sep-Feb)	59 (52.2%)	R	R
Weather condition	1. fine	748 (65.5%)	-0.715 (0.580)	0.489
	2. wet	32 (28.3%)	-0.552 (0.668)	0.576
	3. extreme	7 (6.2%)	R	R
Accident time	1. rush hours (1600–1859; 0700–0959)	39 (34.54%)	0.809 (0.253)	2.245
	2. late night/morning (0000–0659)	5 (4.4%)	0.946 (0.458)	2.576
	3. evening (1900–2359)	11 (9.7%)	1.049 (0.297)	2.856
	4. late morning/afternoon (1000–1559)	58 (51.3%)	R	R
Traffic flow	1. 10000–19999	29 (25.7%)	-0.269 (0.747)	0.764
	2. 20000–29999	45 (39.8%)	0.372 (0.598)	1.450
	3. 30000–39999	39 (34.5%)	R	R
Dependent variable	1. KSI	16 (14.2%)		
	2. slight injury	97 (85.8%)		
Classification accuracy	1. the number of KSI that was correctly predicted: 2 (1.8%)			
	2. the number of slight injury that was correctly predicted: 95 (84.1%)			

Observations: 113
McFadden Pseudo R-Square: 0.149
Likelihood ratio: 13.698 (with 12 D.F., p=0.320)
R: reference case; O.R.: Odds Ratio

By focussing upon the variables of individual accidents, a dataset of 179 incidents has been used for further modelling based on the likelihood of accident severity when a number a driver characteristics and road conditions are known.

A total of 179 accidents have been used in the analysis. These represent all the accidents at the 14 sites over the seven years of Stats19 data that was analysed. The accidents that occurred at sites with no VMS numbered 113 compared to 66 at sites with VMS. Of these 24.3% are classified as KSI (21 observations), 74.4% are classified as slight injury (158 observations) during the period 2000–2006. Tables 8.7 and 8.8 show the statistics summary and estimation results of the binary logistic models of accident severity (KSI vs. slight) with and without VMS signs. The models have pseudo-R2 measures of 0.103 and 0.149 respectively. As for predicting each injury-severity category, the classification accuracy for KSI, slight injury, and no injury was 0.6% and 99.4% and 1.8 % and 84.1% in the second model. With regard to the effect of the explanatory variables it seems that time of day and time of the year (month) have a positive impact on accident severity with positive coefficients of 0.533 and 1.446 respectively (Table 8.7) and that there are greatest impacts in terms of accident severity when there is no VMS at the site. The presence of VMS signs appear to have positive impacts in reducing accident severity, although the results are not conclusive.

5. Conclusions

This chapter investigates impacts of VMS on accident rates and severities on Scottish trunk roads. A before and after analysis of accidents at 14 selected VMS sites in Central and North-East Scotland is presented. The number and location of accidents at the selected sites have been identified. Seven years of Stats19 accident data (2000 to 2006) at these sites was used. The study focuses on VMS signs across four major trunk roads in Scotland that were installed after 2000 plus four control sites. The roads included are the M8 (Edinburgh – West Coast via central Glasgow), M9 (Edinburgh – Stirling), A90 (Dundee – Aberdeen) and the A720 (Edinburgh Southern Bypass), as well as four control sites that are located on similar stretches of road (in terms of flow and accident numbers) but that have no VMS either at the site or on the prolonged approach to the site.

The results of the investigation presented in this chapter show little uniformity in the impacts of VMS on accident rates and they certainly do not confirm the significant accident reductions that have been reported elsewhere in the literature. Indeed, by investigating accidents rates for the sum up of the total number of accidents in the before period, and the total after period show an overall *reduction* of the total accidents of 16.9% after installing the VMS. When investigating the individual sites before and after installing VMS, the split is 50/50 between sites that have experienced an increase in their accident rates and those that have experienced a safer driving environment. However, the % increase in accidents rates (79.88% and a SD 0.948391) is higher than the percentage decrease (-43.92%

and a SD 0.186833). When the control sites are taken into account, the results show that VMS have led to an increase in accidents at 10 of the 12 sites with before and after accident data. From these results it is concluded that the installation of VMS signs might have resulted in an increase in the accident rates on the roads upon which they are placed. However, further analysis of the data of each site in terms of natural fluctuations in accident trends did not show any evidence that the VMS under investigation have contributed to an increase in the true underlying mean μ accident rate at any of the 14 sites due to no statistically significant results being obtained.

A total of 179 accidents, that represent all the accidents at the 14 sites over the seven years of Stats19 data, have further been used to calibrate two sets of models. The modelling results on the other hand suggest that the presence of the VMS reduces accidents severities at the considered sites.

Although the results presented here are by no means conclusive, however they do cast doubt that perhaps the wide ranging benefits to road safety that are frequently attributed to VMS are not as clear as has been reported.

Due to the relatively low number of sites involved in this study, which are all on Scottish trunk roads, the possible ranges of effect now stretch from a possible reduction in accidents to a possible increase. Further research with more data and wider area coverage is therefore urgently needed.

References

Al-Ghamdi, A.S. (2004), *Evaluation of Fog Detection and Advisory Speed System in Urban Transport X – Urban Transport and the Environment in the 21st Century* (Southampton: WIT Press).

Boyle, L. and Mannering, F. (2004), 'Impact of traveller advisory systems on driving speed: some new evidence', *Transport Research Part C*, 12(1): 57–72.

Carson, J. and Mannering, F. (2001), 'The effect of ice warning signs on ice-accident frequencies and severities', *Accident Analysis and Prevention*, 33(1): 99–109.

Chatterjee, K., Hounsell, N., Firmin, P. and Bonsall, P. (2002), 'Driver response to variable message sign information in London', *Transport Research Part C*, 10(2), 149–69.

Conference of European Directors of Roads(2003), Action FIVE – Framework for Harmonised Implementation of Variable Message Signs in Europe.

Cooper, B.R. and Sawyer, H. (2005), Assessment of M25 Automatic Fog-Warning System – The Final Report Federal Highway Administration, Washington D.C.

Erke, L., Sagberg, F. and Hagman, R. (2007), Effect of route guidance variable message signs (VMS) on driver behaviour. *Transport Research Part F*, 10(6): 447–57.

Highways Agency (www.highways.gov.uk/knowledge/334.aspx) .

Highways Agency Variable Message Signs (2005), 'A Guide to VMS and their use', V.1.2.

Karlberg O (2002), 'Roads, Weather, Action Traffic', *Technology International*, Acc. No. 00938796.

Rämä, P. and Kulmala, R. (2000), 'Effects of variable message signs for slippery road conditions on driving speed and headways', *Transport Research Part F*, 3(2): 85–94.

Walker, C. (2007), 'An Investigation into Scottish Trunk Road Accident Rates and Trends following the Installation of Variable Message Signs (VMS) 2000–2006. Unpublished MSc Dissertation. Napier University.

www.trafficscotland.org/traffic.aspx?action=layermap&type=8 - Online NADICS VMS map

Chapter 9

Transantiago: The Fall and Rise of a Radical Public Transport Intervention

Juan Carlos Muñoz, Juan de Dios Ortuzar and Antonio Gschwender

Introduction

Santiago de Chile is the fifth largest conurbation in South America. In December 2004 it had approximately six million inhabitants living in 1.5 million dwellings spread over 1,400 km². The city's transport system featured almost a million private cars, 8,000 buses serving 380 routes and a publicly owned underground system (Metro) with three lines extending 46 kms; it also had some 11,100 shared taxis (*taxi colectivos*) organised on 341 lines providing services on fixed routes with a variable fare and variable frequency. The city also had some 21,400 normal taxis and 6,000 executive/special taxis. It is interesting to mention that neither the Metro, nor the buses or shared taxis, received any operational subsidies.

On the other hand, on a typical working day 16.3 million trips were made, 10 million of which used motorized transport modes (DICTUC 2003); the total number of motorised trips grew significantly between 1991 and 2001, when large-scale O-D surveys were conducted (Ortúzar et al. 1993; Ampt and Ortúzar 2004). This increase may be explained by the impressive performance of the Chilean economy, which saw the proportion of the population living under the poverty line drop from 48% in 1988 to 13% in 2005. Unfortunately, as in many other cities, economic growth has resulted not only in more trips but also in an increase in the share of trips taken by car. Indeed, the car modal split rose from 18.5% to 38.1% in this period, while bus and Metro trips rose only slightly, such that their combined modal split shrank from 68.1% to 49.5%.

However, public transport decline was not only attributable to economic growth. As in many other cities in developing countries, the level of service provided by the Santiago bus system was fairly deficient. On a survey taken in 2001 respondents rated it as the worst among several city services (electricity, heating fuel, banks, telephones, etc.), while ranking Metro and shared taxis as 'very good' and 'reasonable' respectively (Adimark 2001). Some of the many reasons for this dissatisfaction can be traced back to the medium term history of bus services in the city. In the early 1980s the system was privatised and completely deregulated with dramatic consequences (Darbéra 1993; Fernández 1994). For example, bus ownership was atomised (individual firms averaged only some two buses each); also, the driver's salary was directly linked to the number of fares he sold, pushing drivers to compete at street level with other buses, even those from the same company. This resulted in dangerous races to busy stops, or waiting for a red light in congested areas to prolong the stay at a busy junction (buses could be boarded anywhere), or to skip stops with few passengers, refuse entrance to schoolchildren (as they paid only one-third of the adult fare). Bus bunching, a well-known phenomenon in congested streets, accentuated some of these practices which obviously had a negative effect on the quality of service and safety.

As for the buses themselves, lack of proper maintenance led to heavy pollution and the fragmented ownership and use of makeshift, unofficial, terminals made inspection difficult. The reintroduction of limited regulation in the 1990s (street franchising) led to some rationalization of the bus fleet and fare levels, but the service and ownership structures remained untouched. Also, although the average vehicle age was only five years (buses could only remain in service until they were ten years old), the quality of the ride was poor as buses were actually lorries with a bus chassis, so they had mechanical gears, an inappropriate suspension and a steep stair access. Needless to say, a system based on such vehicles was hopeless for people with a mobility handicap. Although drivers were blamed for these defects by the public, they were as much the victims as the culprits. The way their wages were calculated pushed them to compete fiercely, discriminating against students and violating safety rules. However, they spontaneously created a headway control system using observers at strategic intersections that kept track of passing buses and informed drivers on the time intervals separating them (Johnson et al. 2006). Also, they often worked shifts of 14 hours or more, handling tickets and money as they drove, had no formal contracts, endured frequent assaults (sometimes ending in death) in low-income areas, suffered a bad public reputation and were even expected (by the owners) to take about a third of their income by pocketing lower 'fares' charged to passengers willing to ride without a ticket.

Another feature of the system was its high operating costs. Most routes passed through the CBD connecting terminal points on the periphery, with an average length of more than 60 km (counting both directions). The advantage of such a network was that most passengers could travel almost anywhere without transfers, but since frequencies are necessarily the same along a route, service was oversupplied almost everywhere. These extra kilometres not only boosted costs but also meant more pollution, particularly in the peripheral areas where many roads are still unpaved. On the other hand, as fares were not integrated, a new fare had to be paid each time a passenger boarded a bus or entered the Metro, making transfers expensive. Also, as earnings were directly related to demand, drivers chose to work independently of each other giving rise to excessive daily off-peak frequencies[1] and limited night services. Furthermore, lack of integration meant that the Metro accounted for less than 7% of trips. Underutilization of the system

---

1   The incremental cost (fuel, lubricants, tyres, drivers' wages, etc.) of an additional 60 km bus run could be recovered if just 50 passengers, or less than one passenger/km, boarded the vehicle (SECTRA 2003).

was particularly true for the lowest-income groups concentrated in Santiago's outer areas, who faced the extra cost of having to take feeder buses or shared taxis to their closest stations (Gómez-Lobo 2007). Clearly then, the system as it stood before Transantiago suffered from a range of serious structural problems that urgently needed to be addressed.

Finally, the bus companies were actually owner cooperatives which operated like a cartel, coordinating their members' bids in the various tendering processes that occurred since Chile regained democracy in 1990. Attempts by the government to modernise the system were often obstructed (even the powerful Pinochet dictatorship had failed to take on the cartel) and in 2001 the companies brought Santiago to a standstill by blocking major intersections with their vehicles. However, on this occasion the cooperative leaders were taken to jail and the government regained the upper hand with ample public support. This was a crucial moment that revealed the system could actually be changed.

The diagnostic above was shared by most observers of Santiago's public transport system. Suggestions on what to do about it were inspired in part by successful experiences in other South American cities, particularly Curitiba and Bogotá. The approach taken in Curitiba aimed at achieving a sustainable city; a planned city since the 1940's, it provides a wide variety of public transport services that function well together. Although fare integration is quite limited, the city plan includes segregated bus corridors running down the centre of wide streets. Curitiba is considered a success story and deserves the worldwide admiration it has received, but it must be kept in mind that it has only 1.8 million inhabitants. Even so, many urban centres around the world have partially followed its lead, but its long-term integrated land-use and transport plan has proven difficult to replicate elsewhere.

Bogotá chose to develop a bus rapid transit (BRT) system, called Transmilenio, along its two main avenues in the 1990s (by 2007 it had been extended to two more corridors). The city invested heavily on dedicated on-surface infrastructure and stops, with articulated buses provided by private operators. The new system provides fast, reliable, safe and efficient services and has an integrated fare structure embracing its own buses plus those of a few feeder operations. Although it received no direct subsidies initially, the addition of new corridors has run into financial difficulties. Furthermore, Transmilenio has remained totally un-integrated with the rest of the old bus system, which easily outnumbers it in both vehicles and routes. Thus, Bogotá's impressive project showed that although BRT could be implemented in mass corridors it offered few answers to more system-wide problems. This kind of operating scheme has also been successfully implemented in several other cities worldwide (e.g. Quito, Jakarta and Brisbane).

The Transantiago Plan

The basic design

The main goal of this, as we will see, radical intervention was to maintain and hopefully increase the public transport share of trips in the city. For this, the bus system had to be modernised and the quality of service significantly enhanced. However, the government placed certain constraints on this goal by requiring the system to be environmentally, socially and economically sustainable. Environmental sustainability was important because a drastic change was the only foreseeable way to reach the pollution-reduction targets defined by the government for the transport system less than a decade earlier (CONAMA 1997). On the other hand, economic and social sustainability meant that Transantiago would have to be subsidy-free and charge an average fare similar to that of the old system.

The new system was designed as a network of feeder and trunk services in which the Metro would function as the backbone (SECTRA 2003). For this, the city was divided into ten areas, each of them with a single firm running feeder services into the trunk lines and the Metro. Five other firms would run the trunk services over major corridors of the city. This design was intended to minimise on-the-street competition and confine it to the bidding process, where all participants had to be registered corporations. The trunk and feeder structure was chosen because, among other criteria, it would reduce the number of bus-km and the fleet size (Gschwender 2005, pp. 10–11) and therefore reduce operating costs and bus externalities such as pollution, noise and accidents (the buses in Santiago were previously involved in approximately 120 deaths/year, Díaz et al. 2006).

The new setup meant, however, that passengers would have to transfer far more often between lines (including the Metro); since the system contemplated an integrated fare this would not add to the cost for passengers. It was expected that fare integration would significantly boost Metro usage (approximately 100%, although most of the new trips were expected in off-peak periods since then the frequencies of overlapping bus services would drop), reducing bus fleet requirements even further.

The fleet and frequencies for each line were determined using state-of-the art heuristic-based methods for route design and public transport assignment (Malbrán et al. 2004). The basic data included the 2001 O-D survey (DICTUC 2003) and a detailed bus survey conducted that same year for the morning peak (SECTRA 2002). As the design was based on the morning peak, the fleet size and frequencies for other periods were determined in relation to it. For example, the evening peak hour demand was arbitrarily assumed to be 80% of that for the morning rush hour.

Self financing eventually implied that peak period services (both buses and Metro) were designed to run at very high occupational rates (on average six passengers/m^2) for certain route sections. Clearly, if this financial constraint was relaxed the system would require more (and probably some of them smaller) buses and higher frequencies yielding lower occupation rates.[2]

To further reduce incentives to on-street competition, drivers' wages could not be linked to the number of passengers transported directly by each one. This, plus the fact that the companies would receive the same payment for a concessionary fare as for a full-fare, was expected to ensure non-discriminatory services for all passengers. Working conditions for drivers were also expected to improve and labour standard regulations complied with (*i.e.*, an eight-hour maximum working day, and 45 hours per week).

The buses themselves were intended to be modern vehicles equipped with facilities for the disabled and capable of accommodating more passengers. The new buses should be put into service gradually so that the new technologies could be absorbed smoothly by the system. The remainder of the fleet in the early stages would be composed of the newest vehicles from the old system.

The Transantiago design also incorporated an information system that would furnish users with valuable advice both before and during their trips on how best to make their journey. It would monitor the location of every bus via GPS and control bus headways through a communication system installed in each vehicle. Furthermore, it would be set up to provide next bus arrival information via message displays at stops, cellular phones and the Internet.

Cash would be eliminated from the system through the implementation of a smart contactless debit card intended for use by all passengers, thus freeing drivers from handling money and minimising the likelihood of assaults. The money generated by the system would be administered by a financial and technological manager (the AFT, a private company) that would collect the funds and distribute them among operators on a twice-monthly basis. It would also be responsible for distributing the cards, creating a card loading network and installing card readers in every bus.

On the other hand, an awards and penalties scheme similar to the one used by Transmilenio in Bogotá was drawn up. It involved defining a list of infractions and their corresponding penalties in the operators' contracts. The revenues generated by the scheme would be paid over to the 'best operators' through the awards system based on headway regularity, service quality, fare evasion and user satisfaction.

Finally, the Transantiago plan called for a network of segregated bus-only corridors and well-designed bus stops that would speed up service by reducing bus-car and bus-bus interactions, and shorten boarding and alighting times. Unfortunately, while the plan was still in the design phase the government decided to postpone these investments, giving priority to the construction of new Metro lines that would extend the network from 46 kms in 2004 to 83 kms by 2006, and

---

2   Unfortunately the models used in the design did not incorporate an explicit penalty for transferring (over and beyond the waiting and walking time involved in such move), neither did they have as a variable the (dis)comfort implied by having to travel in crowded conditions.

partially subsidising and guaranteeing a set of new urban highways in Santiago, four of which (155 km) were inaugurated during the same period. This decision was widely criticised by transport specialists in the country.

Business model

The Transantiago business model aimed at meeting the following requirements:

1. Companies should have incentives to transport more passengers. Although competition was eliminated from the streets, firms were expected to make efforts to improve their levels of service through newer routes, higher frequencies, more reliable and regular services, etc.

2. Company revenues should be related to their operating costs. Thus, revenues should vary with changes in input costs such as fuel, wages, etc. They should also reflect variations in fleet size and distance travelled; otherwise firms would have no interest in increasing frequencies or adding new services.

3. Demand risks should be kept low. This requirement was considered important to attract new and hopefully foreign operators.

4. A mixture of incumbent and new operators was sought. Although public opinion was against any participation by the incumbent operators (i.e. former members of the owner cooperatives) in the Transantiago process, in the end they were allowed to take part as the Transport Ministry had no legal grounds on which to limit their involvement; also, barring them risked triggering a serious social conflict. Finally, a gradual renovation of the fleet was preferred to renewing it all at once, as mentioned above, and modernization was particularly desired for the trunk units.

In the business model design each of the ten feeder units and five trunk units was assigned a referential demand level and a broad operational plan (services and capacity for different periods over the course of a week), based on output of the strategic network design model (Malbrán et al. 2004). This referential demand incorporated monthly seasonality and was assumed to grow by 1.7% each year. Firms bidding for a particular unit requested a certain charge per passenger given the referential scenario. This allowed identification of each firm's financial needs.

However, the government was reluctant to transfer the total demand risk onto the shoulders of the bidders. For a start, most firms interested in the process were doubtful about the referential demand, especially non-incumbent and foreign operators. Moreover, by partitioning the system into 15 units, the total risk perceived by each firm was higher than the risk level faced by a single entity concentrating the total demand. Thus, it was decided that the system, as a whole, would absorb 90% of the risk of each unit and each firm would only assume the remaining 10%. If demand turned out to be 20% lower (higher) than the referential level, the firm would receive 80% (120%) of its declared financial needs in terms of expected revenue in the first month and 98% (102%) each month thereafter (if demand remained constant). Although such deviations from expected revenue might appear small, it was argued that since firms were heavily debt-financed a 2% rise or fall in receipts could have a significant impact on their bottom lines.

These revenue calculations assumed that the cost structures and input costs of each firm would remain constant. The effects of cost changes were accounted for in two ways. First, monthly revenue was indexed to the monthly evolution of key input costs, and second, it was also adjusted according to a correction formula defined on the assumption that 55% of an operator's costs were proportional to the distance travelled, 35% were proportional to the number of buses and 10% were fixed. It was expected that these adjustments would encourage companies to expand, since a 10% increment in both fleet and distance travelled would increment revenues by the same percentage, while the cost increment would be slightly lower. In addition, more service should trigger more demand which, as mentioned earlier, would also increase revenue. On the other hand, to avoid an oversupply of buses during certain periods the frequency of each service was required to lie within a range defined by the government. If the load factor for a given service exceeded a certain threshold (85% or 90%), the operator would have to put on more buses, while if it was too low, the frequency in the defined range should be reduced.

To further reduce the financial risk assumed by the bidders, additional measures were adopted: (a) a minimum income was guaranteed, varying between 60% and 85% of the reference income depending on the type of concession (main lines with/without new buses and feeder lines); (b) the concession period could be extended up to 24 months until the expected present value of revenue was reached; (c) revenue adjustments were applicable in the event of reductions in patronage due to a fall in commercial speeds; and (d) a compensation fund was set up to stabilise user fares (and hence minimise the impact of fare changes on patronage). Finally, to assure long-term financial sustainability it was established that if fares reached a certain upper limit, measures would be introduced to rationalise the use of cars in the city (*i.e.* introduce a road pricing scheme) in order to boost public transport use.

The awards and penalties scheme described earlier implied a direct incentive to maintain a good level of service, although it would affect only a small proportion of operator revenues. Unfortunately, it was decided that the incentives and the revenue correction formula would go into effect only after the first year of operation. It was assumed that the system needed to stabilise to some degree before these elements of the plan could work properly.

Two of the trunk units were requested to have a completely new full fleet, so their operators could work them for 13 years. These two units were pivotal to the whole system as they served the most important corridors in the city and would need large fleets. It was widely assumed that they were set aside for new operators. The remaining three trunk units were awarded for only three years, but for two of them the operator could extend this period to 13 years if an entire new fleet of buses was acquired. Operators interpreted these three units as being reserved for incumbents, with more open competition reserved for the third unit after three years. As for the feeder units, they were franchised for five years and most of them were expected to be awarded to incumbents as well.

Finally, the plan was also affected by the debt assumed by Metro for constructing a new line (US$ 1,600 million) that was inaugurated a year before Transantiago started operating. Metro was committed to financing both the rolling stock and one-third of the infrastructure costs. Unfortunately, this burden (some US$ 500 million) together with the related operating costs were off-loaded onto Transantiago in the form of an annual payment that increased in piecewise linear fashion with the number of passengers Metro transported. Thus, the lack of an operational subsidy for Transantiago meant that public transport users would pay a significant part of the investment needed for the most recent Metro extension.

Bidding process

The invitation to tender for the Transantiago project was advertised abroad and attracted bidders from Colombia, Spain and France as well as some new Chilean investors. Most of the incumbent bus companies also participated. The tender specifications provided that any one bidder could be adjudicated no more than two trunk units and a maximum of four units in all. Each participant was required to indicate the charge per passenger for the bus services provided on the units it was bidding for. The bid amounts had to fall within a valid range bounded by a lower limit that would ensure the offer was serious and an upper limit that would guarantee that system costs remained under control. In addition, bidders could specify a desire to be awarded no more than a certain maximum of each type of unit due to fleet size or financial capacity limitations.

Because of the narrowness of the valid bidding range all units (except one small feeder unit that in the end was not awarded) were assigned at the range's lower limits. Ties were broken on the basis of three factors: (a) a direct contribution to the compensation fund of the system (declared by the bidder); (b) a commitment regarding expenses per driver on wages and employee benefits, and (c) a specified number of extra kilometres to be run by the operator (this last one only in the case of trunk services). The assignment of units to bidders was made using a greedy heuristic aimed at minimising future system costs (Muñoz and Molina 2007).

As for the AFT, the tender was won by a consortium of Chile's largest four banks, the country's biggest retailer and its largest and most respected computer technology firm. The widespread introduction of a smart card was apparently attractive for the local banks, which saw it as an opportunity to offer financial services and reach a large number of people, many of whom had no other bank products because of their low income. The tender process for the information system was delayed, but eventually assigned to a conglomerate led by a large Indian company. The government announced that it was satisfied with the success of the three tender processes.

The Period between Design and Implementation

Transantiago was originally designed to start in one go. The government talked of *Big Bang*, as a day when every element of the system would go into smooth operation. However, it was soon realised that this involved too many risks and, instead, a transition period was defined during which every part of the system that could be implemented separately would be excluded from the Big Bang. Since the nuclei of Transantiago was the new services and the integrated fare, these aspects could not be unbundled from the rest. It was also decided that the entire city should change routes simultaneously as phasing in the new plan by geographic areas or corridors would require the temporary coexistence of both systems, an impossible task; among other things, the incumbent operators were notorious for trying to sabotage new services by resorting to aggressive gangster-like tactics and an incipient effort by the authorities to integrate buses and Metro in the 1990s, an initiative known as Metrobus, had not been successful.

The transition period was set to begin one year before the official start of the complete system. During that time no changes would be made either to services or fares, which would continue to be paid in cash in a non-integrated system, but new buses could start to operate. The one-year period began when the new firms took control of all bus services in the city but this involved a major problem since the old system used many more buses than Transantiago. The new operators were required to rent buses during the transition year with the exception of those awarded the two major trunk lines; this had been done to clear the way for new operators, widely anticipated to be foreign.

Since the new buses had to satisfy strict custom specifications, they were not expected to arrive immediately and were scheduled to go into service over the course of the year, gradually replacing the older buses as they arrived. The number of new buses requested for this period exceeded the bus production capacity of the three firms based in South America (who offered the most inexpensive buses that fit the required specifications), so an eventual collusion on the price of new buses was avoided. Vehicles had to be equipped with GPS and smart card readers several months prior to launching the information system. It was further required that the old fares could be paid using smart card on buses destined to remain in operation well in advance of the system's start-up. Secondary elements, such as full implementation of appropriate bus terminals (non-existent in the old system), were left for sometime after the official launching date.

Implementation: The Fall of the System

Shortly after the tendering process ended the Minister of Public Works, Transport and Telecommunications, who was the main responsible for the Transantiago project, resigned due to an unrelated conflict. Unfortunately, with only one year left before a new Chilean President was to take office, the replacement Minister decided to slow down work on Transantiago, postponing important decisions until the new administration took office. This unfortunate combination of events meant that during a most crucial one-year period, progress on the plan came almost to a standstill. The various stages of the original work schedules set for the bus operators and the AFT were completely delayed. The new Minister also decided to reduce the scope of the information system, leaving all on-line control over bus headways in the hands of the bus companies. Finally, new firms were allowed to rent some of their buses, thus relaxing the requirement of a totally owned fleet. All these decisions were to have dramatic consequences as we will see below.

In March 2006 a new government, but from the same political coalition, was sworn in. The person chosen as Transport Minister (thus ending an eight-year period without a Ministry separated from Public Works) was a 40-year-old lawyer with an MBA, with no background in public transport systems or transport engineering, who spent the first three months on the job familiarising himself with the problems he inherited. The inauguration of Transantiago was slated to take place as early as August and no later than October of that same year. The project was by then well behind its original schedule and delaying it further would have damaged its credibility.

Yet as October approached, almost none of the key elements of the Transantiago design were in place. The AFT had not yet equipped the buses with the necessary technology, making use of the smart card impossible. Nor had it implemented either the smart card distribution or the loading network. The segregated bus-only streets and lanes were not near to being constructed (severe problems with compulsory buying of private property in the selected streets had been encountered delaying construction indefinitely), so the increased bus speeds assumed in the system design could not be guaranteed. In the light of these problems the government decided to postpone the official launching of the system (Big Bang) until 10 February 2007. This date was an appealing choice since it falls in the middle of the summer holidays when traffic and public transport demand drops sharply.

Unfortunately, as 2007 began the situation had almost not improved at all. As of mid-January the smart card was operational in only a few buses and when 10 February arrived many of them still did not have the technology installed to validate card payments. The operators protested at the failure to implement the card system, and raised doubts about its effectiveness for recording payments. Segregated bus lanes had been little more than painted on some of the main arteries, but building of the much needed bus-only streets was still not complete at the time of writing

Confronted with this scenario, the new Minister made three decisions: (a) during the first three months operators would not be paid per passenger but rather on the basis of their reference demand; (b) the integrated fare would be flat and equal to the bus fare just before Transantiago was inaugurated (US$ 0.7); (c) finally, a trip could not include more than three transfers nor extend beyond 90 min (in contrast to 70 min as originally planned).

The first of these decisions had a series of consequences both immediate and unfortunate. Perhaps the most important one was that as operators no longer had an incentive to provide services, since their revenue was now guaranteed, they considerably reduced the size of the fleet in operation from the original plan. This was aggravated by the delay in introducing the GPS technology, which was crucial to monitor their operating commitments. This was finally compounded by a series of elementary management errors (some believe this was actually sabotage) by some of the incumbent companies, such as drivers unable to get to terminals in time to begin their shifts, rented buses in bad condition and not properly inspected, etc. All this led to massive queues at bus stops and transfer terminals, unacceptably long waits, extreme crowding on Metro services, and a general feeling of chaos that after the first nine months of operation had sadly not abated.

On the other hand, implementing a flat fare was not a bad decision as it enabled passengers to learn the new routes. However, an operational deficit started to grow because the system had been designed to keep the average fare constant, and in the old system 15% of the passengers paid two fares. In addition, the new flat ticket price implied a reduction of approximately 10% in the old Metro fare, and many passengers found they could make two trips in the 90 min window but paying just once. This situation was further aggravated when this time window was extended to 120 min after many users complained they had to pay two peak-hour fares because their trips had become longer under the new regime.

Operating speeds were significantly affected by the lack of specialised infrastructure. For the most part, buses have to share the road with private cars and loading times were long because of the large increase in the number of boardings due to the additional transfers and reduced frequencies. This last problem was particularly acute on trunk routes served by the new 160-passenger articulated vehicles (which had been deemed the flagships of the system), as passengers had to board through the front door and there was almost no buffer capacity to 'store' those waiting to pay.[3] The fall in operating speeds lowered the capacity of the system even further and the reduced fleets took longer to complete their trips, increasing waiting times and load factors.

Although most residents of Santiago tend to blame the system design for the insufficient number of buses, it remains to be seen how the system will function when the full complement of vehicles called for in the plan are in operation and the necessary specialised infrastructure is finally built. All the above problems have been seriously compounded by a massive propaganda war led by the main newspapers, which are all in opposition hands, which the government has lost without putting up a real fight.

An important source of problems has been the delay in installing the GPS technology. Bus regularity has been poor, increasing passenger waiting times and reducing system reliability especially at off-peak periods (and particularly at night)

---

3   This has been partly solved by the increasing use of specialised stops where passengers pay in advance and enter the bus through all doors on arrival.

when frequencies are lower. Bus bunching reached epic proportions and convoys of several buses on the same route became a regular sight.[4] The AFT claimed that implementation of the GPS system in all buses was completed by August 2007, but the headway control system was not in operation by December 2007, as the software originally provided by the AFT was inadequate and had to be replaced.

In this scenario of unreliable, slow, infrequent and crowded buses, passengers turned to the Metro wherever they could. Metro trips also increased because of the initial lack of a comprehensive smart card charging network outside Metro stations. Later in 2007, this network increased and now reaches almost 1,500 points in the city, but still it has been poorly informed. Thus, for a very long time more than 80% of the users found it necessary to go to the Metro just to recharge their cards. All this meant that even though a near-doubling of Metro demand was assumed in the original design, during the early days of Transantiago the underground system struggled to handle the rush at peak periods on some sections of the network and average load factors exceeded seven passengers/m² at times.

Operational performance also suffered as boarding and alighting times at Metro stations increased significantly, with passengers forcing doors and delaying trains. The system's operating speed dropped about 20% but partially recovered after the arrival of new trains and some successful measures aimed at speeding boarding at critical stations (Metro 2007). On the other hand, the socioeconomic mix of Metro users drastically changed with the advent of Transantiago. Previously it was used mainly by medium to high income groups, but fare integration has made it affordable to the masses; this had an important social and distributional impact since the majority of public transport infrastructure investment had historically been allocated to Metro line extensions. However, many frequent Metro users shifted to private transport after judging the new level-of-service unacceptable. As for disabled users, they have been unable to board either the new buses or the Metro during peak periods as both systems have been running mostly full.

In contrast to the above, almost all of the plan's objectives regarding drivers' working conditions have been achieved. Drivers now work legal shift lengths, have proper contracts and no longer need to drive aggressively (on-the-street competition disappeared), resulting in a clear reduction in the number of accidents. Students are no longer discriminated against, bus stops are observed and assaults on drivers are a thing of the past.

Nevertheless, some new bus operators have faced several massive strikes that have shaken the whole system as drivers protest their wages, comparing them with those paid by other firms. Some drivers even argue that before Transantiago their incomes were higher, no doubt factoring in the amount they effectively stole by not issuing tickets, and ignore the fact that now they have legal pension schemes, health services and work fewer hours.

---

4   Bunches of five or six buses serving the same route were commonly encountered. We have counted lines of as many as eight buses on the same trunk route after waiting 20 min.

In general Transantiago's environmental goals were not initially achieved, except for the reduction in noise emission levels that are particularly noticeable in the city centre. Atmospheric pollution during 2007 was higher than in previous years, and some have put the blame on the increase in car use in reaction to the difficulties of Transantiago. This accusation is difficult to prove, however, as Santiago has been suffering from a serious natural gas shortage that has forced many industries and electricity generators to shift back from gas to diesel or coal.

Transantiago on the Rise

Once the system started to operate, the Ministry realised that increasing operating speeds was crucial to the smooth functioning of the new system. Thus, some bus-only corridors were swiftly created (with little more than painted lines on the roads) but have been poorly enforced. Also, approximately 100 pre-paid bus stops have been implemented and they should increase further as more congestion points are detected. Since this setup allows passengers to board buses through all doors, it has proved efficient in speeding service, loading buses uniformly (thereby increasing effective capacity) and reducing fare evasion (which was higher than expected in the early months due to the lack of incentives for operators to enforce payment). In areas where specialised bus corridors have been built and enforced, the system has worked considerably better, reaching operating speeds of up to 28 km/hr compared to the meagre 8 km/hr along similar corridors without it.

The tide definitively turned in May 2007 when the Transport Minister was replaced by a more senior figure, with ample expertise in directing large projects and institutions. Under his command, the authority has already increased the total bus fleet from the original 4,500 units considered in the contracts to some 6,400 buses operating in December 2007. The 179 bus lines that existed in February 2007 were already expanded by June 2007 to 219 normal lines and 15 express lines (called 'Super Expresos'), that run only in the peak without intermediate stops and intensely use the urban freeways to the chagrin of car users.

Although the smart card payment system had worked effectively, the Ministry recognized in mid-June that it was running a financial deficit of over 35%. This was due to a combination of factors, as mentioned above: a lower fare, the ability to concatenate multiple trips within two hours while paying a single fare, the approximately 10% of buses not yet prepared to receive fare payments, passengers unable to access buses by the front door, the continuing inability to charge smart cards in the many areas that still have no charging network, angry passengers who simply refused to pay and blatant evasion. The press, meanwhile, placed most of the blame for the deficit on fare evasion, an allegation that deeply offended much of the local population.

In June 2007 the originally planned system of paying operators on a per-passenger basis was at last put into place after the AFT managed to demonstrate that the technological tools for payment records and revenue distribution were operating properly. The first payment to the trunk companies under AFT was 50% of their previous payments, whereas the feeder companies received an average of 90%. These figures increased significantly in the following months as a result of the demand risk control explained above, but they have not reached their previous levels. The new Minister was confident that this new revenue incentive would help to reduce fare evasion and sat down with the operators to renegotiate key aspects of their contracts.

As a result of this renegotiation, several changes were made to the system:

1. As mentioned above, an increase in the total fleet was agreed, from the 4,500 buses of the original design to 6,400 vehicles that were in operation by December 2007.

2. The operators' payment formula was changed to give them a direct pecuniary incentive to fulfil the operation programs and improve headway regularity; this was only possible once the GPS information was available to the authority. The payment per passenger originally planned was modified by the introduction of a 'fulfilment index', that basically measures the proportion of planned vehicle-hours that are successfully provided by the operator. Thus, the final payment still depends on the number of passengers moved but is now multiplied by the fulfilment index (between 0 and 1). So if the operator provides 90% of the planned vehicle-hrs, only 90% of the payment will be received.

3. Up to 6% of the committed number of operative vehicle-hours can be postponed to anytime during the following month, but to receive full compensation for them the operator will need to provide 20% more than the postponed vehicle-hours if they belonged to peak periods, and 10% more if they belonged to off-peak periods. On the other hand, the fare correction factor was activated immediately (it had been originally planned to start on the second year of the plan). These two adjustments have meant that the payment mechanism depends on the number of passengers, the vehicle-kms planned and the vehicle-hours actually provided. It also recognizes cost impacts if the fleet or the kms planned change from month to month.

4. The authority considered it paramount to increase the incentives for operators to diminish fare evasion, search for new services, and improve service quality. In this sense, the 10% demand risk faced by operators was considered too low. It could be argued that keeping most of the demand risk in the hands of the authority was critical for attracting new and foreign investors. However, once the system started operating firm revenues should grow more significantly on the demand they attract. It could also be argued that this growth should be higher for feeder services than for trunk services since the former can better adapt their routes to reach their customers. This is especially important in those areas where many people are captive public transport users. Finally, the demand risk faced by all firms was raised from the original 10% to 35%.

5. The headway control software will be changed, but its implementation will take until well into 2008. If an operator implements its own headway control system and achieves good regularity in the headways before that, it will be rewarded with up to 2% additional income. Moreover, the operators have the possibility of enhancing their income if they manage to increase their demand or decrease evasion.

6. The initial operation of Transantiago showed that the evening peak was probably more complicated for operators than the morning peak as it was longer than originally planned and also more intense. Furthermore, operators had difficulties in bringing drivers to work the third daily shift needed to cover that period. So, to improve the level of service the authority requested to extend the evening peak period by half an hour, and the beginning of the night period (where only some bus lines run at low frequencies) was delayed by two hours. In addition, the evening peak frequencies were increased by 25% to equal the morning peak frequencies. Thus, the negotiated contracts aimed at improving the service between 5:30 pm and 1 am. The changes imply more vehicle-kms which can be provided with the same fleet, *i.e.* without increasing the number of buses. Nevertheless, operators' payments will be adjusted as a result of the additional bus-kms planned. However, in the case of trunk operators, these extra vehicle-kms will be subtracted from those offered in their bid as additional vehicle-kms offered (for free) by each firm. Thus, each firm will see their payment adjusted only if the requirements exceed their offers. Operators would not be paid for passengers transported in buses operating without payment-validating devices, unless they could prove that the AFT was to blame for not installing them.

All these measures imply better incentives for the operators (aligned with passenger interests), but also a higher financial risk. Therefore, several compensations were agreed:

1. Each company was allowed to postpone up to 12 months one of the three payments they were requested to deposit in the compensation fund.

2. During the first year of operation after the renegotiated contracts are signed, the difference of revenues with the pre-contract system will be reduced. On one hand, if the firm deserves more than in the original scheme it will receive only half more; on the other, if it deserves less, it will be allowed to borrow the difference from future payments once the year is over; thus, the payment will have a fixed and a variable component. The fixed part will be the difference between the payment they would have received without renegotiating contracts and that considered in their original contracts. The variable component will be based on the original payment per passenger considered in their winning bids.

3. A guaranteed minimum demand was fixed at 75% of the reference demand, but the actual income will be calculated considering the fulfilment index.

In summary, the authority has created many incentives for operators to operate their buses properly. Their revenues will be significantly affected by their patronage, plan-related operational cost changes will be covered, regular headways will be recognized, and non fulfilment of their operational plans will be punished. As was designed, all these incentives rely on enforcement via GPS information.

Finally, the authority got a special subsidy of US$ 290 million to finance the deficit that had been projected for the first year (2007) of Transantiago. Half of this amount was restricted by parliament to be granted only when the authority finished the contract renegotiations with the bus companies. This was interpreted as a pressure on the Transport Minister to succeed in this task, but can also be interpreted as an incentive for operators to accept the new terms. The authority also declared its intention to provide a subsidy for 2008 if necessary, although it was estimated to be considerably lower.[5]

When Transantiago was finally implemented in February 2007, the project instantly became the main policy issue in the country, with constant attention in the media as the chaotic situation affected just too many people. Every politician took the opportunity to voice a unanimously critical opinion about it and as the government panicked, the opposition saw an opportunity to score a big jump in the polls. All this was sadly in strong contrast to the low level of interest in public transport (especially the bus system) shown by politicians and public opinion previous to the change.[6] The problems experienced by the new system have negatively impacted the government's approval rates, revealing the high expectations of the general public in the project. On the postive side, the political character of public transport planning decisions seems to have been recognised, and previously taboo subjects like nationalising or subsidising the system are starting to be discussed.

In summary, little more than a year after the Big Bang some key aspects of the project have still to be implemented (*e.g.* infrastructure and centralised headway control) and the system has still a long way to go before convincing Santiago residents of its benefits. The renegotiated contracts were a strong signal in the right direction and it is fairly obvious, even in the media, that things are slowly getting better. The surest sign is that the project was, from January 2008, no longer in the news.

---

5   In November 2007 the government suffered a serious setback as some of its own members in the lower chamber allied with the opposition to defeat the bill; intense negotiations were needed to pass the bill at the senate.

6   Even though Santiago's public transport system was partially regulated in the early 90s, the buses remained fully in private hands with little intervention from the authorities. Despite the evident disapproval of users, the system and its problems were little discussed in the media and totally absent from election campaigns.

Conclusions

Transantiago was a highly audacious plan designed to improve the severely criticised, and with reason, public transport system of a major city. It was intended to provide a solution to almost everything that was wrong with the old system. However, the project suffered from a problematic implementation and achieving its main goal, that of improving the quality of service for all users, is still some way down the road. We believe the following are some important lessons that could help others in the future:

- The government launched Transantiago with extremely limited institutional, legal and financial support. Santiago does not have a city-wide system of local government (it is actually divided in 36 boroughs, each with strong power over its geographical area), so even the most trivial modification to the public transport system requires the consensus of a series of actors including five central government ministries, the 36 local authorities, Chile's national environmental commission (CONAMA), etc.[7] Also, the legal framework in which Transantiago operates is weak; as an example, fare payment can only be enforced by the police, greatly complicating efforts to fight fare evasion (effective fare inspection and enforcement tools are sorely needed). Finally, Transantiago was designed with ridiculously limited human resources; perhaps the biggest project in the country's history was managed by a small office fitted with a handful of young engineers working under an enthusiastic but only slightly more experienced professional, with little specialist support. Given this setting, the initial failure of the system is actually no surprise.
- Transantiago had to deal with too many changes in the authorities responsible for it. In the 30 months following the signing of operator contracts in January 2005, Chile saw four different Transport Ministers and the top Transantiago executive was changed with even greater frequency. The lack of continuity resulting from the absence of a single political figure to promote and defend the plan through its various stages adversely affected the work of the small team dedicated to the project. This was very different from other, more successful, public transport experiences in Latin America such as Curitiba, Quito or Bogotá. The lack of political leadership combined with an unclear institutional design in the transport sector led to numerous difficulties in all phases of the project.[8]
- The business model was beset by a number of significant problems described

---

7   Gwilliam (2005) has stated that … 'true creativity in public transport in developing countries is essentially institutional rather than technological', an argument that fully applies to Santiago.

8   Gschwender (2007a) discusses the institutional design of Transantiago and a proposal for improving it.

above. Clearly, incorporating the right incentives in the operators' contracts is a difficult task that requires striking the right balance among opposing forces. For example, incentives are needed both to provide frequent services even when they do not yield operational revenues, and to limit frequencies so that externalities are controlled. Transantiago also suffered from the effects of assigning contracts with no concern for their implementation. A complex and integrated system with so many actors requires a competent team of experts who understand the technical difficulties involved in putting it into operation. There must also be an authority capable of ensuring that the private operators fulfil their commitments on schedule.

- The implementation of Transantiago showed that an integrated system that has been designed as such cannot be inaugurated if some of its key elements are absent. This calls attention to the crucial role played by the authorities during the period before implementation. A bad kick-off of the system risks shifting many public transport users towards the private car which is exactly the opposite of the purpose desired. Those users are very difficult to bring back.
- The government offered a highly unrealistic vision of what Transantiago would be like. In a large city the public transport system should be designed so that vehicles run at capacity during peak periods unless significant subsidies are provided; passengers should not expect to always travel seated in these periods. Also, rationalization of the system requires that people will generally have to transfer to reach their destinations; this is particularly the case in a highly (income) segregated city, where residences and jobs tend to be far apart for low-income groups. The authorities should have communicated clearly and accurately the advantages and disadvantages of the new system.
- Public participation in the process, although it lasted several years, was almost non-existent. The government did not publicise the details of the system until it was ready. The government could have been more receptive to user feedback and even previous operators' experience.
- Public transport operations in Santiago (and probably in several other Chilean cities) should be subsidised. The diminishing fraction of public transport trips over time is alarming given the serious negative externalities associated with the use of private cars such as pollution, accidents, congestion and noise. Furthermore, in Santiago most public transport users belong to the lower socio-economic class. Thus, a subsidy would benefit not only the city as a whole but also its most vulnerable sector. The smart card system allows such a subsidy to be directly targeted at this group; details on these and other technical and economical arguments are given by Jara-Díaz and Gschwender (2005) and Jansson (2005). The absence of subsidies in the design of Transantiago turned out to be a strong constraint as it incorporated maximum bus and train load factors which were inconsistent with the main goal of the plan (*i.e.* significantly enhancing quality of service). It

is revealing that user comfort was never part of the planning discussions. Debate over subsidization must be linked to a definition of the quality of service a system such as Transantiago should provide.

- Transantiago also confirmed the importance of a centralised headway control system and how its absence affects waiting times. Bus bunching is a well-known problem in public transport operations. The system performance in its first months showed that without some form of headway control and with no pecuniary incentives for the companies and bus drivers, bus bunching could reach massive levels.

- The size of some of the new operators may have been unnecessarily large given the limits on economies of scale obtainable in public transport services (Jara-Díaz 2007). A government study has shown that such economies taper off rapidly once a company's fleet of buses reaches 250 vehicles (SECTRA 2003). This is consistent with international literature evidence. The reason behind the government's decision to create larger firms was to avoid having more than one operator providing services for a given origin-destination pair, but now that on-the-street competition has been eliminated, smaller firms could be preferred in forthcoming renewal bidding processes. It should also be noted that large drivers' unions constitute an ongoing threat to the system and several strikes have already taken place at various bus companies.

- Bus terminal properties should not be left in the hands of the private operators given the significant competitive advantage they confer in future tendering processes. They are often found in highly strategic locations that rapidly become scarce resources. The lack of terminal location alternatives poses a sustainability threat to the system.

And on the plus side:

- Transantiago showed that eliminating bus on-the-street competition was possible.[9] The authors are not aware of any other city with serious street-level competition problems that have been solved as effectively and radically as in Santiago.

- It is still early to claim that Transantiago shows that running a cashless system is feasible since fare evasion in some areas of the city is still rather high. However, it is quite remarkable that the system is 100% relying only on a debit card; in fact, smartcard use by poor and relatively less educated people was one of the big worries everybody had about the system and it has worked without almost any problems.

---

9   An immediate consequence of this change is evident in the radically lower number of buses running with their doors open. Before Transantiago this was the norm, leading to several deaths every year (and many more injuries) due to passengers falling from moving buses.

- Transantiago has considerably improved drivers' working conditions. Under the old system, drivers did not declare their employment (meaning they had no access to bank credits) and about half of their salaries came from not issuing tickets to some riders and pocketing their fares. Drivers were compelled to compete with other buses, roaring through the streets causing accidents, pollution and congestion. They worked very long shifts (14 hours or more), were often assaulted, and frequently fought with schoolchildren over concessionary fares. All these situations have radically improved with the new system.
- Despite its many operating problems, the Transantiago process has shown that breaking a very strong public transport cartel and securing the participation of international operators can be achieved. Although limited, the amount of regulation in the previous system (bus operations were subject to tendering processes) somewhat eased this major task; if the system had been totally deregulated, as in the 80s, the government would have had to negotiate the desired changes with the incumbent operators, making the entire process considerably more difficult.

Acknowledgements

This study was partially financed by Project ACT-32 within the framework of CONICYT's *Anillos Tecnológicos* programme. Thanks are also due to FONDECYT (Project 1050672) and to the Millennium Institute on *Complex Engineering Systems* for having supported our research work.

References

Adimark (2001), *Presentación de Resultados Indice Nacional de Satisfacción de Consumidores Segundo Semestre* <http://www.adimark.cl/calidad22001/index.htm>.

Ampt, E.S. and Ortúzar, J. de D. (2004), On best practice in continuous large-scale mobility surveys. *Transport Reviews* 24, 337–63.

CONAMA (1997), *Plan de Prevención y Descontaminación Atmosférica de la Región Metropolitana* <www.conama.cl/portal/1301/article-34930.html>.

Darbéra, R. (1993), Deregulation of urban transport in Chile: what have we learned in the decade 1979–1989? *Transport Reviews* (13): 45–59.

Díaz, G., Gómez-Lobo, A. and Velasco, A. (2006), 'Las micros en Santiago: de enemigo público a servicio público', in A. Galetovic (ed.), *Santiago: ¿Dónde Estamos y Hacia Dónde Vamos?* (Santiago: Centro de Estudios Públicos).

DICTUC (2003), *Actualización de Encuestas Origen-Destino de Viajes, V Etapa.* Final Report to SECTRA, Department of Transport Engineering, Pontificia Universidad Católica de Chile, Santiago.

Fernández, D. (1994), 'The modernization of Santiago's public transport: 1990 1992', *Transport Reviews* (14):167–85.

Gómez-Lobo, A. (2007), 'Transantiago: una reforma en panne', Trabajos de Investigación en Políticas Públicas N° 4, Departamento de Economía, Universidad de Chile, Santiago.

Gschwender, A. (2005), 'Improving the urban public transport in developing countries: the design of a new integrated system in Santiago de Chile', 9th Conference on Competition and Ownership in Land Transport (Thredbo9), Lisbon, Portugal.

Gschwender, A. (2007), 'A Comparative Analysis of the Public Transport Systems of Santiago de Chile, London, Berlin and Madrid: What can Santiago learn from the European Experiences?', PhD Thesis, Bergische Universität Wuppertal.

Gwilliam, K.G. (2005), 'Creative problem solving in developing countries', 9th Conference on Competition and Ownership in Land Transport (Thredbo9), Lisbon, Portugal.

Jansson, J.O. (2005), 'Bus transport system optimization and pricing', 9th Conference on Competition and Ownership in Land Transport (Thredbo9), Lisbon, Portugal.

Jara-Díaz, S.R. (2007) *Transport Economic Theory* (Amsterdam: Elsevier).

Jara-Díaz, S.R. and Gschwender, A. (2005), 'Making pricing work in public transport provision', in Button, K. and Hensher, D.A. (eds), *Handbook of Transport Strategy, Policy and Institutions* (Oxford: Pergamon Press), pp. 447–59.

Johnson, R.M., Reiley, D.H. and Muñoz, J.C. (2006), '"The war of the fare": how driver compensation affects bus system performance', Working Paper, National Bureau of Economic Research, Washington, D.C.

Malbrán, H., Muñoz, G., Thomas, A., Schwarz, D. and Zucker, M. (2004), 'Transantiago: el desafío de un nuevo sistema de transporte público para Santiago de Chile', Proceedings XIII Pan-American Conference of Traffic and Transportation Engineering, Albany, USA.

Metro (2007), 'Solución para el aumento de la capacidad de transporte: operación expresa de Línea 4 del Metro de Santiago', XIII Congreso Chileno de Ingeniería de Transporte, Santiago, Chile.

Muñoz, J.C. and Molina, D. (2009), 'A multi-unit tender award process: the case of Transantiago', *European Journal of Operations Research*, 197(1): 307–11.

Ortúzar, J. de D., Ivelic, A.M., Malbrán, H. and Thomas, A. (1993), 'The 1991 Great Santiago origin-destination survey: methodological design', *Traffic Engineering and Control* 34: 362–68.

SECTRA (2002), *Análisis Modernización de Transporte Público V Etapa – EOD a Buses en el Gran Santiago* <http://www.sectra.cl>.

SECTRA (2003), *Análisis Modernización de Transporte Público VI Etapa – Estructura de Costos del Transporte Público* <http://www.sectra.cl>.

Chapter 10

Unexpected Delay and the Cost of Lateness on I-394 High Occupancy/Toll Lanes

Nebiyou Y. Tilahun and David M. Levinson

1. Introduction

High Occupancy/Toll (HOT) lanes allow vehicles that do not meet occupancy requirements to access High Occupancy Vehicle (HOV) facilites for a fee that may be fixed or dynamically set. Implementation of HOT lanes have increased use of previously under utilized capacity on HOV facilities. Since 1995 HOT facilities have opened up in California (SR-91 and I-15), Texas (I-10 and US-290), Minnesota (I-394), Utah (I-15) and Colorado (I-25). Others such as Washington State and Virginia are currently considering implementation of HOT lane programs.

The I-394 MnPASS lanes in Minnesota opened for use in 2005. The aims of the project were to provide options for travellers and to improve usage of the available capacity on the existing HOV lanes. Any surpluses were also to be used for bus transit service improvement in the corridor (Cambridge Systematics Inc. et al. 2006). Currently tolls are electronically collected and dynamically set to maintain free-flow conditions on the HOT facility while carpool and transit users can access it for free. The fee on I-394 HOT lanes can vary from $0.25-$8.00 with the average toll of $1.10 (September 2006) (NuStats 2006). Single Occupancy Vehicles (SOVs) that want to use the facility have to lease a transponder. MnPASS customers used the system twice a week on average (Munnich and Buckeye 2007). The system had 11,000 subscribers as of June 2007 (Gutknecht 2007). A survey of MnPASS subscribers found very high satisfaction with the system (NuStats 2006). Before and after MnPASS implementation attitudinal surveys also found that the proportion of people that thought the project was a 'good idea" was closely comparable across different income groups (NuStats 2006).

HOT lanes serve to reduce travel time, and increase arrival travel time reliability for their users. Implementation of HOT lanes has also led to reduction in peak delays in general purpose lanes. In Minnesota congestion has been reduced in the entire corridor after MnPASS implementation (Munnich and Buckeye 2007). Similarly, among panel survey participants, the proportion of people who said they were delayed by congestion on a reference trip that they were assigned fell by 8 percent, whereas it rose by 6 percent in the control I-35W corridor from fall 2004 to spring 2006 (NuStats 2006). On SR-91 in California, delays were reduced from a range of 30–40 minutes to less than 10 minutes for SR 91 users in the first six months and rose slightly after a year (Sullivan 1998). On I-15 a reduction of 19% and 23% in travel time in the morning and afternoon peak were observed between 1996 and 1997 (Supernak et al. 1999).

One advantage of value pricing projects is to give travellers the option to get out of unanticipated congestion by paying a premium. While regular delay due to recurring congestion can be planned for, unanticipated delay makes on-time arrival and scheduling difficult. Strategies to combat unanticipated delay such as early departure have their own penalties as they may lead to excessive early arrival at the destination. On Texas's Northwest freeway (US-290), the fluctuation in average daily speeds in the general lanes (ranging from about 15 to over 60 mph) as compared to the HOV facility (between about 45 and 65 mph) highlight the reliability advantage these facilities provide (Burris and Stockton 2004). On I-15 for example, the most cited reason for using the HOT lanes is the need for on time arrival (Supernak et al. 1999; Supernak et al. 2001). On SR-91 on the other hand, congestion avoidance was most cited as the reason for using the toll lanes. The need to be at a destination on time, the penalties of delay as well as the willingness of individuals to pay to ensure timely arrival has been demonstrated in different studies (Gaver 1968; Small 1982; Noland and Small 1998). This willingness to pay is related to the costs of scheduling, or the ability to meet time constraints at both the origin and destination without excessive unanticipated delay.

While studies of travel time reliability have used standard deviation (Black and Towriss 1993) and range of travel time (Brownstone and Small 2005) to measure uncertainty in travel time, the individual traveller uses information gathered from past experience and recollected from memory to make decisions when alternative travel options are available. Hence past experience of delay or on-time arrival is expected to affect current trip decisions. Once the traveller has departed from their point of origin, their ability to meet scheduled arrival times is largely influenced by events out of their control. The availability of HOT lanes gives some of that control back to the traveller by providing an option to forego the delay for a price, provided the traveller has the necessary equipment to use the facility.

In this study individuals are asked to respond to stated preference questions that are based on the traveller's previous experience. Respondents include users of both MnPASS and general lanes. The questions ask the respondents to assume that they are making the same 'trip on the same day, at the same time of day, for the same purpose' and 'under the same time pressures.' We then test whether or not individuals that experienced delay on the actual trip would show a willingness to pay that is higher than individuals that arrived at their destination early or on time. By asking the respondents their anticipated and actual arrival time on the previous trip, we focus on un-anticipated delay only.

Consistent with previous studies (e.g. (Small 1982)), it is expected that excess delay is especially penalized. Travellers are thus expected to adjust their willingness to pay when they have experienced such a penalty than when they have not. The difference in willingness to pay would represent the costs of the anticipated delay. Such differences, if present, could also explain why some people would not consistently use the MnPASS lanes on a daily basis, but would adjust behaviour based on experience. Though previous studies have shown early arrival to have a disutility, here it is lumped together with on-time arrival because the trip is already underway in the context examined.

One characteristic of the I-394 HOT lanes is that the system is entirely electronic and requires prior subscription for any SOV to use the facility. Decisions to pay and use the HOT lanes can thus only be made en-route by those who have an active subscription. The initial access hurdle reduces the possibility that a traveller changes behaviour the next time they anticipate similar traffic conditions. In a stated preference setting this last requirement is not important, but choices between those that have transponders and make the decision regularly and those that don't have the equipment may be different enough to warrant separate investigations. The following section briefly discusses the survey and is followed by the analysis and results of the SP study.

2. The Survey

The data used for this study is part of a three phase pre- and post-MnPASS implementation study. We specifically focus on waves 2 and 3, which have been conducted after the opening of the MnPASS lanes. The mail and phone survey assigned particular trips to respondents on which to record their experiences. After a few weeks, individuals were phoned to gather the information on their travel experience on the assigned trip, their attitude on MnPASS and traffic along I-394. By reciting their trip experience on the reference trip, the respondents are made to recollect what their experience was. A subset of them were then asked stated preference questions that uses the reference trip which are used in this study. A complete survey questionnaire used in these studies is provided in (NuStats 2006).

For our purposes, we focus on those individuals that participated in the SP study. These individuals have provided information on their experiences on their assigned trip including times of departures, expected time of arrival, and actual time of arrival which they had recorded into a worksheet pre-mailed to the respondents. The SP questions were asked by setting up situations under similar time constraints as the one that they have been on, but offering them different free and tolled travel time options on the general purpose and HOT lanes.

Two types of SP questions were asked of the respondents. The first set (method A) has four questions that have randomly generated travel time savings and toll costs. The second set (method B) has a fixed travel time savings, while asking the respondents if they will pay one of eight possible tolls consecutively. The two methods were used to confim results were consistent among methods as well as to be able to derive individual level willingness to pay from method B (NuStats 2006, p. 10). The individuals are told to assume that they are making the same trip as the one they had recorded, and further the trip is on the same day, at the same time, for the same purpose, and under the same time pressure as they were in the reference trip.

The number of question sets presented under method B varies from person to person because as a person switches preference and decides to pay, it is assumed they would pay anything less than offered, or as they switch to reject a particular toll, it is assumed they would reject anything higher since the time savings doesn't change. In order to have a balanced data set, all eight offers are included and offers they would have rejected or accepted are coded accordingly. Each respondent thus has a total of 12 binary sets of choices to make (four from method A and eight from method B) in which they can pay a toll and get some time savings or forego the time savings and travel on the free lanes.

Some of the subjects in this study were also part of a panel and appear across waves of the study. In the analysis here, we have not accounted for persons appearing across waves, but rather treated them as different individuals. Counting this way, there are 901 stated preference respondents in waves 2 and 3. Out of these, several had responded 'don't know' on some of the choice questions. In addition, due to problems encountered during the administration of the survey during wave 2, method B was not administered to a subset of the subjects. 29 people whose trip purpose is not listed are also excluded from the analysis here. The analysis here considers 700 people for whom both method A and method B were completed, and who have responded to all questions. The stated preference questions under method A and method B were as follows:

Now assume you're making the same trip in the future that you recorded in your travel log. It's a trip on the same day, at the same time of day, for the same purpose, and you're under the same time pressures. You enter the freeway, I-394, and have the option of making this trip using MnPASS if you want to.

Method A

If you were to use the general traffic lanes on I-394, your trip would take TOLLTIME+[#] and be free. If you used the MnPASS lane you would pay [$] and your trip would take TOLLTIME, saving [#] minutes. Now under these conditions, which would you choose to:

Use the MnPASS lane, pay [$] and save [#] minutes
Use the general lane for free
Don't know

Method A (rotated)

If you were to use the MnPASS lane on I-394, you would pay [$] and your trip would take TOLLTIME. If you were to use the general traffic lanes, your trip would take

TOLLTIME+[#], [#] minutes longer than in the toll lane, but it would be free. Now under these conditions, which would you choose to:

Use the MnPASS lane, pay [$] and save [#] minutes
Use the general lane for free
Don't know

Method B
Now imagine a different scenario. If you were to use the MnPASS lane on I-394, you would pay [$] and you would save [#] minutes. Under these conditions what would you do?

Use the MnPASS lane, pay [$] and save [#] minutes
Use the general lane for free
Don't know

3. Analysis

The analysis looked at subscribers and non-subscribers separately. The majority of the subscribers were sampled from the subscriber database, while non-subscribers were randomly selected from households that live along the recently opened I-394 corridor. Thirty five people contacted from a transit database but who have reported driving alone as their main mode of travel and the mode used for the reference trip are also included.

The data for each group (subscribers and non-subscribers) is then divided into six categories based on the individuals' travel experience on their assigned trip. Each category is a combination of departure time period (Morning peak (7:00am-9:30am), afternoon peak (4:00pm-6:00pm) and off-peak time durations) and whether the individual arrived at their destination early/on time or if they arrived later than their stated expected time of arrival on their reference trip. Since the SP questions asked the respondents to consider the alternatives while making the 'trip on the same day, at the same time of day, for the same purpose' and 'under the same time pressures', this classification would let us capture the differences in willingness to pay that are informed by past experience, provided the delays were truly unanticipated. To ensure this is the case, we use the difference in expected and actual arrival times rather than the respondents answer about being delayed by congestion (which could be recurrent congestion). Time of day considerations are also important in this classification because the constraints on people's time, as well as traffic conditions under morning-peak, off-peak and afternoon peak travel times are different. The six categories and the number of people in each category are given in Table 10.1.

In addition to the cost and travel time savings that MnPASS offers, the choice to use it also depends on the flexibility in arrival time at the traveller's destination.

Table 10.1   Respondents in each category

Time of travel	Arrival experience	Subscribers	Non-subscribers
Off peak	On time/ early	56	211
	Late	6	40
Morning peak	On time/ early	110	143
	Late	22	39
Afternoon peak	On time/ early	14	39
	Late	7	13
Percentage early/ on time		83.7%	81%
Percentage late		16.3%	19%

It is expected that there would be a lower likelihood to opt for the MnPASS lane under flexible arrival time conditions even when unanticipated delay occurs all other things equal. In the following formulation, a random parameter logit model is used to account for repeated choices across individuals. Choices are assumed to depend on monetary cost, travel time, trip flexibility and purpose. The utility of alternative j for person i is given as:

$$U_{ij} = V_{ij} + b_i + \varepsilon_{ij}$$
$$b_i \sim N(0,\sigma^2)$$
$$V = f(T, C, F, W, A)$$

Where:

T: Travel time (Minutes)
C: Cost (toll)
F: reported flexibility on arrival time for reference trip (0 = have to be at destination on time or within 10 minutes, 1=Flexible)
W: work trip (0 =No, 1=Yes)
A: method A (randomly generated tolls and time savings in SP) (0 =No, 1=Yes)
b_i: random term for person i
$\varepsilon_{ij} \sim$ iid Extreme Value

For each of the time-of-day experience combinations the deterministic part of the utility for person on alternative j which has attributes of time, cost and flexibility is defined as follows:

Off-peak – early/on time: $V_{ij} = g_0 + a_1 * T_{ij} + a_2 * C_{ij} + a_3 * F_i + g_4 * W_i + g_5 * A_{ij}$
Off-peak – late: $V_{ij} = g_0 + b_1 * T_{ij} + b_2 * C_{ij} + b_3 * F_i + g_4 * W_i + g_5 * A_{ij}$
Morning peak – early/on-time: $V_{ij} = g_0 + c_1 * T_{ij} + c_2 * C_{ij} + c_3 * F_i + g_4 * W_i + g_5 * A_{ij}$
Morning peak – late: $V_{ij} = g_0 + d_1 * T_{ij} + d_2 * C_{ij} + d_3 * F_i + g_4 * W_i + g_5 * A_{ij}$
Afternoon peak – early/on time: $V_{ij} = g_0 + e_1 * T_{ij} + e_2 * C_{ij} + e_3 * F_i + g_4 * W_i + g_5 * A_{ij}$
Afternoon peak – late: $V_{ij} = g_0 + f_1 * T_{ij} + f_2 * C_{ij} + f_3 * F_i + g_4 * W_i + g_5 * A_{ij}$

Table 10.2   Stated choice model predicting choice of HOT lane alternative

Description			MnPASS subscribers				Non-subscribers			
			Estimate	Error	t stat	p value	Estimate	Error	t stat	p value
Intercept		g_0	1.325	0.575	2.31	0.022 **	-3.566	0.416	-8.57	0.000 ***
Off peak	time	a_1	-0.256	0.035	-7.30	0.000 ***	-0.320	0.028	-11.36	0.000 ***
Early/on time	cost	a_2	-1.466	0.12	-12.27	0.000 ***	-1.609	0.117	-13.77	0.000 ***
	flexible	a_3	0.360	0.746	0.48	0.630	-1.272	0.467	-2.72	0.007 ***
Off peak	time	b_1	-0.420	0.154	-2.73	0.007 ***	-0.297	0.048	-6.19	0.000 ***
Late	cost	b_2	-1.669	0.41	-4.07	0.000 ***	-1.206	0.163	-7.42	0.000 ***
	flexible	b_3	-0.264	1.917	-0.14	0.890	0.573	0.918	0.62	0.533
AM peak	time	c_1	-0.331	0.03	-11.01	0.000 ***	-0.329	0.031	-10.74	0.000 ***
Early/on time	cost	c_2	-1.558	0.103	-15.14	0.000 ***	-1.478	0.119	-12.39	0.000 ***
	flexible	c_3	-1.193	0.553	-2.16	0.032 **	-0.627	0.542	-1.16	0.249
AM peak	time	d_1	-0.282	0.062	-4.54	0.000 ***	-0.332	0.048	-6.90	0.000 ***
Late	cost	d_2	-1.776	0.225	-7.91	0.000 ***	-1.974	0.251	-7.87	0.000 ***
	flexible	d_3	-0.245	1.205	-0.20	0.839	3.999	1.089	3.67	0.000 ***
PM peak	time	e_1	-0.236	0.079	-3.01	0.000 ***	-0.256	0.051	-5.06	0.000 ***
Early/on time	cost	e_2	-1.335	0.21	-6.36	0.000 ***	-1.093	0.174	-6.27	0.000 ***
	flexible	e_3	0.767	1.189	0.65	0.520	-0.728	0.939	-0.77	0.439
PM peak	time	f_1	-0.758	0.18	-4.21	0.000 ***	-0.531	0.095	-5.60	0.000 ***
Late	cost	f_2	-1.788	0.418	-4.28	0.000 ***	-1.684	0.321	-5.25	0.000 ***
	flexible	f_3	-6.250	2.155	-2.90	0.000 ***	-0.410	1.492	-0.27	0.784
Work trip (1=yes, 0=No)		W	-0.514	0.512	-1.00	0.317	-0.056	0.34	-0.17	0.868
Method A (1=Yes, 0=No)		A	-0.059	0.154	-0.38	0.702	-0.472	0.151	-3.12	0.000 ***
Standard deviation		σ	2.945	0.227	12.99	0.000 ***	3.054	0.197	15.52	0.000 ***
Number of respondents			215				485			
-2logliklihood (final estimates)			1768.8				2396.1			
-2logliklihood (at all 0, $\sigma=1$)			3274.2				5392			

Where:

g_k, a_l, b_l, c_l, d_l, e_l, f_l; $k = 0$, 4, 5 and $l = 1$, 2, 3 are model coefficients to be estimated

The base alternative is taken to be the free alternative, and the estimate model predicts the probability that the individual chooses the tolled lane. The model is fit for each of the six categories allowing different coefficients for time, cost, and arrival time flexibility in each of the categories. The hypothesis is that the willingness to pay on the current trip for those individuals that reported they were delayed in their reference trip is going to be higher than those that reached their destination either on time or early. This difference signifies the cost of anticipated delay that arises due to lateness from expected travel time. It is also expected that individuals would be less likely to pay for trips that have flexible arrival time all other things the same. Table 10.2 has the estimated model for subscribers and non-subscribers. Table 10.3 gives the willingness to pay estimates for subscribers and non-subscribers respectively by past trip experience.

Subscribers

The results indicate that arrival time flexibility did not reduce the odds of choosing the tolled lane regardless of trip experience among subscribers all other things held the same in the off peak duration. During the AM peak, those subscribers who arrived early/on time on their reference trip and had arrival time flexibility were less likely to opt for the tolled lanes than if the respondent had a relatively fixed arrival time all other things equal. This suggests that those who didn't have trip flexibility more readily exercised using the HOT lanes than those that had more flexibility. In the same time slice, when the reference trip experience is late, that distinction disappears and those that had trip flexibility were no less likely to choose the HOT lanes.

In the afternoon peak, when the experience was early or on time, having trip flexibility did not impact choice of the HOT lane. However, the results are very pronounced in the afternoon peak when the traveller has been late on the reference trip. In this group, those that have a fixed arrival time were far more likely to opt for the tolled lane than those that had flexible arrival time, all other things equal.

Willingness to pay (WTP) estimates for subscribers, presented in Table 10.3, suggest a significantly higher willingness to pay among subscribers who were late in the afternoon peak as compared to all other groups. While willingness to pay estimates for subscribers in the other time groups have considerable overlap at the 95% confidence interval, those subscribers that were late in PM peak had a WTP that was $14.80 more than their early/on time counterparts. Though the sample size in this group is small (7 people late and 14 people early), the results are consistent with expectations that afternoon tasks would be constrained by, for instance, closing times at destinations (e.g. child day care) or multiple tasks that have to be done in limited time, making late arrival penalties far more severe than in the morning where people can 'make up' for lost time. Among AM travellers,

Table 10.3   Willingness to pay estimates ($US/hour)

Category			Subscribers		Non subscribers	
Time	Arrival	WTP	Estimate	95% CI	Estimate	95% CI
Off peak	Early/on time	WTP_a	10.47	(8.03, 12.92)	11.94	(10.03, 13.84)
	Late	WTP_b	15.11	(7.51, 22.71)	14.82	(10.40,19.23)
AM peak	Early/on time	WTP_c	12.73	(10.84, 14.61)	13.36	(11.06, 15.65)
	Late	WTP_d	9.54	(5.97, 13.11)	10.10	(7.49, 12.72)
PM peak	Early/on time	WTP_e	10.62	(4.7, 16.55)	13.96	(8.62, 19.29)
	Late	WTP_f	25.43	(18.75, 32.1)	18.95	(12.95, 24.94)
$WTP_a - WTP_b$			-4.63	(-12.51, 3.25)	-2.88	(-7.43, 1.67)
$WTP_c - WTP_d$			3.19	(-0.66, 7.04)	3.25	(0.06, 6.44)
$WTP_e - WTP_f$			-14.80	(-23.7, -5.91)	-4.99	(-12.89, 2.91)

the WTP for those who were late tends to be lower than that for those that were early, while not significantly different (95% CI for WTP_c-WTP_d (-0.66,7.04)), while there wasn't a statistically different WTP among those that were late and those that were early/on time in the off peak period.

Non-subscribers

Non-subscribers who reported arrival time flexibility showed increased probability of choosing the free lane when they are taking an off-peak trip on which they were previously early/on time after controlling for other variables. In the same time group, those that had trip flexibility were no less likely to choose the tolled lane when they were late in the reference trip.

During the AM peak, when the experience on the reference trip had been early/on time, trip flexibility did not have an impact on choice after controlling other variables. On the other hand, among those that were late in the AM peak, those that reported having trip flexibility had a much higher probability of choosing the HOT lane than those that did not have flexibility all other things the same. In the PM peak, regardless of experience, having arrival time flexibility did not reduce the likelihood of choosing the tolled lane. This suggests that time-cost trade-offs rather than arrival time flexibility are the most important determinants in choosing one alternative over the other in the PM peak period.

Similar to the subscriber group, willingness to pay estimates among non-subscribers is largest for those who were late in the afternoon. There is however considerable overlap with willingness to pay between this group and their early/on-time counterparts in the same time window at the 95% confidence interval (see Table 10.3).

Differences in willingness to pay are detected between those that were early/ on time ($13.36/hr) in the AM peak and those that were late in the same time period ($10.10/hr) (see Table 10.3). A similar trend is also seen among subscribers where the WTP in the AM-late group is considerably lower than the AM-early/on time group. That the WTP for the AM-late group among both subscribers and non subscribers is lower that the AM-early/on time group while this trend is absent in all other groups, suggests that among those that were late in this time slot on the reference trip the lateness penalty might not have been very high, and would not necessitate a revision of how they trade time and cost in their decision making. Among non-subscribers, in all other cases, there is considerable overlap at the 95% CI in the willingness to pay estimate within each time category suggesting the experience of delay in the reference trip had little impact on adjusting the time-cost tradeoffs that people make.

Willingness to pay estimates in this stated preference context are also comparable among subscribers and non-subscribers in each of the categories. This seems reasonable as out of 251 panel members who were non-subscribers an overwhelming 78 percent never considered being subscribers, and only 5 percent and 14 percent cited the transponder being too expensive and not wanting to pay to use MnPASS respectively (Cambridge Systematics Inc. et al. 2006) as reasons for not considering it. The remaining 81 percent didn't consider subscribing to MnPASS for non-economic reasons.

The models also show that there is no evidence to suggest that choices over work trips are any different from other trips. In addition, while subscribers show no difference between survey question methods suggesting more consistent choices, non-subscribers are more willing to opt for the tolled alternative under method B than they are under method A all other things equal. Additional individual variables such as sex and income were found to not improve the overall fit of the model and were dropped. The models also pick up a significant person to person variation among both subscribers and non subscribers (σ=2.945 for subscribers, σ =3.054 for non subscribers – Table 10.2). The magnitude of the standard deviation in both groups suggests that in some cases the subject effects can dwarf the effects from the time, cost and flexibility considerations.

One implication of this model is that costs of unreliability/unanticipated delays are more severe for afternoon rush hour travellers than either morning rush hour travellers or off-peak travellers. That the willingness to pay is highest among subscribers who were late in the PM as compared to subscribers in any other time of day/trip experience category, and that this same category (afternoon peak-late) also has the highest willingness to pay among non-subscribers as well, suggests that delays in this time window are more penalized and that their effect is more likely to inform trip choice decisions in the future.

While not directly comparable because we are dealing with unanticipated delay, these findings are in tune with findings on SR-91 that afternoon peak toll road volumes were consistently larger than morning peak volumes especially since congestion in the free lanes were also worse (Sullivan 1998). Yet it contrasts with findings on I-15 that afternoon delays were more tolerated and more people chose to use the free alternative than the HOT alternative as compared to the AM peak (Supernak, et al. 2001).

4. Conclusion

This study examined differences in choice behaviour for individuals that have had different travel experiences in the past. The analysis is based on the I-394 MnPASS HOT lane project recently implemented in the Twin Cities. Using a Stated Preference survey, individuals are asked about a trip they have taken before, and asked if they would opt for the free route or pay and go on the HOT lanes under similar time constraints and trip conditions but different travel time and toll structures.

By segmenting the data we are able to compare how trip experience affects current choices made by travellers. Costs of unexpected delay are found to be most severe in the afternoon peak where the willingness to pay of travellers who have been delayed is highest. The basic hypothesis, that individuals would be willing to exchange more money per time savings after experiencing an unexpected delay bears out in the afternoon peak for subscribers, but not in the morning or off-peak cases. While willingness to pay estimates for non-subscribers is highest in the afternoon peak previously delayed group, the estimate overlaps considerably with the non-late group.

That the willingness to pay is higher among subscribers who were late as compared to subscribers in any other time of day/trip experience category suggests that delays in this time window are more penalized and that their effects are more likely to inform trip choice decisions in the future.

References

Black, I. and Towriss, J. (1993), *Demand Effects of Travel Time Reliability.* Centre for Logistics and Transportation, Cranfield Institute of Technology.

Brownstone, D. and Small, K. (2005), 'Valuing time and reliability: assessing the evidence from road pricing demonstrations', *Transportation Research Part A: Policy and Practice* (39): 279–93.

Burris, M. and Stockton, W. (2004), 'HOT Lanes in Houston – Six Years of Experience', *Journal of Public Transportation*, 7(4): 1–21.

Cambridge Systematics Inc., Short-Elliott-Hendrickson Inc. and LJR Inc. (2006), *I-394 MnPASS Technical Evaluation. Final Report.* Cambridge Systematics Inc. and Short-Elliott-Hendrickson Inc. and LJR Inc.

Gaver, D. (1968), 'Headstart Strategies for Combating Congestion', *Transportation Science*, 2: 172.

Gutknecht, K. (2007), 'MnPASS two-year anniversary shows slow, but steady, growth', *Mn/DOT Newsline*.

Munnich, L. and Buckeye, K. (2007), 'I-394 MnPASS High-Occupancy Toll Lanes: Planning and Operational Issues and Outcomes (Lessons Learned in Year One)'. 86th Annual Meeting of the Transportation Research Board. *Compendium of Papers CD-ROM*. (Washington, D.C.).

Noland, R.B. and Small, K. (1998), 'Simulating Travel Reliability', *Regional Science and Urban Economics*, 28: 535.

NuStats (2006), *MnPASS Evaluation Attitudinal Panel Survey Wave 3: Final Report*. NuStats and Humphrey Institute of Public Affairs, University of Minnesota.

Small, K. (1982), 'The Scheduling of Consumer Activities: Work Trips', *The American Economic Review*, 72: 467–79.

Sullivan, E. (1998), *Evaluating the Impacts of the SR 91 Variable-Toll Express Lane Facility: Final Report*.

Supernak, J., Golob, J., Golob, T., Kaschade, C., Kazimi, K., Schreffler, E. et al. (2001), *I-15 Congestion Pricing Project Monitoring and Evaluation Services. Task 13. Phase II Year Three Overall Report*.

Supernak, J., Golob, J., Golob, T., Kaschade, C., Schreffler, E. and Kazimi, K. (1999), *I-15 Congestion Pricing Project Monitoring and Evaluation Services. Phase I: Overall Report*.

Chapter 11

Integrated Network Improvement and Tolling Schedule: Mixed Strategy versus Pure Demand Management

Barbara W.Y. Siu, Hong K. Lo

1. Introduction

Amongst transportation problems that plague contemporary urban areas, the most prevalent of which may be traffic congestion. Traffic congestion occurs on roadways when traffic grows to beyond about 90% of their capacity (Papacostas and Prevedouros 2001). As a result, the level of service, which is usually a measure of speed or delay, deteriorates to an unacceptable level. Congestion countermeasures are basically classified into supply and demand measures. Supply strategies include the development of new or expanded infrastructure. Actions in this category are to expand roadway capacity, introduce new highway links, improve junction control, etc., so that the demand is better served, and delays and queuing are lessened. On the other hand, demand strategies include congestion pricing, parking pricing, restrictions on vehicle ownership and use, and other incentive and disincentive policies. Actions in this category aim to modify travel behaviour so that travel demand is lessened or switched to other modes, other times, or other locations that have more capacity to accommodate it. In this study, we consider link capacity expansion and road pricing as the supply and demand measures to be included in the integrated strategy.

The use of road pricing for demand management is well-studied. The revenue collected, among many possibilities, can be used to finance transport infrastructure improvements. In this way, supply and demand strategies for transportation management are not as distinct as they may seem. In particular, synergy can be achieved if these two strategies are mixed in an optimal manner rather than introduced separately. Indeed, financing transport infrastructure via tolling is not a new concept. The approach of build-operate-transfer (BOT) in highway construction and management has been adopted extensively since the 18th century. A brief discussion of the history and examples of BOT projects can be found in Chen and Subprasom (2007). Issues of joint consideration of tolling and highway expansion or construction have been analysed in the transportation literature, such as equity, price control and financial viability (Chen and Subprasom 2007), competitive equilibrium with multiple private operators (Yang and Meng 2000; 2002), etc. Previous studies typically analysed a particular highway segment under the BOT scheme. Our study developed herein provides a general framework that incorporates cases that: 1. The network operator can be either a private entity aiming at profit maximization or the government aiming at maximizing social welfare; 2. All network links are considered as candidates for pricing and expansion rather than pre-selecting a particular highway segment for the analysis; 3. The phasing of network upgrades (new links or capacity expansions) over time is considered rather than treating the problem as an one-off investment over a concession period.

As both costs and effects of any transportation management strategy will accrue over a long period of time, subject to ever-changing demand patterns, gradual network upgrades, varying road pricing scheme and location costs, it is important to incorporate the time dimension in the analysis for the development of a long-term, well-managed growth in transport infrastructure over time. In particular, by introducing the time dimension to the development of time-dependent transport supply and demand management (TS-DM) strategies, Lo and Szeto (2002) showed that they can significantly improve the overall network performance, as network expansion and tolling can be arranged into phases optimally over time (Lo and Szeto 2004; 2005; Szeto and Lo 2005; 2006; 2008). The time-dependent TS-DM problem can be conceptualized as a bi-level program, in which the upper level specifies the objective to be achieved across time by optimizing the TS-DM strategy, subject to constraints of demand growth, physical capacity, and economic considerations. The lower level problem contains the time-dependent combined model, describing the equilibrium travel pattern with respect to the time-dependent TS-DM strategy of the upper lever problem. Some example objectives to be optimized in the upper level problem include travel cost minimization, reserve capacity maximization, consumer surplus maximization under elastic demand, and multi-objective optimization including user cost, construction cost, etc. (Yang and Bell 1997).

In this study, to take into account the long-term effect of integrated tolling and transportation improvement schemes on the overall network performance, in addition to the typical route choice equilibrium assignment, the lower-level problem models the re-location choices of travellers, including both their residence and job locations, in order to minimize their total travel and activity costs. In this time-dependent bi-level formulation, the final output is a set of optimal link capacity expansion and tolling schedule over the planning horizon, which incorporates anticipated population and zonal attraction changes in the future. The TS-DM strategy such formed may serve as a prescriptive tool or reference for government agencies to plan for long-term network management strategies. Moreover, as the TS-DM strategy is specified over time and segmented into phases, which provides flexibility for recourse planning should reality (i.e., the forecast population and land use changes) turn out to be not exactly as predicted. In addition, such a set up permits the development of a probabilistic approach to cater to future uncertain scenarios, which could be an extension to this study. In this study, based on this extended combined model, we study the performance of the mixed TS-DM strategy vis-à-vis that of pure demand management. Hopefully, this will shed light on the marginal benefit of infrastructure improvement on top of demand management, and to provide a more balanced view against the belief that demand management alone is sufficient in solving congestion problems, which has been gaining popularity recently.

One note of caution, however, is that although the formulation can be applied to bigger network scenarios, in the numerical example, we choose to use a small network for ease of results exposition and illustration. After all, this study focuses more on model formulation rather than on policy analysis. Therefore, even though we tried our best to use reasonable parameters in the numerical example, we emphasize that the results obtained are for illustration purposes. They should not be interpreted as accurate indicators for the general level of benefits of TS-DM strategies. We anticipate the benefit of TS-DM strategy to vary from scenario to scenario.

The organization of this chapter is as follows: Section 2 describes the lower level time-dependent combined trip-distribution/traffic assignment problem; Section 3 outlines the bi-level formulation in determining the time-dependent transportation supply and demand management strategy; Section 4 illustrates the formulation with a small network example with some sensitivity analysis; and Section 5 concludes the chapter.

2. Time-Dependent Combined Model

This section develops the lower-level time-dependent combined model. Given a time-dependent TS-DM strategy, to model the resultant changes in demand and activity travel pattern over time, combined models are essential for this purpose. Boyce (1980) developed the methodology in combining trip distribution and traffic assignment into a single model. Lam and Huang (1992) introduced extensions to accommodate multiple user classes. In this study, we further introduce the time dimension in the formulations. The time scale considered in the model is typically 5–10 years. The equilibrium condition holds at each discretized time frame in the planning horizon. The interaction across time mainly involves the overall population growth over time, the competing modes' supply over time, network capacity expansions accumulated over time (assuming that network capacity once added would not be demolished), finance related transactions and rates over time, and the locations' holding capacities over time (once developed, the amount of land available will diminish). Introducing the time dimension in this modelling framework is not only appealing from a theoretical perspective, but more importantly, it enables the analysis of practical and important questions about the effects of a TS-DM strategy over time, including issues such as inter-generation equity (Szeto and Lo 2006), robustness of the TS-DM strategy under uncertainty (Szeto and Lo 2005), and means for implementing the strategy over time (Szeto and Lo 2008). On the other hand, segmenting the planning horizon into connected discrete phases allows for timely review and modification or recourse, if needed, of the TS-DM strategy, making the result more flexible than one-off designs based on a particular scenario forecast.

In this model, the population is separated into locators and non-locators (Lam and Huang 1992). Locators are those who have neither fixed employment nor residence locations; they choose their residence and employment locations, and the corresponding routes simultaneously. Non-locators, on the other hand, have fixed residence locations and decide on their employment locations and the corresponding route choices. In addition, the whole population is stratified by income and modeled as different classes.

2.1 Notations

a	Link index
τ	Period index, $\tau \in [0, T]$
n	Period length in years
$x_a^{(\tau)}$	Daily flow on link a in period τ
$C_a^{(\tau)}$	Capacity of link a in period τ
t_a^0	Free-flow travel time of link a
a_1, a_2	Link travel time function parameters
$y_a^{(\tau)}$	Capacity expansion decision in period τ to be effective in $\tau + 1$
$\rho_a^{(\tau)}$	Link toll implemented on link a in period τ
$l^{i(\tau)}$	Location cost of zone i in period τ
$l_0^{i(\tau)}$	Basic location cost of zone i in period τ
θ^i	Location cost function parameter associated with zone i
δ_{ap}^{ij}	Route-link incidence parameter, equals 1 if link a is on route p between OD pair ij 0 otherwise
$c_p^{ij(\tau)}$	Daily travel cost on path p between OD pair ij in period τ
$C_a^{(\tau)}$	Daily total cost of commute on link a in period τ, defined in (3)
k	Income class
$T_p^{ijk\,(\tau)}$	Trips from zone i to j via path p by locators of income class k in period τ
$T_p^{ijk\,(\tau)}$	Trips from zone i to via path p by non-locators of income class k in period τ

$P^{k(\tau)}$	Class k locator population in period τ
$O^{ik(\tau)}$	Class k non-locator population residing in zone i in period τ
$\beta^{k(\tau)}/\tilde{\beta}^{k(\tau)}$	Logit function parameter for class k locators/non-locators in period τ
$\gamma^{k(\tau)}, \lambda^{ik(\tau)}$	Lagrange multipliers for equations (6) and (7)
$V^{ik(\tau)}$	Location attraction of residential zone i to income class k in period τ
$W^{jk(\tau)}$	Location attraction of destination zone j to income class k in period τ
$K^{i(\tau)}$	Capacity of zone i in period τ
i	Annual inflation rate (%)
r	Annual discount rate (%)
$\varphi(r,\tau)$	Converts daily toll revenue to period value and discount to time 0
B_C, B_M	Unit construction and maintenance cost parameter
$\kappa, \kappa_{ya}^{(\tau)}, \kappa_{\rho a}^{(\tau)},$ $\omega_p^{ijk(\tau)}, \tilde{\omega}_p^{ijk(\tau)}$	Lagrange multipliers for constrains (21), (19), (20), (13) and (14) respectively

2.2 Travel cost

To simplify notations, travel time is expressed in monetary terms throughout this chapter. In this study, we adopt the customary BPR travel time function:

$$t_a^{(\tau)} = t_a\left(x_a^{(\tau)}, C_a^{(\tau)}\right) = t_a^0\left[1 + \alpha_1\left(\frac{x_a^{(\tau)}}{C_a^{(\tau)}}\right)^{\alpha_2}\right] \tag{1}$$

where t_a^0, $C_a^{(\tau)}$ are link a's free-flow travel time and capacity at time τ respectively. α_1, α_2 are coefficients of the BPR function. Furthermore, capacity of link a, $C_a^{(\tau)}$, at time τ can be modified by capacity expansion $y_a^{(\tau)}$, which will be in effect in the next period (i.e. $\tau+1$):

$$C_a^{(\tau+1)} = C_a^{(\tau)} + y_a^{(\tau)} = C_a^{(0)} + \sum_{t=0}^{\tau} y_a^{(t)} \tag{2}$$

In addition to travel time, we consider link toll $\rho_a^{(\tau)}$ as the demand management measure for congestion; hence, the total cost of commute on link a, $c_a^{(\tau)}$ at time τ is

$$c_a^{(\tau)} = t_a^{(\tau)} + \rho_a^{(\tau)} + l^{i(\tau)} + l^{j(\tau)}, \tag{3}$$

where $l^{i(\tau)}, l^{j(\tau)}$ are the associated location costs/benefits if link a originates from zone i and/or terminates at zone j; these two terms are null if link a is neither a starting nor terminating link on a path. Note that the link cost $c_a^{(\tau)}$ is a function of the traffic flow $x_a^{(\tau)}$. The path travel cost is then the composite travel cost, travel time plus toll, expressed as:

$$c_p^{ij(\tau)} = \sum_a \delta_{ap}^{ij} \left(t_a^{(\tau)} + \rho_a^{(\tau)} \right) \tag{4}$$

2.3 Combined model

The time-dependent combined trip-distribution/traffic assignment model can be formulated as the following Mathematical Program (MP):

$$
\begin{aligned}
\min_{T,\tilde{T}} \; S = & \sum_\tau \sum_k \sum_{ij} \sum_p \left(1/\beta^{k(\tau)} \right) T_p^{ijk(\tau)} \left(\ln T_p^{ijk(\tau)} - 1 \right) \\
& + \sum_\tau \sum_k \sum_{ij} \sum_p \left(1/\tilde{\beta}^{k(\tau)} \right) \tilde{T}_p^{ijk(\tau)} \left(\ln \tilde{T}_p^{ijk(\tau)} - 1 \right) \\
& + \sum_\tau \sum_a \int_0^{x_a^{(\tau)}} c_a^{(\tau)}(x,\cdot)\, dx
\end{aligned}
\tag{5}
$$

subject to

$$\sum_{ij} \sum_p T_p^{ijk(\tau)} = P^{k(\tau)} \tag{6}$$

$$\sum_j \sum_p \tilde{T}_p^{ijk(\tau)} = O^{ik(\tau)} \tag{7}$$

$$x_a^{(\tau)} = \sum_k \sum_{ij} \sum_p \delta_{ap}^{ij} \left(T_p^{ijk} + \tilde{T}_p^{ijk} \right) \tag{8}$$

The last term in (5) involves the integral of the total cost on link a over the link flow variable only, with the other parameters (toll and location costs) kept constant.

As in typical combined models, the parameters β^k and $\tilde{\beta}^k$ calibrate the trip distribution and traffic assignment of class k travellers (Sheffi 1985).

The Lagrangian for the MP - is:

$$
\begin{aligned}
L = &\sum_{\tau}\sum_{k}\sum_{ij}\sum_{p}\left(1/\beta^{k(\tau)}\right)T_p^{ijk(\tau)}\left(\ln T_p^{ijk(\tau)} - 1\right) \\
&+\sum_{\tau}\sum_{k}\sum_{ij}\sum_{p}\left(1/\tilde{\beta}^{k(\tau)}\right)\tilde{T}_p^{ijk(\tau)}\left(\ln \tilde{T}_p^{ijk(\tau)} - 1\right) \\
&+\sum_{\tau}\sum_{a}\int_0^{x_a^{(\tau)}} c_a^{(\tau)}(x,\cdot)\,dx \\
&+\sum_{\tau}\sum_{k}\gamma^{k(\tau)}\left(P^{k(\tau)} - \sum_{ij}\sum_{p}T_p^{ijk(\tau)}\right) + \sum_{\tau}\sum_{k}\sum_{i}\lambda^{ik(\tau)}\left(O^{ik(\tau)} - \sum_{j}\sum_{p}\tilde{T}_p^{ijk(\tau)}\right)
\end{aligned}
\tag{9}
$$

The KKT optimality conditions are:

$$
\nabla_{T_p^{ijk(\tau)}}L = \frac{1}{\beta^{k(\tau)}}\ln T_p^{ijk(\tau)} + c_p^{ij(\tau)} + l^{i(\tau)} + l^{j(\tau)} - \gamma^{k(\tau)} = 0
\tag{10}
$$

$$
\nabla_{\tilde{T}_p^{ijk(\tau)}}L = \frac{1}{\tilde{\beta}^{k(\tau)}}\ln \tilde{T}_p^{ijk(\tau)} + c_p^{ij(\tau)} + l^{i(\tau)} + l^{j(\tau)} - \lambda^{ik(\tau)} = 0
\tag{11}
$$

Rearranging (10) and (11), we have:

$$
\begin{aligned}
T_p^{ijk(\tau)} &= \exp\left(\beta^{k(\tau)}\gamma^{k(\tau)}\right)\exp\left(-\beta^{k(\tau)}l^{i(\tau)}\right)\exp\left(-\beta^{k(\tau)}l^{j(\tau)}\right)\exp\left(-\beta^{k(\tau)}c_p^{ij(\tau)}\right) \\
&= Q^{k(\tau)}V^{ik(\tau)}W^{jk(\tau)}\exp\left(-\beta^{k(\tau)}c_p^{ij(\tau)}\right) \\
\tilde{T}_p^{ijk(\tau)} &= \exp\left(\tilde{\beta}^{k(\tau)}\lambda^{ik(\tau)}\right)\exp\left(-\tilde{\beta}^{k(\tau)}l^{i(\tau)}\right)\exp\left(-\tilde{\beta}^{k(\tau)}l^{j(\tau)}\right)\exp\left(-\tilde{\beta}^{k(\tau)}c_p^{ij(\tau)}\right) \\
&= \tilde{A}^{ik(\tau)}\tilde{V}^{ik(\tau)}\tilde{W}^{jk(\tau)}\exp\left(-\tilde{\beta}^{k(\tau)}c_p^{ij(\tau)}\right)
\end{aligned}
\tag{12}
$$

For notational simplicity, the first three terms on the RHS in both expressions of are written as $Q^{k(\tau)}, V^{ik(\tau)}, W^{jk(\tau)}, \tilde{A}^{ik(\tau)}, \tilde{V}^{ik(\tau)}, \tilde{W}^{jk(\tau)}$, respectively. Furthermore, making use of the constraints (6) and (7), we obtain $Q^{k(\tau)}$ and $\tilde{A}^{ik(\tau)}\tilde{V}^{ik(\tau)}$ as:

$$
Q^{k(\tau)} = P^{k(\tau)}\left[\sum_{k}\sum_{ij}\sum_{p}V^{ik(\tau)}W^{jk(\tau)}\exp\left(-\beta^{k(\tau)}c_p^{ij(\tau)}\right)\right]^{-1}
$$

$$
\tilde{A}^{ik(\tau)}\tilde{V}^{ik(\tau)} = O^{ik(\tau)}\left[\sum_{k}\sum_{ij}\sum_{p}\tilde{W}^{jk(\tau)}\exp\left(-\tilde{\beta}^{k(\tau)}c_p^{ij(\tau)}\right)\right]^{-1}
$$

Therefore, the flows of class k locators and non-locators on path p between OD pair ij are obtained by the following logit functions:

$$T_p^{ijk(\tau)} = P^{k(\tau)} \frac{V^{ik(\tau)} W^{jk(\tau)} \exp\left(-\beta^{k(\tau)} c_p^{ij(\tau)}\right)}{\sum_k \sum_{ij} \sum_p V^{ik(\tau)} W^{jk(\tau)} \exp\left(-\beta^{k(\tau)} c_p^{ij(\tau)}\right)} \qquad (13)$$

$$\tilde{T}_p^{ijk(\tau)} = O^{ik(\tau)} \setminus \frac{\tilde{W}^{jk(\tau)} \exp\left(-\tilde{\beta}^{k(\tau)} c_p^{ij(\tau)}\right)}{\sum_k \sum_{ij} \sum_p \tilde{W}^{jk(\tau)} \exp\left(-\tilde{\beta}^{k(\tau)} c_p^{ij(\tau)}\right)} \qquad (14)$$

Based on these results, the MP – essentially is solving the traffic distribution-assignment problem according to the logit model. For locators of class k in period τ, we know from (13) that travellers choose their residence location i, employment location j, and route p simultaneously based on the residential and employment attractions (via $V^{ik(\tau)}, W^{jk(\tau)}$ and hence $l^{i(\tau)}, l^{j(\tau)}$) and travel cost, $c_p^{ij(\tau)}$, which includes both travel time and toll. On the other hand, in a similar manner, non-locators' decisions are effected by employment attraction and travel cost only, as in (14).

2.4 Location cost function

The location cost is formulated to be related to the level of zonal activity congestion, composed of a fixed term and a variable. The fixed term describes the intrinsic cost/ benefit of that zone. The variable part is related to the zonal congestion. For residential zones, more residents in a zone imply a more congested or unpleasant living environment and a lower chance of finding satisfactory housing for locators, leading to decreased zonal attraction or increased location cost. As for employment zones, since zonal employment is more or less fixed, more workers working in a zone implies a lower chance of finding jobs there. Other forms of location cost functions may be adopted in this modelling framework. In this study, we extend the location cost function in Yang and Meng (1998) to allow for different income classes. When this model is to be applied in real network, the exact forms and corresponding parameters can be calibrated against the base year data and then forecasted for the time periods in the planning horizon. This, however, does not say that defining and calibrating the location cost function are trivial tasks. In addition, the concept of hedonic pricing may be applicable here. In the interest of space and simplicity, we adopt a simple location cost function for the purpose of this study, but we note that it is an important topic that deserves more studies. Following the same notations as in the previous sections, we use $l^{i(\tau)}$ to measure the location cost of residential zones and $l^{j(\tau)}$ for employment zones:

$$l^{i(\tau)} = l_0^{i(\tau)} + \theta^i \left[\frac{\sum_j \sum_p \left(T_p^{ijk(\tau)} + \tilde{T}_p^{ijk(\tau)} \right)}{K^{i(\tau)}} \right]^2$$

$$l^{j(\tau)} = l_0^{j(\tau)} + \theta^j \left[\frac{\sum_i \sum_p \left(T_p^{ijk(\tau)} + \tilde{T}_p^{ijk(\tau)} \right)}{K^{j(\tau)}} \right]^2$$

(15)

The fixed components $l_0^{i(\tau)}$, $l_0^{j(\tau)}$ are assumed to be negative, denoting the benefit of living/working in zone i/j. The parameters θ^i, θ^j calibrate the activity congestion effects. $K^{i(\tau)}$, $K^{j(\tau)}$ are proportional to the total opportunity (or capacity) within the zone in period τ. The location cost functions are modified by parameters $\beta^{k(\tau)}$, $\tilde{\beta}^{k(\tau)}$ in (12) to reflect the different perceptions or effects of such cost to different income classes.

The time-dependent combined model described above forms the platform for modelling travellers' long term equilibrium travel and location choices by internalizing traffic congestion and zonal activity congestion. Using it as a platform, we can evaluate and optimize the performance of the transportation network in response to a certain objective. The optimization objective can take several forms, such as the total discounted travel time over the planning horizon, total discounted social welfare, total discounted profit, etc. The problem of transportation network management via TS-DM takes the form of a bi-level program and can be solved accordingly, as discussed below.

3. Mixed TS-DM Strategy under Total Cost Recovery

The time-dependent combined model developed in Section 2 provides an evaluation platform to study transportation management strategies. Traditionally, transportation supply and demand management measures are considered as separate congestion countermeasures. In this study, we aim at developing a formulation to jointly determine the optimal network capacity enhancement and tolling strategy. Moreover, by introducing the time dimension into our formulation, the optimal schedule of network expansion and tolling can be determined. The objective function for transportation network management may take different forms, such as travel cost minimization, reserve capacity maximization, consumer surplus maximization, or multi-objective optimization including user cost, construction cost, etc. (Yang and Bell 1997). The objective function considered in this study is to minimize the total system travel cost. Moreover, in order to achieve financial viability of network capacity enhancements, we impose the constraint of total cost recovery by tolling over the entire planning horizon. For this purpose, we set the total net present value (total discounted toll revenue less total discounted infrastructure costs) over the planning horizon to be zero. The Net Present Value (NPV) is defined as:

$$NPV = \sum_{\tau}\sum_{a} \varphi(r,\tau) x_a^{(\tau)} \rho_a^{(\tau)} - \sum_{\tau}\sum_{a} B_C t_a^0 y_a^{(\tau)} \left(\frac{1+i}{1+r}\right)^{n\tau}$$

$$-\sum_{a} B_M t_a^0 \left[\sum_{i=0}^{nT+(n-1)} \left(\frac{1+i}{1+r}\right)^i C_a^{(0)} + \sum_{t=0}^{T-1} \sum_{i=n(t+1)}^{nT+(n-1)} \left(\frac{1+i}{1+r}\right)^i y_a^{(t)} \right]$$

(16)

where $\varphi(r,\tau)$ is a function which converts the total travel cost at time τ to time 0 (starting time) with r as the discount rate. The first term in (16) is the total toll collected over the entire time horizon; the second and third terms are the total construction and maintenance costs, respectively, with B_C and B_M as the unit construction and maintenance cost parameters at year 0, subject to an inflation rate of $i\%$ per year. The three terms are discounted to year 0 to obtain their present values.

For the case of fixed total population studied here, we consider the objective function to be the discounted total system travel cost (TSC), defined as:

$$TSC = \sum_{\tau}\sum_{a} \varphi(r,\tau) x_a^{(\tau)} \left(t_a^{(\tau)} + \rho_a^{(\tau)} \right)$$

(17)

Hence, the bi-level program is:

$$\min_{y,\rho} \; TSC$$

(18)

subject to

$$y_a^{(\tau)} \geq 0 \quad \forall a \in A, \tau \in [0,T]$$

(19)

$$\rho_a^{(\tau)} \geq 0 \quad \forall a \in A, \tau \in [0,T]$$

(20)

$$NPV = 0$$

(21)

where x_a is obtained from $(T,\tilde{T})$ by solving the lower level program (5) – (8). For each schedule of (y,ρ), the lower level program (5) to (8) yields a set of uniquely determined $(T,\tilde{T})$.

Condition for Optimality

By examining the first-order optimality conditions of the bi-level program (18)-(21), we have the following proposition:

PROPOSITION 1: *For any link with positive link capacity expansion at time* τ *and such a link is tolled after the improvement under the principle of total cost recovery, the marginal reduction in total system travel time due to such expansion balances its unit marginal costs of construction and maintenance, i.e.*

$$\sum_{t>\tau} \varphi(r,t) x_a^{(t)} \frac{\partial t_a^{(t)}}{\partial y_a^{(\tau)}} + B_C t_a^0 \left(\frac{1+i}{1+r}\right)^{n\tau} + B_M t_a^0 \sum_{j=n(\tau+1)}^{nT+(n-1)} \left(\frac{1+i}{1+r}\right)^j = 0 \qquad (22)$$

The proof is provided in Appendix A, as derived from the Karash-Kuhn-Tucker first order optimality conditions. Restating this result, if the capacity of a link is expanded at time τ and is tolled afterwards for total cost recovery, the marginal reduction in total system travel time due to such capacity expansion, i.e., the first term on the LHS of , balances the unit marginal cost (both construction and maintenance) associated with the expansion, i.e., the second and third terms on the LHS of (22). Note that condition (22) holds at the link level even the optimization is accomplished for the entire network. Essentially, for links that can contribute larger reductions in total travel time, they receive a higher budget for expansion, which is sensible. Moreover, (22) provides a tight condition to rationalize the allocation of budget to be spent on each link.

4. Numerical Example

To illustrate the formulation in Section 3 (i.e., mixed TS-DM strategy under total cost recovery), we construct the numerical example of a small network over the planning horizon of 30 years (in three 10-year periods). The formulation is applicable to general networks. The small network chosen is for simplicity of illustration and tractability of results. The network consists of two origins (nodes 1, 2) and two destinations (nodes 5, 6), and is connected by 7 links, as shown in Figure 11.1. The initial link capacities, free-flow travel times are detailed in Table 11.1. The population is stratified into two classes ($k = 1,2$), and each class is composed of both locators and non-locators, with $\beta^{1(\tau)} = \beta^{1(t)} = 0.2$ and $\beta^{2(\tau)} = \beta^{2(t)} = 0.5$. The total population is growing over time as in Table 11.2, but with non-uniform growth rates for different sectors of the population. In addition to zonal population growths over time, zonal attraction is varying over time as well, as detailed in Table 11.3. As described in Section 2.4, the zonal attraction is dependent on the intrinsic attraction and total opportunities. In this example, we consider that zones 1 and 6 are intrinsically more attractive than zones 2 and 5. However, the total opportunities in Zones 1 and 6 are not expanding over time, whereas zones 2 and 5 are actively expanding to accommodate the escalating demand. Furthermore, the inflation rate is $i = 1\%$; discount rate is $r = 4\%$; α_1 and α_2 in the travel time function (1) are taken to be 0.15 and 4, respectively, as

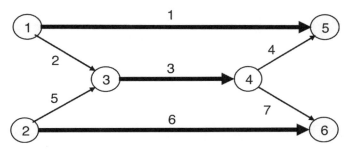

Figure 11.1   The example network

Table 11.1   Link characteristics

Link	Free Flow Time	Capacity
1	30	20
2	10	10
3	10	20
4	10	10
5	10	10
6	30	20
7	10	10

Table 11.2   Population composition over time

Zone	T = 0					T = 1					T = 2				
	Locator		Non-Locator			Locator		Non-Locator			Locator		Non-Locator		
	k=1	k=2	k=1	k=2	Sum	k=1	k=2	k=1	k=2	Sum	k=1	k=2	k=1	k=2	Sum
1	10	10	10	10	20	10	20	15	10	25	15	30	20	15	35
2			10	10	20			10	15	25			15	15	30
Total	60					80					110				

Table 11.3   Coefficients of the location cost functions over time

Zone	T = 0			T = 1			T = 2		
	/	/	/	/	/	/	/	/	/
1	-10	30	1	-10	30	1	-10	30	1
2	-5	30	1	-5	50	1	-5	80	1
5	-2	30	1	-2	50	1	-2	80	1
6	-5	30	1s	-5	30	1	-5	30	1

are typical for the BPR function. The unit construction cost B_C is $500, unit maintenance cost per year B_M is $5.

By solving the bi-level program in Section 3, the optimal TS-DM strategy obtained is summarized in Table 11.4. Note that the capacity expansion stated is to be implemented in the next period, hence no expansion decision is made in T=2, which is the end of the planning horizon. As shown in Table 11.4, the optimal TS-DM strategy is a sequence of network link expansions over time rather than a one-off scheme with all improvements to be implemented in the first period. Although one may think that implementing the expansions earlier will allow commuters to benefit from them for a longer time within the planning horizon, the tradeoff is that the maintenance expenditure will go up also which translates into higher tolls. But more importantly, as the population will relocate over time to optimize their total transportation and activity costs, the network congestion or bottlenecks will be changing over time as well. One-off network upgrade schemes my lead to sub-optimal utilization of the expansions over the planning period. The proposed mixed TS-DM strategy offers a more precise and effective way in managing the capacity expansions by providing them at places and, equally important, at times when they can be optimally utilized.

Table 11.4   The Optimal TS-DM strategy

link	T = 0		T = 1		T = 2		Surplus
	Expansion	Toll	Expansion	Toll	Expansion	Toll	(Deficit) ($)
1	–	3.34	–	1.89	–	1.79	214,992
2	30.26	5.04	5.14	1.35	–	0.51	37,917
3	46.97	2.40	14.05	0.69	––	0.35	(101,427)
4	21.53	0.04	9.22	0.00	––	0.59	(133,731)
5	16.68	0.04	8.92	0.23	–	0.78	(96,184)
6	0.56	1.34	–	1.28	–	1.45	73,334
7	25.43	3.04	4.84	1.34	–	0.73	5,098

Total System Travel Time		Total Discounted surplus ($)	0
($)	13,110,944		
(per capita average)	177,454		
Total System Travel Cost			
($)	14,163,989		
(per capita average)	192,722		

It should be emphasized that the network-wide tolls serve dual purposes: congestion management and cost recovery of the capacity expansions. The optimal toll pattern is different for all three phases within the planning horizon, depending on the link use pattern derived from the OD trip matrix. Since total cost recovery is achieved for the whole network, not for each individual link, we can see that some links

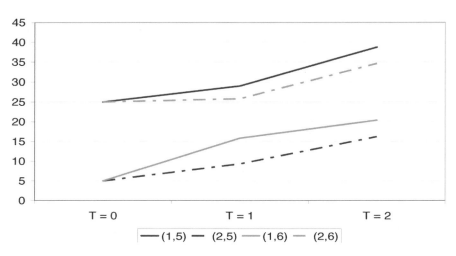

Figure 11.2   The time dependent OD Trip matrix under the optimal TS-DM strategy

have surpluses, while others have deficits. Thus, cross-subsidies among links can be used in an optimal way to finance the capacity expansions so as to achieve the optimal result for the whole network. As for traditional BOT schemes, construction or capacity enhancement and tolling are often considered on a link by link basis, which precludes cross-link subsidy, and therefore the possibility of achieving a better network-wide optimal result.

4.1 Interaction between transportation provision and zonal attractions

The trip end totals for the optimal TS-DM strategy under total cost recovery are provided in Table 11.5, with the time-dependent OD matrices shown in Figure 11.2. Despite the symmetric network (see Figure 11.1 and Table 11.1) as well as the almost symmetric and uniformly growing population and location attractions (see Table 11.2 and Table 11.3), it is interesting to note that the OD demands over time as shown in Figure 11.2 do not exhibit the same trend – certain OD pairs attract proportionally more trips. This is primarily due to the impact of time-dependent TS-DM strategy on zonal accessibility and consequential changes in location choices. By inspecting the trip end totals in Table 11.5, we find that locators are in fact relocating their homes and changing employment locations in response to the location attraction changes. Non-locators who are not moving their homes also optimize their composite costs by modifying their work locations over time. Decisions on residential and employment locations as well as route choices under the time-dependent TS-DM framework involve inseparable interactions between link capacity expansions and tolling, which

Table 11.5   Trip ends by income class, locators and non-locators

Zone	Class	T = 0	T = 1	T = 2
1 (intrinsically more attractive)	Locator (k=1)	5.00	5.86	8.65
	Locator (k=2)	5.00	13.98	20.51
	Non-locator (k=1)	10.00	15.00	15.00
	Non-locator (k=2)	10.00	10.00	15.00
	Sum	**30.00**	**44.84**	**59.16**
2 (expanding over time)	Locator (k=1)	5.00	4.14	6.35
	Locator (k=2)	5.00	6.02	9.49
	Non-locator (k=1)	10.00	10.00	20.00
	Non-locator (k=2)	10.00	15.00	15.00
	Sum	**30.00**	**35.16**	**50.84**
5 (expanding over time)	Locator (k=1)	5.00	5.07	7.78
	Locator (k=2)	5.00	10.40	16.33
	Non-locator (k=1)	10.00	12.81	16.41
	Non-locator (k=2)	10.00	10.05	14.46
	Sum	30.00	38.33	**54.97**
6 (intrinsically more attractive)	Locator (k=1)	5.00	4.93	7.22
	Locator (k=2)	5.00	9.60	13.67
	Non-locator (k=1)	10.00	12.19	18.59
	Non-locator (k=2)	10.00	14.95	15.54
	Sum	**30.00**	**41.67**	**55.03**

together impact the transportation cost, intrinsic location attraction, zonal development (changes in total opportunity), and population changes. These relationships should be jointly considered and carefully modeled, by means of the time-dependent TS-DM framework.

The importance of stratifying the whole population into locators and non-locators can be demonstrated in Figure 11.3 and Figure 11.4. Figure 11.3 shows the result for the case where the city is composed of purely locators, whose income class distribution maintained to be the same as in Table 11.2. In contrast, Figure 11.4 is produced by changing the locator population in Table 11.2 to non-locators and split them evenly between the two residential zones. This contrast in results, as illustrated in Figure 11.3 and Figure 11.4, shows that even with the same total population, different location behaviour produces very different location choices as reflected in the differences in the OD trip matrix, which has substantial consequential effect on the resultant optimal TS-DM strategy to be adopted.

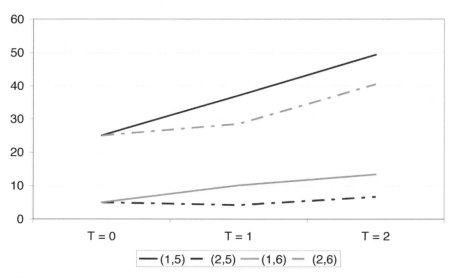

Figure 11.3   OD Trip Matrix (pure locators)

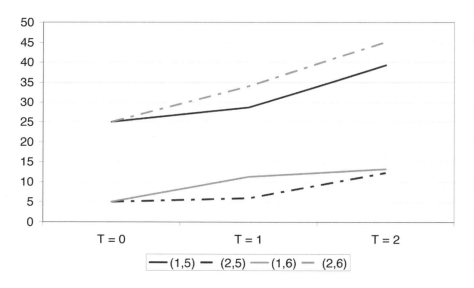

Figure 11.4   OD Trip Matrix (pure non-locators)

4.2 Effectiveness of integrating transportation supply and demand management

In order to illustrate the effectiveness of jointly considering transportation supply and demand strategies as compared with pure demand strategies, which are gaining popularity recently, we compare two cases. One is the pure demand management and another is the 'do-nothing' scenario which serves as a benchmark. Pure demand strategies rely on road pricing alone to alleviate congestion, which involves the traditional system optimal formulation, wherein the total system travel time is the objective. The toll is merely used as a device to achieve the system optimal solution. That is, the toll revenue is not part of the objective function, even though the toll does increase the cost of travel to users. Two measures are generated for this case: TST refers to the total system time, whereas TSC refers to the total system cost, which includes both the total system time and the total toll collected. The two extra cases help demonstrate the synergy bought about by utilizing the toll revenue for network capacity expansion versus the traditional pure demand management strategy. As the formulations for these two cases are relatively straightforward, due to space limitation, they are not provided here.

Table 11.6 and Figure 11.5 illustrate that using the toll revenue for network capacity expansion outperforms the pure demand management strategy. Despite high tolls being charged in the pure demand scheme, the total system travel time and total system travel cost are 48% and 43%, respectively, higher than those in the 'Mixed TS-DM' strategy. This finding confirms the superiority of integrating transportation supply measures into the traditional demand management strategies for managing traffic congestion. In fact, a carefully scrutinized investment of toll revenue into network capacity expansion can generate win-win situations. At zero net cost to the network operator (government), there is a notable reduction in total travel time/cost and toll level.

The comparison between these three cases depends on the initial congestion, as expected. To illustrate the sensitivity of the initial congestion, we construct Figure 11.6, in which the initial network link capacities are double those as shown in Table 11.1. Hence, the congestion level is lower. We can see that the three strategies perform similarly in terms of travel time (note the absolute value on the left axis). In fact, when the initial network is large enough, only small scale capacity expansions are required to achieve optimality. In such a case, the maintenance cost of the inherently large network dominates the total costs, with the network toll mainly serves the purpose of cost recovery rather than congestion control. In Figure 11.6, the benefit of re-investment of the toll revenue into the road network is evident. The pure demand and mixed TS-DM strategy gives almost the same total system travel time. However, users are charged 2.6 times higher in the pure demand strategy than in the mixed strategy. Indeed, an investment of $0.34 million in expansion can achieve the same effect, with road users paying a lower toll and the investment fully recovered by the end of the planning horizon.

In contrast, in Figure 11.7, the initial network is the same as in Table 11.1 except that the capacities of links 1 and 6 are reduced to 10 units (i.e., the network is initially

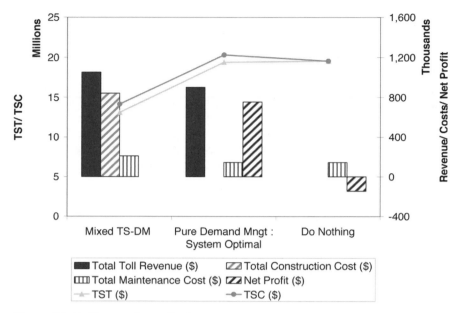

Figure 11. 5   Comparison of schemes

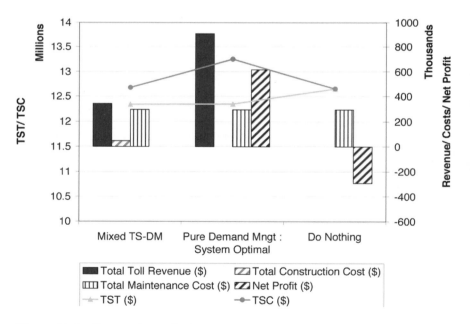

Figure 11.6   Comparison of schemes (large initial capacity)

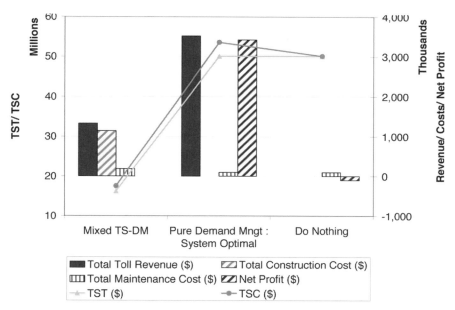

Figure 11.7   Comparison of schemes (small initial capacity)

more congested and becoming even more congested over time as the population grow). We can see the drastic improvement in the overall network performance introduced by the mixed TS-DM strategy. In this scenario, the additional network capacity becomes vital. Albeit the demand management strategy collects 2.7 times the toll as in the mixed strategy, the total system time and cost are still about 3 times higher.

4.3 Optimality of the TS-DM strategy

To further understand the performance of the mixed TD-DM strategy, we conduct a sensitivity analysis of its optimality. The objective is to find an optimal TS-DM strategy such that the total toll revenue collected is constrained to a certain value, subject to the condition of total cost-recovery. In other words, we pre-specify the maximum allowable toll revenue to be collected as a constraint, which might be necessary due to policy considerations. We then optimally allocate the network capacity expansion such that the associated construction and maintenance costs are to be fully recovered by the toll revenue. From the government's perspective, the toll charge collectible from her citizens may be restricted, in view of the affordability of individuals, or other political pressures. Thus, the maximum allowable toll revenue becomes the overall budget constraint in the optimization. With the basic network, the total discounted maintenance cost is around $0.14 million (column 2 in Table 11.6) and therefore the total toll collected starts from $0.15 million in

Table 11.6   Comparison of schemes

	Mixed TS-DM	Pure Demand Mngt : System Optimal (TST minimization)	Do Nothing
Toll Revenue ($)	1,053,045	901,449	0
Construction Cost ($)	842,764	0	0
Maintenance Cost ($)	210,280	146,024	146,024
Net Profit ($)	(0)	755,424	(146,024)
TST ($)	13,110,944	19,415,227	19,556,924
TSC ($)	14,163,989	20,316,676	19,556,924

Figure 11.8. The total network travel cost TSC (travel time plus toll) of the mixed strategy drops sharply in the beginning as the toll revenue constraint gradually relaxes. Subsequently, the system performance reaches the minimum and then it reverts back to an increasing trend. The minimum point corresponds exactly with the optimal TS-DM strategy as described by the first column in Table 11.6, which does not impose such a toll revenue constraint. This result is of no coincidence. For simplicity of exposition, the value of time is taken to be one in this example. Before the minimum point, the per dollar relaxation in the toll revenue constraint (i.e. infrastructure cost) drives down the total system travel time by more than one unit; on the other hand, the reduction is less than unity beyond the minimum point. At the optimal point, a unit investment results in a unit reduction in total system time. This result is precisely described by condition (22) of Proposition 1. Despite the fact that capacity expansion typically reduces travel time, over investment in capacity expansion translates into higher tolls under the cost recovery requirement, which in turn drives up the total system travel cost TSC. Thus, even empowered with the option of capacity expansion, the notion of 'the more, the better' does not uphold. In the end, the cost-efficiency of the investment in capacity expansion does matter. Meanwhile, as shown to the right of the minimum point, the curve does not rise abruptly, which implies that the loss in efficiency due to over-investment is not growing sharply. Hence, slight miscalculations in the expansion scheme would not introduce substantial detrimental effects.

Taking advantage of this analysis, we compare how the mixed TS-DM strategy performs as compared with the traditional pure demand management. Under the pure demand management strategy, the network link tolls are optimally calculated so as to give the minimum discounted total travel time (TST); similar to the above, the total toll revenue for this case is also constrained exogenously. The upper two curves in Figure 11.8 show the total discounted travel time (TST) and travel cost (TSC) under the pure demand management strategy. Since the total demand is fixed, TST remains constant after reaching a minimum, so there is no further benefit in terms of TST even if higher tolls are allowed. Essentially, the network location and travel choices are already optimal over the fixed network. As compared with the mixed strategy, one can see that the pure demand management

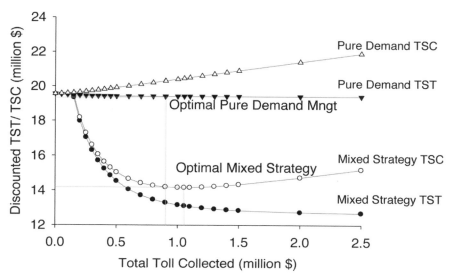

Figure 11.8   Sensitivity of the overall system performance

strategy never outperforms the mixed TS-DM strategy, in terms of TST and TSC. Figure 11.8 elucidates our contention: by re-investing the toll revenue optimally in the network, one can achieve significant improvements in the network performance (TST) as well as user costs (TSC).

4.4 Sensitivity analysis

In this section, the sensitivities of the TS-DM strategy for different time segments in the planning horizon and different location cost functions are analysed. We reiterate that the sensitivity analysis conducted is based on the hypothetical network example as shown in Figure 11.1. The purpose here aims at highlighting the sensitive parameters, and therefore the effort or level of refinement needed for their data collection and calibration when this framework is applied in real world scenarios.

4.4.1 Time segment length   In the aforementioned numerical study, the time segment for each planning time frame (n) is set to be 10 years. In this subsection, the segment length is shortened to every 5 years, with the population and location attractions as shown in Table 11.2 and Table 11.3 interpolated correspondingly for these new or shortened time segments (or extrapolated for the last period). We label the time index as $T=0$, which matches the same time as the original problem setting, and we insert time indices, making the subsequent ones as T= ½, 1, 1½, 2, …. denoting, respectively, year 5–9, year 10–14, etc.

When comparing the optimal TS-DM strategies in Table 11.7 and the original strategy with 10-year time segment in Table 11.4. We observe a consistency in the capacity expansion plan, although to slightly different extents. Again, more capacity expansion is to be implemented in the earlier periods in order to save construction cost, which is increasing over time, as well as to allow the benefit of the additional capacity to be realized at an earlier time. A slightly different tolling strategy is produced; the reason can be inferred from the new predicted OD demand matrices in Figure 11.9. Although the OD demands in Figure 11.9 and Figure 11.2 display similar overall trends, there are notable differences in the estimated OD demands over the future time periods, inferring different link use patterns. Recall that the link tolls serve the dual purposes of both cost recovery as well as congestion control; this explains why the new tolling strategy does not resemble the original one in Table 11.4. A minor point to note is that the overall demand is higher in the current context, since the demand growth is interpolated for periods ½, 1½, and extrapolated for T=2½, which is higher than that of the original period 0, 1 and 2 in Table 11.2. For the sake of fair comparison, we can focus on the average travel time (or cost) per capita in Table 11.4 and Table 11.7. There is about a 3% reduction in both quantities when the time segment is reduced from 10 years to 5 years.

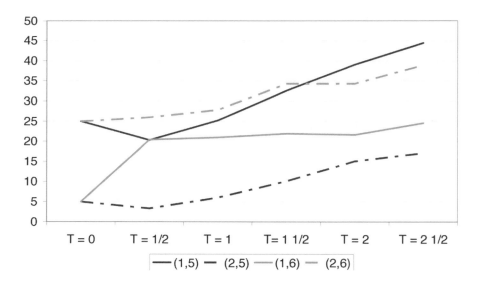

Figure 11.9   OD Trip Matrix under optimal TS-DM strategy with 5-year time frame

Table 11.7   The optimal TS-DM strategy under the 5-year time frame

Link	T=0		T=½		T=1	
	Expansion	Toll	Expansion	Toll	Expansion	Toll
1	0.18	3.17	0.06	1.42	0.75	2.46
2	27.73	5.00	7.08	0.02	8.21	0.41
3	36.82	2.32	12.73	1.27	14.66	1.68
4	3.42	0.00	10.35	2.67	13.16	1.18
5	9.08	0.00	5.66	0.02	6.44	0.33
6	2.62	1.17	0.30	0.16	0.92	1.21
7	33.40	3.00	2.39	0.10	1.50	0.09

Link	T=1½		T=2		T=2½	
	Expansion	Toll	Expansion	Toll	Expansion	Toll
1	2.11	3.98	-	1.31	-	5.09
2	1.16	0.27	-	0.40	-	0.00
3	8.89	2.98	-	0.40	-	0.00
4	8.86	0.45	-	0.11	-	4.68
5	7.73	0.43	-	0.18	-	0.80
6	0.00	2.73	-	0.08	-	3.82
7	0.02	0.15	-	0.01	-	3.53

Toll Revenue ($)	1,114,174
Construction Cost ($)	979,643
Maintenance Cost ($)	134,531
TST ($)	13,647,608
(per capita average)	172,331
TSC ($)	14,761,782
(per capita average)	186,394

This result indicates that the length of time segment has an effect on formulating the TS-DM strategy. It has less an effect on capacity expansion than on the tolling scheme. Indeed, for tolling consideration, it appears that one would benefit from having a more refined time scale for the analysis, which is consistent with the practice.

4.4.2 Location cost function   In this subsection, the coefficients θ^i and θ^j in the location cost function (15) are modified to reflect different degrees of the location cost/ benefit to be affected by activity congestion. For the case of θ^i and $\theta^j = 5$ (location cost worsen more quickly with zonal congestion than the base case), Table 11.8 and Figure 11.10 are produced. On the other hand, for θ^i and $\theta^j = -5$, Table 11.9 and Figure 11.11 are produced to model the case when location costs are less sensitive to activity congestion. When examining Table 11.4, Table 11.8 and Table 11.9, one can see that the three cases give very close TSC (i.e. objective value), which suggests that travellers would distribute themselves to achieve the same optimal TSC, despite changes to the location cost functions. A progressive

Table 11.8   Optimal TS-DM strategy ($\theta^i = \theta^j = 5$)

Link	T=0		T=1		T=2	
	Expansion	Toll	Expansion	Toll	Expansion	Toll
1	-	3.20	-	2.17	-	1.51
2	20.52	5.04	-	1.87	-	0.08
3	47.01	2.27	13.90	0.48	-	0.35
4	31.69	0.04	13.81	0.01	-	0.98
5	26.31	0.03	14.21	0.18	-	1.39
6	0.59	1.20	0.01	1.67	-	1.14
7	15.37	3.04	0.02	2.12	-	0.19
Toll Revenue ($)	1,053,163					
Construction Cost ($)	842,858					
Maintenance Cost ($)	210,305					
TST ($)	13,110,781					
TSC ($)	14,163,991					

Table 11.9   Optimal TS-DM strategy ($\theta^i = \theta^j = 0.5$)

Link	T=0		T=1		T=2	
	Expansion	Toll	Expansion	Toll	Expansion	Toll
1	-	3.35	0.04	1.66	-	1.59
2	32.57	5.03	6.54	1.29	-	0.62
3	47.02	2.42	13.91	0.74	-	0.35
4	17.65	0.04	7.87	-	-	0.44
5	14.51	0.03	7.27	0.24	-	0.56
6	0.56	1.35	0.03	1.23	-	1.46
7	29.37	3.04	6.04	1.17	-	0.98
Toll Revenue ($)	1,053,231					
Construction Cost ($)	842,907					
Maintenance Cost ($)	210,324					
TST ($)	13,110,756					
TSC ($)	14,163,987					

trend can be observed in the capacity expansion plan as well as the tolling scheme when reading through Table 11.9, Table 11.4 and Table 11.8 ($\theta^i = \theta^j$), increasing from 0.5, 1 to 5)), where location costs are becoming more and more sensitive to activity congestion. The same trend can be seen in the OD demand patterns too (Figure 11.11, Figure 11.2 and Figure 11.10).

The result illustrates that the optimal TS-DM plan exhibits a certain degree of sensitivity to location attraction function, but the final objective value is not as sensitive when the other variables (population, basic location attraction etc.) remain unchanged.

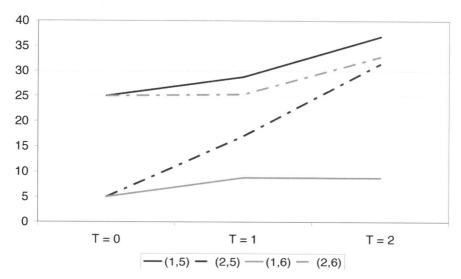

Figure 11.10 OD Trip Matrix ($\theta^i = \theta^j = 5$)

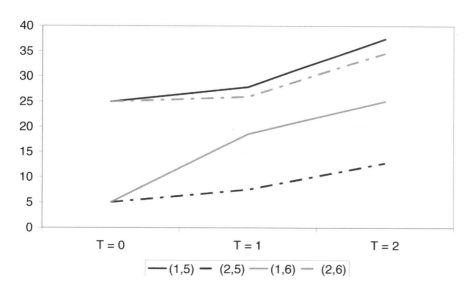

Figure 11.11 OD Trip Matrix ($\theta^i = \theta^j = 0.5$)

5. Concluding Remarks

This study formulated the planning of time-dependent TS-DM strategies for transportation management in the form of a bi-level program. The lower level problem of this bi-level program consists of the time-dependent combined trip distribution and assignment model, which accommodates residential and work location choices of locators and non-locators as well their route choices. The objective of the upper level problem is to minimize the discounted total system travel cost by determining the optimal link capacity expansion and tolling plan, subject to the total cost recovery constraint. The technique developed herein is applicable for other objective functions and constraints in the upper level problem. Within this framework, the formulation provides flexibility in analysing transportation management strategies, such as pure supply management (via capacity expansion), pure demand management (via road pricing), or mixed supply and demand management strategies.

The bi-level optimization program, expressed in the form of a mathematical program with equilibrium constrains, is known to be intrinsically hard to solve. Solution difficulty of this model increases with the number of discrete time segments modeled in the planning horizon as well as with the network size. In the interest of space, this chapter focused on the discussion of the formulation while leaving out detailed discussions of the solution method, which is not the focus here. Nevertheless, the formulation developed herein can be solved by a number of methods, such as descent algorithms, penalty methods (e.g., Dempe 2000), SQP Methods (e.g., Jiang and Ralph 2000), or other heuristics.

In the small network example provided, we demonstrated the strength of the time-dependent TS-DM strategy in determining the optimal tolling and capacity expansion schedule while considering future changes in population and its composition as well as changes in zonal attractions over time. The result illustrated that the decisions on residential and employment locations as well as route choices involve intricate interactions between link capacity expansions and tolling as a result of the TS-DM strategy adopted, which impacts on transportation costs, intrinsic location attraction, zonal development (changes in total opportunity), and population changes. Moreover, from the result in the numerical example, the result indicated that investment in link capacity enhancement together with tolling are much more effective than demand management alone in reducing traffic congestion. Substantial improvements can be gained in both travel time as well as travel cost via the implementation of the mixed strategy. The results obtained support our contention set out in this study, namely, by including network capacity enhancement as an integral part of the network management strategy, one can achieve superior results as compared with the pure demand management strategy.

Implementing transportation supply and demand strategies in an integrated manner is indeed a promising way for ensuring sustainable transportation provision and management. It provides transportation network management agencies with information on how to best toll network links as well as to decide when and where, and to what extent network capacity investment should be made over time. Yet, as the network management plan is developed over the planning horizon, forecasts in population growth, zonal attractions, inflation, changes in costs, etc. play critical roles in this planning process. By segmenting the planning horizon into discrete phases, it provides flexibility for recourse planning, should reality (i.e., the forecast population and land use changes) turn out to be not exactly as predicted. Sensitivity analysis of the solution under various uncertain but influential factors is an important extension to this study. In addition to the sensitivity analysis presented in this chapter, the forms of the location attraction function, value-of-time estimates, logit-split parameters, etc deserve attention too. In some cases, how to incorporate recourse strategies in the planning of mixed TS-DM strategies in a probabilistic and dynamic framework would be interesting and important further studies.

Acknowledgements

We are grateful for the constructive comments of the referee. The study is supported by the Competitive Earmarked Research Grants HKUST6154/03E and #616906 from the Research Grants Council of the HKSAR.

Appendix A Proof of Proposition 1

First, we rewrite the bi-level program (18) to (21) to an equivalent single-level optimization by replacing the lower level by its KKT conditions (Chapter 5, Dempe 2002):

$$\min_{y,\rho,T,\tilde{T}} \quad TSC$$

subject to (19), (20), (21), (6), (7), (10), (11) .

From the first order conditions, we obtain the following relationships: For $y_a^{(\tau)}$:

$$\sum_{t>\tau}\varphi(r,t)x_a^{(t)}\frac{\partial t_a^{(t)}}{\partial y_a^{(\tau)}} - \kappa_{ya}^{(\tau)} + \kappa\left[-B_C t_a^0\left(\frac{1+i}{1+r}\right)^{n\tau} - B_M t_a^0\sum_{j=n(\tau+1)}^{nT+(n-1)}\left(\frac{1+i}{1+r}\right)^j\right]$$
$$+\sum_{t>\tau}\sum_k\sum_{ij}\sum_p\left(\omega_p^{ijk(t)} + \tilde{\omega}_p^{ijk(t)}\right)\frac{\partial c_p^{ij(t)}}{\partial y_a^{(\tau)}} = 0 \tag{23}$$

For $\rho_a^{(\tau)}$:

$$(1+\kappa)\,\varphi\left(r,\tau\right)x_a^{(\tau)} - \kappa_{\rho a}^{(\tau)} + \sum_k \sum_{ij} \sum_p \left(\omega_p^{ijk(\tau)} + \tilde{\omega}_p^{ijk(\tau)}\right)\frac{\partial c_p^{ij(\tau)}}{\partial \rho_a^{(\tau)}} = 0 \tag{24}$$

Furthermore, making use of , we have:

$$\frac{\partial c_p^{ij(\tau)}}{\partial y_a^{(\tau)}} = \delta_{ap}^{ij}\,\frac{\partial t_a^{(\tau)}}{\partial y_a^{(\tau)}} \quad \text{and} \quad \frac{\partial c_p^{ij(\tau)}}{\partial \rho_a^{(\tau)}} = \delta_{ap}^{ij} \tag{25}$$

where $\kappa_{ya}^{(\tau)}$, $\kappa_{\rho a}^{(\tau)}$, κ are Lagrange multipliers for constraints (19), (20) and (21), and $\omega_p^{ijk(\tau)}$, $\tilde{\omega}_p^{ijk(\tau)}$ are Lagrange multipliers for constraints (10) and (11).

Combining (25) into the last term of (23), we have:

$$\sum_{t>\tau}\varphi\left(r,t\right)x_a^{(t)}\frac{\partial t_a^{(t)}}{\partial y_a^{(\tau)}} - \kappa_{ya}^{(\tau)} + \kappa\left[-B_C t_a^0\left(\frac{1+i}{1+r}\right)^{n\tau} - B_M t_a^0 \sum_{j=n(\tau+1)}^{nT+(n-1)}\left(\frac{1+i}{1+r}\right)^j\right]$$
$$+\sum_{t>\tau}\frac{\partial t_a^{(\tau)}}{\partial y_a^{(\tau)}}\sum_k\sum_{ij}\sum_p\left(\omega_p^{ijk(t)} + \tilde{\omega}_p^{ijk(t)}\right)\delta_{ap}^{ij} = 0 \tag{26}$$

By the same token, combining (25) into (24), we have:

$$(1+\kappa)\,\varphi\left(r,\tau\right)x_a^{(\tau)} - \kappa_{\rho a}^{(\tau)} + \sum_k \sum_{ij} \sum_p \left(\omega_p^{ijk(\tau)} + \tilde{\omega}_p^{ijk(\tau)}\right)\delta_{ap}^{ij} = 0 \tag{27}$$

Rewriting (27) as

$$\sum_k \sum_{ij} \sum_p \left(\omega_p^{ijk(\tau)} + \tilde{\omega}_p^{ijk(\tau)}\right)\delta_{ap}^{ij} = -(1+\kappa)\,\varphi\left(r,\tau\right)x_a^{(\tau)} + \kappa_{\rho a}^{(\tau)}$$

and substituting into (26), we obtain:

$$\sum_{t>\tau}\varphi\left(r,t\right)x_a^{(t)}\frac{\partial t_a^{(t)}}{\partial y_a^{(\tau)}} - \kappa_{ya}^{(\tau)} + \kappa\left[-B_C t_a^0\left(\frac{1+i}{1+r}\right)^{n\tau} - B_M t_a^0 \sum_{j=n(\tau+1)}^{nT+(n-1)}\left(\frac{1+i}{1+r}\right)^j\right]$$
$$+\sum_{t>\tau}\frac{\partial t_a^{(\tau)}}{\partial y_a^{(\tau)}}\left[-(1+\kappa)\,\varphi\left(r,\tau\right)x_a^{(\tau)} + \kappa_{\rho a}^{(\tau)}\right] = 0$$

Simplifying, we obtain:

$$-\kappa\left[\sum_{t>\tau}\varphi\left(r,t\right)x_a^{(t)}\frac{\partial t_a^{(t)}}{\partial y_a^{(\tau)}} + B_C t_a^0\left(\frac{1+i}{1+r}\right)^{n\tau} + B_M t_a^0 \sum_{j=n(\tau+1)}^{nT+(n-1)}\left(\frac{1+i}{1+r}\right)^j\right] - \kappa_{ya}^{(\tau)} + \sum_{t>\tau}\kappa_{\rho a}^{(t)}\frac{\partial t_a^{(t)}}{\partial y_a^{(\tau)}} = 0$$

For a link with a positive $y_a^{(\tau)}$ and $\rho_a^{(t)}$ $(t > \tau)$, its associated Lagrange multipliers for constraints (19)-(20) are zero, i.e., $\kappa_{ya}^{(\tau)} = \kappa_{\rho a}^{(t)} = 0$, then the last two terms vanish.

$$\sum_{t > \tau} \varphi(r,t) x_a^{(t)} \frac{\partial t_a^{(t)}}{\partial y_a^{(\tau)}} + B_C t_a^0 \left(\frac{1+i}{1+r}\right)^{n\tau} + B_M t_a^0 \sum_{j=n(\tau+1)}^{nT+(n-1)} \left(\frac{1+i}{1+r}\right)^j = 0 \qquad (28)$$

This concludes the proof.

References

Boyce, D.E. (1980), 'A framework for construction network equilibrium models of urban location', *Transportation Science*, 14(1): 77–96.

Chen, A. and Subprasom, K. (2007), 'Analysis of regulation and policy of private toll roads in a build-operate-transfer scheme under demand uncertainty', *Transportation Research A*, 41: 537–58.

Dempe, S. (2002), *Foundations of Bilevel Programming* (The Netherlands: Kluwer Academic Publishers).

Huang, H.J. and Lam, W.H.K. (2005), 'A stochastic model for combined activity/ destination/route choice problems', *Annals of Operations Research* 135: 111–25.

Jiang, H. and Ralph, D. (2000), 'Smooth SQP Method for Mathematical Programs with Nonlinear Complementarity Constrains', *SIAM Journal on Optimization* 10(3): 779–808.

Lam, W.H.K. and Huang, H.J. (1992), 'A combined trip distribution and assignment model for multiple user classes', *Transportation Research B*, 26(4): 275–87.

Lo, H. and Szeto, W.Y. (2002), 'Planning transport network over time: a preliminary investigation', *Proceedings of the 7th International Conference of the Hong Kong Society for Transportation Studies*.

Lo, H. and Szeto W.Y. (2004) 'Planning transport network improvements over time', in *Urban and Regional Transportation Modeling: Essays in Honor of David Boyce* (Massachusetts: Edward Elgar), pp. 157–276,

Lo, H. and Szeto, W.Y. (2009) 'Time-dependent transport network design under cost-recovery', *Transportation Research B*, 43(1): 142–58.

Papacostas, C.S. and Prevedouros, P.D. (2001) *Transportation Engineering and Planning (Third Edition)*, (New Jersey: Prentice Hall).

Sheffi, Y (1985), *Urban Transportation Networks* (New Jersey: Prentice Hall).

Szeto, W.Y. and Lo, H. (2005), 'Strategies for road network design over time: robustness under uncertainty', *Transportmetrica* 1(1): 47–63.

Szeto, W.Y. and Lo, H. (2006), 'Transportation network improvement and tolling strategies: the issue of intergeneration equity', *Transportation Research Part A* 40: 227–43.

Szeto, W.Y. and H. Lo. (2008), 'Time-dependent transport network improvement and tolling strategies', *Transportation Research Part A*, 42(2): 376–91.

Yang, H. and Bell, M.G.H. (1997), 'Models and algorithms for road network design: A review and some new developments', *Transport Reviews* 18(3): 257–78.

Yang, H. and Meng, Q. (1998), 'An integrated network equilibrium model of urban location and travel choices', *Journal of Regional Science* 38(4): 575–98.

Yang, H. and Meng, Q. (2000), 'Highway pricing and capacity choice in a road network under a build-operate-transfer scheme', *Transportation Research Part A* 34: 207–22.

Yang, H. and Meng, Q. (2002), 'A note on "highway pricing and capacity choice in a road network under a build–operate–transfer scheme"', *Transportation Research Part A* 36: 659–63.

Chapter 12

Traveller Responses to the Stockholm Congestion Pricing Trial: Who Changed, Where Did They Go, and What Did It Cost Them?[1]

Joel P. Franklin, Jonas Eliasson, and Anders Karlström

Introduction

Among transport economists and traffic planners, congestion pricing has long been advocated as an efficient means to reduce road congestion. Yet, up until recent years, the idea had rarely been implemented, with Singapore and Trondheim the only examples of congestion pricing systems that vary by time of day.[2] In the last few years, however, new congestion pricing systems have been introduced in various forms, with London and Stockholm being the most ambitious systems in the sense that the congestion charges apply to the entire urban core. With the Stockholm system now in place, we have a chance to measure some real effects of congestion pricing on daily travel patterns.

The effects of the Stockholm system were studied in an extensive evaluation program. This evaluation program was particularly important since the fate of the charges would be decided by a popular referendum. The evaluation covered not only effects on traffic volumes and travel times, but also effects on emissions, perceived urban environment, traffic safety, delivery traffic, public transport, taxis etc., generating almost 30 different sub-reports (available at www.stockholmsforsoket. se), The results from the evaluation were summarized prior to the referendum by an expert panel (Algers et al. 2006). Drawing upon this report, Eliasson et al. (2008) summarize the main effects and conclusions from the trial.

---

1 This project was funded by the Royal Institute of Technology's Center for Transport Studies, VINNOVA, The Swedish National Road Administration, and Stockholm Municipality. We acknowledge helpful comments and support by Lena Smidfeld Rosqvist, Annika Nilsson, Anders Levander, Muriel Beser Hugosson, and Ulf Tunberg. Computational assistance was provided by Aron Tesfaghebrel.

2 Oslo and Bergen also have cordon pricing systems, but they charge a flat rate throughout the charging period.

While the widely published traffic measurements showed a stable decrease of 20–25% less traffic across the charging cordon during charged hours, less is known about the nature of the 'disappearing' traffic—which traffic 'disappeared' and what happened to it. The purpose of this chapter is to examine the changes in travel patterns that occurred as a result of the Stockholm congestion charges.

We start by analysing how the car drivers' travel patterns were changed by the charges, particularly with regard to how they affected people of different income level and gender. Next, we use models of travel choice to investigate in more detail who changed behaviour, particularly by either changing mode or adjusting departure time. Lastly, we quantify the benefits and burdens of the congestion charges on those who adjusted travel behaviours and those who did not, using a welfare analysis.

Background

The congestion charges in Stockholm were first introduced as the centrepiece of the 'Stockholm Trial'. The Stockholm Trial consisted of two parts: (i) a congestion charging scheme that was in place from 3 January to 31 July 2006, and (ii) expanded public transport that was in place from 31 August 2005 to 31 December 2006. Initially, the trial was meant to consist only of a congestion charging scheme. Later, it was decided that the charging scheme should be complemented by public transport enhancements—several new bus lines, additional capacity on commuter trains and subways, and more park-and-ride facilities.

History of the congestion charging trial

The stated purpose of the Stockholm Trial was to 'test whether the efficiency of the traffic system could be enhanced by congestion charges' (City of Stockholm 2005). The objectives of the charges were to 'reduce congestion, increase accessibility and improve the environment' (both the perceived living environment and the measurable emissions from car traffic). A target was set to reduce traffic across the cordon by 10–15%. This target was loosely based on previous studies on how congestion charging systems should be designed.

The congestion charging scheme was originally meant to be a 'full-scale trial for several years' and was a part of an agreement between the Social Democratic, Left, and Green parties on the national level following the election in the autumn of 2002. For various reasons—most importantly legal complaints regarding the technology procurement process—the period of the trial became considerably shorter than was initially planned.

The Stockholm Trial was followed in autumn of 2006 by referendums in the City of Stockholm and in about half of the neighboring municipalities. The referendum result within the City of Stockholm ended with a majority for keeping the charges, but when adding in the suburbs, a majority of the voters in the county was against

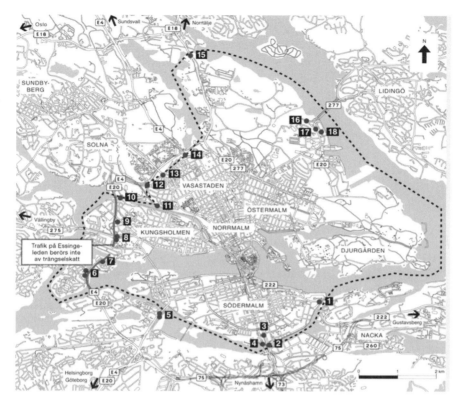

Figure 12.1 The Stockholm congestion charging cordon and toll locations

the charges. However, the results could be viewed as unrepresentative, since many municipalities did not arrange a referendum at all. Finally, it was decided by the new national government, elected at the same time as the congestion charging referendum, that the congestion charges should be reintroduced permanently, starting in August 2007.

While the congestion charges were an extremely hot topic leading up to the referendum in 2006, the debate has been remarkably calm—virtually non-existent—since the reintroduction in August 2007. Opinion polls also show stable support for the charges: in December 2007, 48% of Stockholm County residents were positive to the charges, 27% were negative and the rest had no opinion. It seems as if the congestion charges are becoming more and more accepted as part of the Stockholm traffic planners' toolbox.

Table 12.1   Schedule of toll prices

Time Period	Toll Amount (SEK)
06.30 – 06.59	10
07.00 – 07.29	15
07.30 – 08.29	20
08.30 – 08.59	15
09.00 – 15.29	10
15.30 – 15.59	15
16.00 – 17.29	20
17.30 – 17.59	15
18.00 – 18.29	10
18.30 – 06.29	0

Design of the Congestion Charging System

The charging system consists of a cordon around the inner city of Stockholm with time-differentiated charges. The area inside the cordon is about 30 square kilometres (see Figure 12.1). There are 18 toll stations located at Stockholm city entrances and exits. Vehicles are identified by automatic number plate recognition (ANPR). During the trial, transponder (tag-and-beacon) technology was used as an additional way to identify vehicles, but the ANPR technology—originally introduced only for legal reasons—turned out to work so well during the trial that the transponders were abolished when the charges were reintroduced in 2007.[3] There is no opportunity to pay at the toll station. Instead, around 80% of the payments are made automatically through direct debit, and the rest are paid retroactively, either at local shops (e.g. 7-Eleven) or through bank transfers.

The cost for passing a toll station is SEK 10, 15, or 20, depending on the time of day (see the schedule in Table 12.1). The cost is the same for entering or exiting the cordoned area. The maximum amount payable per vehicle and day is SEK 60. No congestion charge is levied in the evenings or at night, nor on Saturdays, Sundays, public holidays or the day before a public holiday. Various exemptions (for e.g. buses, foreign cars, alternative-fuel cars and for traffic between the island of Lidingö and the rest of the county) means that about 25% of the passages are free of charge.

---

3   There is still a possibility to voluntarily use transponders for drivers who want an even more reliable identification. This is relevant mainly for drivers to and from the island of Lidingö, an island whose only connection to mainland Sweden goes through the charged area. Because of this, traffic to and from Lidingö passing through the charged area in less than 30 minutes is exempted from traffic. This creates an incentive for Lidingö drivers to make sure that they are not missed when crossing the cordon, since the system would then not view them as exempted.

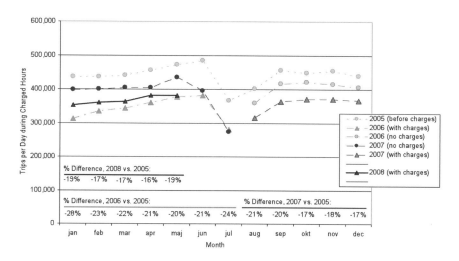

Figure 12.2   Traffic across the cordon, charged hours, 2005–2008

No congestion tax is levied on the Essinge Bypass past Stockholm (the grey road that passes toll stations 6 through 10 in Figure 12.1). This is the only free-of-charge passage between the northern and southern parts of Stockholm County, which are separated by a waterway. The Essinge Bypass was heavily congested even before the charges, so from a pure traffic management perspective, there is a strong argument for also charging vehicles on the bypass. The opposition from the surrounding municipalities was so strong however, that it was decided that the Essinge Bypass should be free of charge.

Change in Total Traffic Flows

The effects of the congestion pricing system on auto trips into and out of the central city were more or less as we should expect: with the charges in place, traffic decreased, as shown by Figure 12.2. When they were removed again at the end of the trial, on 1 August 2006, traffic immediately jumped back to its old level—almost.[4] Surprisingly, there was a stable remaining traffic reduction of around 5–10% compared to the 2005 level (and that level had been stable for around 15 years). Due to road works and problems with the measurement equipment, the size of the residual effect is a bit uncertain, but there was certainly a difference. One explanation could be that something else was affecting traffic levels—increased fuel prices, for example. But this, along with other alternate explanations, was

4   The periods between when the charges were abolished and when they were reintroduced are less certain, due to technical problems with the measurement equipment.

checked meticulously with econometric methods, and the increased fuel prices could at most explain 1% of the traffic decrease.

Instead, we hypothesize that some car users developed new travel habits during the trial, which persisted even afterwards: some car drivers found alternative modes or destinations that were actually better than they had thought before they had ever tried them. Another similar hypothesis is that there was a small but persistent 'shift' in travel habits in the sense that those commuters who used to go by car, say, three times per week instead went by car, say, two times per week. We know from other sources that many people are mixed-mode users: if some of these can decrease their shares of car trips only somewhat, it will matter a lot in the aggregate—and the effect will perhaps be persistent.

When charges were reintroduced in August 2007, traffic was once again down 20% compared to 2005 levels, i.e. around the same traffic levels as during the trial. Traffic has been slowly creeping up, but this does not seem to depend on car users 'getting used to' the charges and returning to their old habits—it can be shown that the traffic increase can be more than explained by increasing population and car ownership, as well as by inflation and an increasing share of exempted alternative-fuel cars (up from 2% of cordon crossings early 2006 to 11% in the middle of 2008, and steadily increasing), causing the charge level to drop in real terms.

Where Did the Car Drivers Go?

If traffic into and out of the city centre decreased with the introduction of the toll, what exactly happened to these travellers? In this section, we examine what sorts of strategies were used by travellers in coping with the new toll. In other words, we describe what proportion of the 'disappearing' trips shifted to other routes, modes, times of day, or other options. In doing this, we consider separately the case for work trips and the case for discretionary trips, which tend to have different kinds of constraints.

Data

The main source of information for the analysis in the rest of this chapter is a two-wave panel trip survey carried out in 2004 (before the charges) and 2006 (when the charges had been introduced). The 2004 wave was conducted mainly in September 2004 (with some observations in October), while the 2006 wave was conducted in March 2006. Originally, the second wave was meant to be conducted exactly one year after the first, but the introduction of the charges was postponed when the procurement was appealed. Hence, the second wave had to be postponed. This introduced a difficult problem when comparing the surveys, since there was a significant seasonal effect—an unusually warm September 2004 and a unusually cold and snowy March 2006. This resulted in a higher total number of trips in 2004, a higher share of walk/bicycle trips, and probably several other changes as

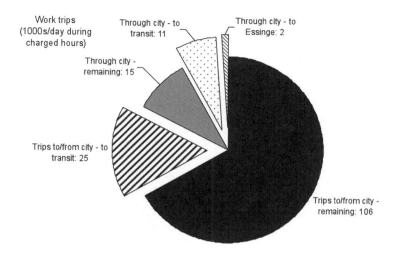

Figure 12.3   Work trips by car across the cordon, divided by O-D relation and remaining/disappearing

well. Moreover, quite a number of people change residential or workplace location or undergo other changes during an 18-month period, and there is a tendency for people with long work trips to be more likely to move or change jobs, making it difficult to sort out the effect of the charges from other effects.

In an attempt to adjust for these effects as far as possible, we make two adjustments. First, for work trips, we re-scale the total number of (work) trips 2004 to match the total number of (work) trips in 2006 for each of three aggregated origin-destination relations: north-south, north-centre and south-centre. Second, we re-scale the number of walk/bicycle trips 2004 to match the 2006 numbers, assuming that walkers/cyclists are drawn from car and public transport in the same proportion as they are in the O-D relations that are not affected by the charges. The second adjustment means that we will define away car drivers switching to walk/bicycle because of the charges, but because of the snow, the number of walk/ bicycle trips in March 2006 was so low that this cannot affect the main picture.

Discretionary trips, on the other hand, are probably even more affected by seasonal variation than work trips—especially the total number of trips and the share of walk/bicycle trips. Fortunately, the seasonal effect on car trips to/from the city does not seem to be very large, so these numbers are left without adjustment. The north-south traffic, on the other hand, exhibits a much stronger seasonal variation. Cross-checking against traffic measurements, we can deduce that the discretionary north-south car trips must be around 20% greater in September than

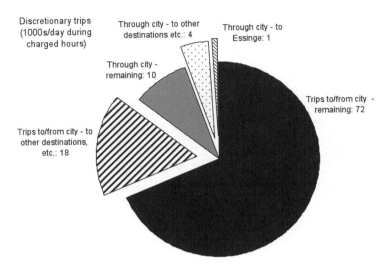

Figure 12.4   Discretionary trips by car across the cordon, divided by O-D relation and remaining/disappearing

in March solely due to seasonal variation. Hence, we adjust the 2004 north-south trips (both through and around the inner city) by this number.

Adaptation strategies

Using the travel survey as described above, we first analyse the pattern of work trips in relation to the origin-destination relations. Figure 12.3 shows work trips, divided into trips with origin or destination in the city centre and 'through trips', going between the north and the south of Stockholm County through the city centre.

Out of all work trips by car across the cordon, 24% 'disappear'. This translates into 27% 'disappearing' trips across the cordons, since some of the trips cross the cordon twice. This is fairly consistent with traffic measurements. Out of the disappearing 24%, 16 percentage points were trips to or from the centre switching to transit, seven percentage points were through trips switching to transit and one percentage point was trips switching to the non-charged Essinge Bypass (continuing to go by car). Hence, route switching was only a minor adaptation strategy: almost all disappearing work trips by car seem to have switched to transit. We will analyse departure time change in a later section.

Turning to discretionary trips, the trip decrease is roughly the same as for work trips—22% of the discretionary trips 'disappeared', making up 24% of the discretionary trip cordon crossings.

It turns out to be hard to assess where the disappearing discretionary trips went instead. This is partly due to large seasonal variation, but also to the fact that

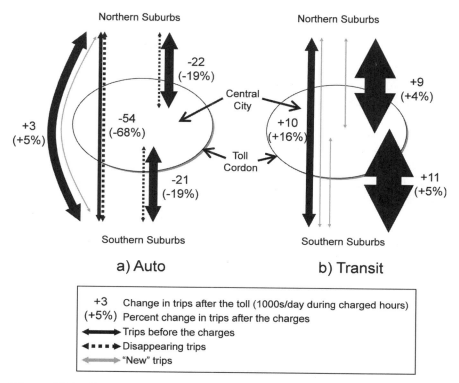

Figure 12.5   Changes in private trip streams

discretionary travel patterns are not 'stable'—the adaptation possibilities are much more multi-faceted, and trips are not 'replaced' on a simple one-to-one basis. The 'disappearing' discretionary trips did not end up on public transport—the number of transit trips decreased about on par with the expected seasonal variation between 2004 and 2006. A small part of the through trips switched to the Essinge Bypass. The most common adaptation strategies seem to be choosing other destinations and decreasing trip frequencies, possibly by combining trip purposes and increasing trip chaining. This is illustrated in Figure 12.4.

Of the 22% disappearing discretionary trips, only a few (one percentage point) switched to the Essinge Bypass, while the large majority (22 percentage points) cannot be 'tracked' easily. Part of this is due to the confounding effect of the seasonal variation—the overall number of trips in March is considerably lower than in September, even in O-D relations which are not affected by the charges—and part of this is due to trips not being 'replaced' by other trips in a traceable way. Figure 12.5 shows how the overall car and transit streams (counting private trips only) were altered by the charges. Black arrows show private traffic streams before the charges, while red arrows show decreases and green arrows increases.

Who Changed Departure Time and Mode?

The design of the Stockholm Trial was intended to spur two specific kinds of changes in travel behaviour: mode choice and departure time choice. The simultaneous public transport enhancements were meant to entice drivers to leave the car at home, and the differentiated toll levels during the course of the day were designed to discourage trips during the most congested part of the peak period and to encourage off-peak trips. Congestion is heavy in Stockholm only for a couple of hours per day, so it is desirable to increase peak spreading to reduce congestion during peak hours. As explained earlier, the charges were highest during peak hours.

On the other hand, it can be argued that it is precisely during peak hours (and in particular morning peak hour) that it will be most difficult to affect people's departure time. This is because the cost in terms of travel time is highest during peak hour, and those that easily could have chosen another departure time probably already make their trip off-peak. Empirical evidence also suggest that people are less flexible during the morning peak hour (Saleh and Farrell 2005).

The empirical evidence that the trial affected departure time is mixed. Karlström and Franklin (2008) found weak support that the charges affected departure time for morning commutes. On the other hand, Schollbach et al. (2008) also studied departure time during and before the trial using a GPS data set. Hence, their data set only included a small number of individuals (N = 48), but *all* types of trips by car for those individuals. Using the GPS data set it is also possible to analyse the exact timing of crossing the toll station, making it possible not only to analyse departure time change, but also peak spreading and payment avoidance. However, they found no evidence of changes in departure time. In this section, we will take a closer look at changes in departure time for morning commuting trips as a response to congestion charges using the travel survey data described earlier.

The degree of effect

A descriptive analysis reveals that there is a high degree of persistence in the departure time for the morning commuting trips. In fact, in March 2006, during the trial, almost 70% departed within 15 minutes of their departure time in the fall of 2004, before the trial (Karlström and Franklin 2008). Moreover, about 25% report the exact same departure time on both occasions.

If departure time for work in the morning changes, the departure time *from* work in the afternoon may also be affected. Let us consider the individuals who in both in 2004 and 2006 travelled to work in the morning (06:00–09:30), and home in the afternoon (14:00–19:00), using transit and car.[5] Figure 12.6 shows the bivariate density plot of departure time changes in minutes for those individuals (1138

---

5   As explained earlier, due to the strong seasonal effects, we have excluded the slow modes (walk and cycle) from the analysis.

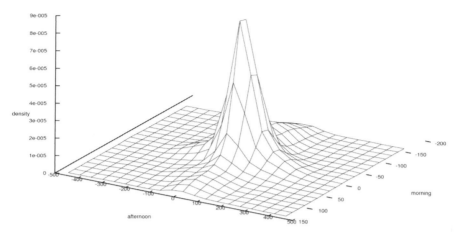

Figure 12.6   Bivariate density of observed departure time changes in the morning and in the afternoon (measured in minutes)

observations). First, a high degree of persistence in departure time, in particular in the morning, is clearly visible. Second, there is little evidence of a fixed number of working hours per day. It is likely that there are seasonal effects involved in the number of working hours per day. In fact, the number of working hours is lower in spring of 2006 compared with fall of 2004, both because of later departure time to work and earlier departure from work. As we will see later, it is probably only a small percentage of individuals who switch due to the congestion charges. If a small number of individuals changes their daily scheduling, it is not likely to be apparent in a density plot like Figure 12.6. Still, it is interesting that there is a rather weak link between changed departure time in the morning and changed departure time in the afternoon. In particular, the data shows little evidence of an eight-hour working day. The link between morning departure time and afternoon departure time is probably rather complex.

Given the arguments above and the descriptive analysis, it seems that the effect on departure time is likely to be small. But how small, and can it be detected at all? To assess this question we will employ different techniques. We will first estimate a joint model of departure time change and mode choice change. To account for possible selection bias, we will then employ a propensity score matching estimator to further strengthen our results.

A joint model of mode and departure time choice

Since mode choice and departure time are two different adjustments to the congestion charges, it is useful to model them simultaneously. This allows us to assess the substitution between mode choice change and departure time change. For instance, are men and women likely to adopt different adjustments? Let us

Table 12.2   Joint model for changing mode and departure time for initial car-drivers

	Model 1		Model 2	
Attribute	**Value**	**Std. Error**	**Value**	**Std. Error**
Travel Time	−0.02	0.01	−0.02	0.01
Variables for Car and Same Departure Time:				
Constant	1.37	0.60	1.71	0.37
Flexible Working Hours	-0.67	0.23	-0.58	0.21
Variables for Car but Changed Departure Time:				
Constant	0.11	0.61	0.50	0.37
Crossed the Cordon	0.65	0.27	0.66	0.26
Variables for Transit Variables:				
Female and Crossed the Cordon	1.66	0.40	1.63	0.41
Male and Crossed the Cordon	1.46	0.39	1.44	0.40
Flexible Working Hours	−0.27	0.34	–	–
Log-Likelihood	-519.87		-521.00	
McFadden's rho	0.056		0.054	
Log-Likelihood at alternative specific constants only: -551.05				
Number of observations: 635				

therefore consider the initial car drivers among morning commutes, and consider the switch to transit, together with the choice of changing departure time. The definition of 'same/changed' departure time will be defined using a 15-minute threshold. That is, if the individual departure to work is within 15 minutes of the original departure time, it will be considered to be the same departure time. Otherwise, it is considered to be a changed departure time. Our model is therefore a three-alternative discrete choice model. The first choice is to stick with car mode, with the same departure time. The second alternative is also car, but with changed departure time. The third alternative is switching to transit.

The estimation results of such a three-alternative multinomial logit (MNL) model are reported in Table 12.2.[6] While the overall goodness-of-fit is not

---

6   The MNL model is subject to the independence of irrelevant alternatives (IIA) assumption. Here, it may be argued that the IIA assumption may be violated. We have relaxed the IIA assumption by also estimating a nested logit model and a error component nested logit model, but we could not reject the simple MNL model.

impressive, each of the variables has the expected sign, if such exists. For instance, having flexible working hours decreases the probability of having the same departure time,[7] and travel time has a negative sign. Also, crossing the cordon has a significant positive effect on switching to transit. This is expected: other studies have shown that there is about a 15–20% effect on mode choice (switching to transit from car) due to the congestion charges.

For our purposes, we note that the variable for being tolled while sticking with car and changing departure time is significant. To quantify the effect on departure time, we employ sample enumeration and calculate the probability of changing departure time with and without toll. The estimated effect is 4.4%, interpreted as the increased probability of choosing changed departure time (and stick to the car mode) if subject to a toll, compared to the situation without the toll.

We also note that there seem to be small differences between the genders. As is evident from the estimates of changing to transit (when subject to crossing the cordon), the differences between the genders seem to be small. Likewise, we have also estimated gender-specific effects for the alternative of changing departure time (not reported here). Again, the effect is rather similar for both genders. If anything, it seems that men are more likely to change departure time, while women are more likely to switch to transit. However, these differences are not statistically significant.

While the estimated results support the hypothesis of changed departure time in response to the congestion charges, we note that we find rather weak evidence in Karlström and Franklin (2008). Here, we analyse the departure time change, but not whether the change is for an earlier or later alternative. Moreover, here we estimate the effect on departure time jointly with the effect on mode choice. However, both studies are subject to a potential selection bias problem. Whether an individual is subject to the toll or not is not random. In fact, the individuals have chosen the mode—and departure time—before the trial. In this sense, using a dummy variable for crossing the toll cordon as a regressor is problematic, since the regressor may be correlated with the error term. To deal with this problem, below we will employ a propensity score matching estimator (Rosenbaum and Rubin 1983).

In the terminology of the propensity score literature, we will use the term *treated* for an individual who crosses the toll cordon by car before the trial. The details of the propensity score matching estimator can be found in, for instance, d'Agostino (1998), and Karlström and Franklin (2008). In short, each treated individual is matched with individual(s) with similar characteristics in the control group (untreated population), and the difference in the dependent variable (changes in departure time) is estimated. We will estimate the average treatment effect of the treated (ATT).

---

7   For comparison, we included the model where this variable is also associated with the transit alternative (Model 1), but since it was not significant; we also report the model where it is deleted (Model 2).

Table 12.3   Estimates of average treatment effects on the treated

Group	Proportion Changing Departure Time [a]		ATT [b]	One-Tailed Significance [c]
	Untreated	Treated		
Initial Transit Riders and Car Drivers	0.343	0.376	+0.032	p<.10
Initial Car Drivers Only	0.363	0.376	+0.013	p<.03

[a] Changing Departure Time is determined by differences in departure time of at least 15 minutes, when crossing the toll cordon.
[b] ATT = Average Treatment effects on the Treated.
[c] Significance was determined by bootstrap (drawing with replacing), using 100 simulations.

Note that our dependent variable is the binary variable 'changed departure time among car drivers' (initial car drivers sticking with the car mode). Using the ATT estimator we can compare the proportion changing departure time between the treated group (car drivers crossing the toll cordon) and the untreated group. We will consider two different definitions of 'untreated', viz. (i) all other transit riders and car drivers, and (ii) all other car drivers only. Including transit riders in the control group is useful since it increases the sample size. On the other hand, seasonal effects may be asymmetrical between car drivers and transit riders, in which case it is more useful to only include car drivers in the control group.

The estimates of the average treatment effect of the treated (ATT) are found in Table 12.3. Interestingly, using either control group we are able to detect a departure time change which is small but statistically significant. Note that our earlier estimate of 4.4% is now reduced. In particular, note that the precision in the estimate is highest for the smallest estimate, in which we use other car drivers only (and not transit riders) in the control group. In this case, we conclude that there are about 1% of car drivers change departure time (according to the 15-minute threshold definition) when crossing the toll cordon. This effect is small, but statistically significant.

To summarize, we have investigated the departure time change on individuals crossing the toll cordon by car. We have focused on the morning peak, primarily because that is when peak spreading would be most desirable. On the other hand, there are also the trips where we, on *a priori* grounds, believe the effect would be the smallest, and therefore the most difficult to detect. Still, using two different methods, we conclude that there is a small but statistically significant time departure time change due to the toll. A conservative estimate seems to be about one to three percent, and probably in the lower range of that interval.

What Did It Cost?

We can now say a variety of things about whose behaviour was affected by the toll, what those people did instead, and what motivating factors were behind those adjustments. Now we can take this a further step and begin to estimate the size of the burden to these people – both to those who paid the toll and those who adapted by changing their behaviour. We essentially approach this as a welfare analysis, where we estimate the benefits and burdens of the toll's direct and indirect effects in quantitative terms, then convert them to monetary units where necessary. We use the same data in this section as in the earlier analyses of departure time and mode choice switching behaviour, that is to say we isolate the analysis to morning commute trips for those who did not move homes and did not change workplaces between 2004 and 2006.

This is by no means the only effort to quantify the welfare effects of the Stockholm toll system. An *ex ante* study was conducted by Eliasson and Mattsson (2006), but that used simulated data, not empirical observations of travel choices. More recently, two studies on the welfare effects are in press: one by Eliasson (2008) performing a benefit-cost analysis of the system as a whole, but this did not focus on equity considerations; and one by Karlström and Franklin (2008), which includes a welfare and equity analysis, but with important differences from this study. First and most importantly, that study assumed a constant value of time for all travellers, an assumption also made by the Swedish government in performing official benefit-cost analysis, but which is dubious in the face of real choices that people of different income levels take. Second, that latter study made no accounting for the potential economic benefits from the collected toll revenue; instead, the tolls paid simply disappeared.

This analysis advances our understanding of the Stockholm Trial's welfare effects by taking into account varying value of time, by examining differences both across income levels and across groups with different incidence of the tolls, and by considering a range of positive effects that might arise from use of the collected toll revenue.

Despite these advancements, due to data limitations, this is still not a full accounting of all possible costs and benefits of the congestion pricing trial. First, in this section we only take into account commute-to-work trips. The accounting for these trips is far simpler than for other trips, since both work and home location change less easily than locations for other activities, such as shopping or recreation. Indeed, as we saw earlier, the most common adaptation for commuters was to change mode, and hence that adaptation is our focus in this section. Second, travel time data for trips on transit did not account for potential time savings for buses due to the toll. Therefore, those who travelled by bus in both 2004 and 2006 will be considered to have been unaffected, either by a price change or by travel time changes. Third, our travel time estimates from the regional travel model represent the peak period as a whole, and therefore are not sensitive to changes across the time periods with different toll levels. As a consequence, we cannot properly account for the effects of changing departure time.

Given the data restrictions above, we restrict the analysis here to tolls paid, changes in auto travel time savings, the burden of adjusting from auto to bus to avoid the toll, and a set of three simple scenarios for refunds of toll revenues: 1) no refunds, 2) equal lump sum refunds, and 3) tax reductions proportional to income. Our measure of welfare is stated in units of Swedish Crowns (SEK) per year. Hence, travel time savings were converted using estimates of value of time. We used a range of values of time, depending on income level and gender, based on a study of value of travel time from the Stockholm region (Transek AB 2008).

By allowing the value of time to vary, the results of this study are somewhat different from a previous analysis of the welfare effects of the Stockholm Trial (Karlström and Franklin 2008), wherein the value of time was taken to be constant across all individuals. In our assumptions here, the value of time increases monotonically across the five income categories, for both men and women. The values of time are higher for men than for women for the first three (i.e. lowest) income categories, which encompass the bulk of this study's sample, but for the highest two income categories, women have a higher value of time than men.

To estimate the burdens of switching modes, we took the assumption of the Rule of Half, setting the adjustment cost to be equal to one-half of the cost of the toll and the effects of travel time savings that are avoided by switching from auto to transit. In essence, this assumes that the demand for auto trips, as a function of generalized costs (i.e. both monetary costs and time costs) is a straight line (Lakshmanan et al. 2001). The same assumption is commonly made in cost-benefit analysis for transport projects, and indeed has been employed previously in the ex-ante evaluation of the Stockholm Trial (Eliasson and Mattsson 2006).

Following the estimate of welfare effects by tolls paid, travel time changes, and adjustment costs, some further adjustments were made. First, the welfare effects were converted in SEK per year, assuming 220 work days per year after standard weekends, holidays, and vacation time are deducted. We also used an adjustment factor for vehicle occupancy of 1.27, so all of the tolls paid were divided by this number to reflect the real charge on individuals, rather than on vehicles.

Finally, the earlier study by Karlström and Franklin (2008) found that about 8–11% of travellers who were not actually affected by the toll still chose a different mode in 2004 than in 2006. That is to say, there are apparently other reasons, besides the toll, for people to not take the same mode on the survey day in 2004 as on the survey day in 2006. We should therefore account for the possibility that there are many travellers who vary their choice of commute mode on a regular basis. We do not know who, in particular, varies their mode more often than others, so we simply apply an adjustment factor to the entire study sample, resulting in a scaling down of the full set of welfare results. In particular, we multiply the results by a factor of 88% (set somewhat below 90% to be conservative) to account for those who do not drive every day.

Table 12.4   Average welfare effects by toll effect sub-group

Group	Average Welfare Change (SEK/year/person)	Weighted Proportion of Sample
All	−78	100.0%
By toll effect sub-group:		
tolled	−1616*	5.7%
tolled-off	−992*	2.7%
un-tolled	+65*	89.9%
tolled-on	−1063*	1.7%

Note: * = significantly different (>95%) from the average welfare change for pooled toll effect sub-groups.

Overall welfare effects

The average welfare effects are summarized in Table 12.4. On average, the change in welfare across the study sample, after sample weighting, was −78 SEK per year. Note that this is substantially lower than the figure of −189 SEK per year reported by Karlström and Franklin (2008). This is entirely due to the use of updated estimates for values of travel time, rather than by the previous government-approved estimates, and allowing those values to vary depending by demographic group. The value of time in the previous study was 65 SEK per hour, while in this study they range from 83 to 452 SEK per hour, depending on income level and gender. Thus, according to these estimates, the value of travel time savings goes much further in mitigating the burden of paying a toll.

The average value of −78 SEK per year is not actually very indicative of any single person's effects. This is because the question of whether one originally drove to work or took public transport has a huge effect on the result of the welfare estimate, just as does the question of whether one continued to do so after the toll was implemented. We can see this by breaking down the sample into the four subgroups: 1) the 'tolled', who were observed to take auto in both study years and whose trip crossed the cordon line, 2) the 'tolled-off', whose trips went across the cordon but switched from auto to transit, 3) the 'un-tolled', including both those who took public transport in both years and those whose trip did *not* cross the cordon, and 4) the 'tolled-on', who switched from transit to auto even though the trip crossed the cordon.

These labels for the four possible traveller responses have been widely used in congestion pricing literature (e.g. Zettel and Carll 1964), but the last label, 'tolled-on', perhaps requires some clarification: we do not suppose that those who switch from transit to auto are doing so for the virtue of paying a new toll itself, but rather that they are perhaps attracted to the auto alternative by some reduction in congested travel times, which for these individuals is more valuable than the amount of the new toll. Yet even these descriptions should not be taken too literally; for any given person in the sample, the choice to take auto or transit on the survey days was affected by a great many things besides travel time and out-of-pocket costs, so there may well be other reasons for someone switching modes or taking the same mode on both years' survey days.

Comparing each subgroup, we find the average welfare effects shown in Table 12.4. Now, we see that those who initially drove are either paying an average of –1616 to keep driving, or are burdened by –992 to switch to transit. These are much larger than the average value of –78, largely because that overall average is weighted down by the un-tolled group, which constitutes nearly 90% of the weighted sample. In essence, we see here that an unfortunate minority of residents—those who previously drove to work—are significantly burdened, while for the vast majority who did not, there is a small benefit. This, perhaps, explains the vocal opposition that is often expressed against congestion pricing proposals throughout the world.

Aside from the tolled sub-group, the tolled-on were worst-off. We would expect these to do worse than the tolled-off, but it is perhaps surprising that the tolled-on had such negative effects. If these people would do so much worse than the un-tolled, then why switch to paying the toll? The likely answer is that these people switched to the tolled option for reasons outside what we know. They may, in fact, be regular car-drivers who only happened to be taking a rare trip on transit on the 2004 survey day; or they may have had circumstances change such that in 2006, driving was unavoidable. It is also possible that for some of these, we have miscalculated the travel time savings benefits, which for some individuals probably outweigh the value of the toll. Whatever the case, we do not see a significant amount of these—they represent the smallest toll effect sub-group, with only 1.7% of the total sample.

Effects across income categories

One of the major criticisms of congestion pricing is that it is regressive, since those with the least income have the hardest time affording to pay the toll (Richardson 1974). At the same time, there is a strong counter-argument to be made that congestion pricing can be regressive if the drivers are, by and large, those with the highest incomes, and those with lower incomes take transit. An advantage of the approach here is that we can examine the average effect either on income categories as a whole, or on income categories among drivers, transit riders, or even those who switch.

These average effects for income and toll effect sub-groups are shown in Table 12. 5. Asterisks mark the income categories whose effects are significantly different from the pooled income categories. The most notable result here is actually the absence of significant differences. These results agree with the earlier study by Karlström and Franklin (2008), even though this study takes into account a varying value of time across income levels. The only significant trend here is among the un-tolled, where the income categories are significantly different from the pooled income categories. There is also a trend of increasing benefit with income, but an

Table 12.5   Average welfare effects by income category

Income Category	Average Welfare Change, SEK/year/person (Weighted Proportion of Sample)				
	All Sub-Groups	Toll Effect Sub-Group			
		Tolled	Tolled-Off	Un-Tolled	Tolled-On
< 25 000					—
	−50*	−1789	−1009	+2*	
	(16.4%)	(0.2%)	(0.4%)	(15.7%)	(0.0%)
25–40 000					
	−138	−2256	−1288	+28*	−1425
	(24.7%)	(1.2%)	(0.5%)	(22.5%)	(0.4%)
40–55 000					
	−39	−2439*	−474	+58	−165
	(27.4%)	(0.9%)	(0.5%)	(25.8%)	(0.1%)
55–70 000					
	−12	−332	−830	+100*	−1016
	(17.7%)	(1.3%)	(0.5%)	(15.1%)	(0.8%)
> 70 000					
	−152	−1617	−1280	+219*	−1017
	(12.9%)	(1.9%)	(0.7%)	(10.1%)	(0.3%)

Note: * = significantly different (>95%) from the average welfare change across all income categories.

important note here is that all five income categories did indeed see an average benefit. In other words, for the only subgroup where income played a significant role, everyone was better off anyway.

Also, although there are not significant differences between income levels, there are some differences in the average numbers, but these do not follow a clear trend from low to high incomes. The reason for this is likely that other factors, such as distance travelled and amount of toll paid (based on time of day), and number of times crossing the toll cordon, varied more widely *within* each income categories than *between* categories. It appears that individual circumstances have a greater effect on welfare than income level.

The role of toll revenues

In assessing the true equity effects of a toll system, it is important to understand the role of collected toll revenues. Currently, the collected revenue from the Stockholm congestion charging system is deposited into the national government's general fund. As stated earlier, the toll revenue has been earmarked for road construction, yet this decision has been subject to change in the past, with the previous government intending to the use the funds to support public transport in Stockholm. Even if the revenues are certain to go toward roadway projects, the distribution of benefits among the population is far from clear.

Table 12.6   Average welfare effects by refund scenario

Group	Average Welfare Change, SEK/year/person		
	No Refunds	Refund Scenario	
		Lump Sum	Tax Reduction
All	−78	+180	+173
By toll effect sub-group:			
tolled	−1616*	−1416*	−1344*
tolled-off	−992*	−727*	−734*
un-tolled	+65*	+328*	+316*
tolled-on	−1063*	−822*	−807*
By Income Category:			
< 25 000	−50*	+244*	+124
25–40 000	−138	+110	+45
40–55 000	−39	+224	+192
55–70 000	−12	+234	+273
> 70 000	−152	+84	+322

Note: * = significantly different (>95%) from the average welfare change for pooled groups.

Yet, the use of revenues can be extremely important to the equity effects of a toll system, as evidenced by prior studies (e.g. Eliasson and Mattsson 2006). Therefore, while we cannot be definitive about the redistributive effects of toll revenue disbursements, we can at least identify some bounds, by testing two theoretical scenarios for refunding toll revenues. The first is deliberately progressive, a lump sum refund to all in our study population; the second, deliberately regressive, with an across-the-board reduction in the income tax rate.

Adding the effects of each of these refund schemes to the total welfare effects found above, we arrive at the average welfare effects shown in Table 12.6. Importantly, all of the effects are now positive, and this holds true for both a lump sum and a tax reduction. Thus, we see an affirmation of one of the core arguments for congestion pricing: that by reducing externalities, we can see a net positive effect. Moreover, the empirical evidence supports a theoretical result from Small suggesting that all income levels could see a benefit on average, as long as revenues are appropriately returned (Small 1983).

In comparing the two refund scenarios, we see the expected result that the lump sum scenario is progressive, with the lowest income categories receiving the greatest benefit, while the tax reduction scenario is regressive, with the highest income categories gaining the most. Certainly, the refunds themselves for the two scenarios should be progressive and regressive, respectively, but what this tells us is that these original tendencies are not overwhelmed by the pattern of costs due to the congestion charging system itself, as represented by the 'No Refund' scenario. Treating the two refund scenarios as bounds, the conclusion we can reach is that a wide range of uses for the toll revenues could maintain a positive average effect for all income categories, even if some uses would be more progressive than others.

Table 12.6 also shows the average welfare effects of the refund scenarios for each toll-effect subgroup: the tolled, the tolled-off, the un-tolled, and the tolled-on. The two scenarios are not notably different from each other, and they show substantial improvements over having no refund at all. Yet, the differences between the sub-groups are still significant in the same way as if there were no refund at all. The same sub-groups still see a net loss, even with the refund, although the magnitudes are not as great; and the un-tolled see an even greater benefit. Hence, while the role of refunds can be expected to mitigate regressive effects across income levels, they may do little to assuage the objections of drivers.

Discussion

The Stockholm Trial has offered a unique opportunity to observe the travel adjustments made in response to a price increase for driving, how these varied across different demographic groups, and how the benefits and burdens were borne by these groups. In the above analyses, we have seen changes in choice of mode, departure time, route, and destination, each to a different degree. In some cases, such as with mode and departure time choice, we can say with high confidence that these changes were responses to the toll, not simply incidental changes due to unobserved factors. With others, such as destination and route choice, we can at least see changes in total travel patterns between those before the tolls and those during.

Combining the results from the various analyses above, we can estimate the relative proportions adjusting in each manner for those directly affected by the toll, shown in Figure 12.7.

Out of the approximately 25% trips across the cordon that disappeared, around 10 percentage points were work trips switching to transit and one percentage point was work trips switching to the Essinge Bypass. Six percentage points were discretionary trips switching to other destinations or abolishing the trip (possibly by trip chaining or combining trip purposes), and under one percentage point switching to the Essinge Bypass. The remaining five percentage points are disappearing professional traffic—deliveries, taxi, craftsmen etc. Since we do not have travel surveys for this type of traffic, we cannot decompose it further. That professional traffic is affected at all by the relatively low charges may come as a surprise, but there is significant evidence in the interview studies carried out with professional drivers that they in fact tried to plan their routes and trip chains in order not to cross the cordon unnecessarily often, and moreover to decrease the number of trips altogether.

Another observation is that route and mode changes were far from the only adaptation strategy—in fact, for discretionary trips, hardly anyone changed mode, instead preferring to adapt in other ways. The fact that these trips were obviously not 'replaced' in a simple one-to-one fashion may be an important observation: our impression is that many people, traffic experts not least, seem to be unconsciously

Trips

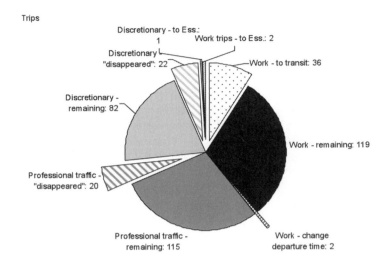

Figure 12.7   Summary of shares of trips remaining and shifting, by purpose

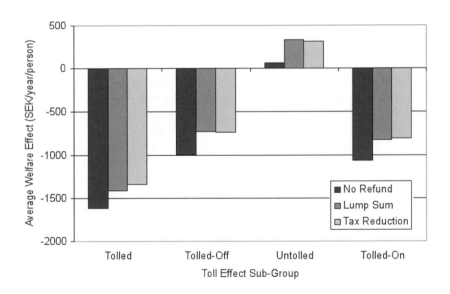

Figure 12.8   Average welfare effects for toll effect sub-groups by refund scenario

stuck with the assumption that there is a more or less fixed number of trips to be made, and that the effect of the charges should be possible to sort neatly into categories like 'mode change', 'destination change' and 'departure time change'. For discretionary trips, the adaptations seem to be much more multi-faceted, to the point that it is hard to say what really happened.

Our welfare analysis of morning commute trips found that the distribution of benefits and burdens due to paying the toll, enjoying travel time savings, or adjusting to it by changing travel mode, did not show significant differences between income groups. This appears to be the case whether value of time is considered to be constant (Karlström and Franklin 2008) or considered to be increasing with income, as we assumed here. The most important factor for determining benefits or burdens was whether a person's trip in 2004 was affected by the toll, and how they responded. As we can see in Figure 12.8, the un-tolled were the only group with a net benefit, even after accounting for either of two schemes for refunding toll revenue. However, this group represents nearly 90% of the population, resulting in an average net loss for the population as a whole of only 78 SEK per year, which is quite small, or a net *positive* effect of more than twice that magnitude if the toll revenues are refunded.

References

Algers, S. et al. (2006), *Facts and results from the Stockholm Trial, Final Version.* (Stockholm, Sweden: City of Stockholm).

City of Stockholm (2005), *On Stockholm's Trial* (Information Brochure, English Version), (Stockholm, Sweden: City of Stockholm).

d'Agostino, R.B. (1998), 'Propensity score methods for bias reduction in the comparison of treatment to a non-randomized control group', *Statistics in Medicine,* 17: 2265–81.

Eliasson, J. (2008), 'Cost-benefit analysis of the Stockholm congestion charging system', *Transportation Research Part A: Policy and Practice,* 43(4): 468–80.

Eliasson, J. et al. (2008), 'The Stockholm congestion charging trial 2006: Overview of the effects', *Transportation Research Part A: Policy and Practice* 43(3): 240–50.

Eliasson, J. and Mattsson, L.-G. (2006), 'Equity effects of congestion pricing: quantitative methodology and a case study for Stockholm', *Transportation Research Part A: Policy and Practice,* 40: 602–620.

Karlström, A. and Franklin, J.P. (2009), 'Behavioral adjustments and equity effects of congestion pricing – analysis of morning commutes during the Stockholm trial.' *Transportation Research Part A: Policy and Practice,* 43(3): 283–96.

Lakshmanan, T.R. et al. (2001), 'Benefits and costs of transport: classification, methodologies, and policies', *Papers in Regional Science,* 80: 139–64.

Richardson, H.W. (1974), 'A note on the redistributional effects of road pricing'. *Journal of Transport Economics and Policy,* 8: 82–5.

Rosenbaum, P.M. and Rubin, D.B. (1983), 'The central role of the propensity score in observational studies for causal effects', *Biometrika,* 70: 41–55.

Saleh, W. and Farrell, S. (2005), 'Implications for congestion charging for departure time choice: Work and non-work schedule flexibility', *Transportation Research Part A: Policy and Practice,* 39: 773–91.

Schollbach, F. et al. (2008), 'Analysis of changes in travel behavior due to the congestion charge in Stockholm (Working Paper). (Stockholm: Royal Institute of Technology).

Small, K.A. (1983), 'The incidence of congestion tolls on urban highways', *Journal of Urban Economics*, 13: 90–111.

Transek AB (2008), 'Jämställdhet vid val av transportmedel', [Equality in Mode Choice], (Solna, Sweden: Transek AB).

Zettel, R.M. and Carll, R.R. (1964), *The Basic Theory of Efficiency Tolls: The Tolled, the Tolled-Off, and the Un-Tolled* (Washington: Highway Research Board).

Chapter 13

Travel Demand Management Measures: Technical Answers or Political Gains? Closing Remarks

Gerd Sammer and Wafaa Saleh

Overview

This book presents a number of contributions on specific research areas in the field of travel demand management (TDM). Each chapter describes an investigation and research findings on the impacts of TDM measures, including road pricing/congestion charging. It is clear from scrutiny of the chapters presented and topics addressed in this volume that there is a large amount of research on the development, success, failure and opportunities for travel demand management in the transport system.

There are still a number of areas for further actions and improvements, in particular with reference to climate change, clean urban transport and congestion avoidance. Also, upcoming questions such as estimation of long-term effects, appropriate evaluation procedures for TDM including criteria of sustainability, equity and health, effectiveness of marketing and voluntary travel behavioural changes, public, pedestrian and bicycle transport and their potential for substitution of car trips etc. need further investigations. Setting targets for reducing traffic or prospective traffic growth requires vision and very careful planning and consideration of the political agenda. Many activities of the European Commission and of national and local governments, in Europe and worldwide, aim to achieve this vision and support these developments. But, on the one hand, it has to be mentioned that the political decision and implementation process of TDM measures is rather difficult, especially when pricing measures or restrictive measures for cars are to be included. On the other hand the effectiveness of TDM is strongly dependent on the 'principle of carrot and stick' towards car users.

Themes and Chapters

The main aim of this book therefore is to share experiences and discussions of a number of topics and research areas which have been neglected in the past.

The contributors in this volume address issues such as investigations of the desirable and undesirable impacts of TDM measures, and the implications of pricing measures, such as parking pricing, public transport fare structures and subsidies. In addition, international experiences with TDM measures have been highlighted in order that lessons can be learned and experiences can be exchanged. Finally, other TDM measures and the implications of their implementation are considered.

There are still a number of areas for further actions and improvements. These include: boundary issues of TDM; more experiences with measures other than road pricing; and the contribution of TDM to the reduction of greenhouse gases and the implementation processes.

Future Development

Some TDM measures are claimed to improve the transportation options available to consumers while others provide incentives to change trip scheduling, route, mode or destination or reduce the need for physical travel through more efficient land use, or transportation substitutes. What are needed therefore are technically feasible and politically-supported market reforms that have vision and give careful consideration to the short and long term impacts of TDM measures in order to encourage more efficient travel behaviour.

Many TDM measures solve one or two problems, but aggravate others. For example, building park and ride (P & R) schemes may help to attract a proportion of car users, but tends to increase total mileage driven and can, in some cases, attract those who previously used public transport for their whole journey. Public transport measures such as bus lanes and improved fare structures help achieve some modal shift objectives, but the limited capacity of public transport services might hinder the desired goal. Implementing traffic calming measures and intelligent transport systems may reduce speeds, improve safety and improve the environment in some local and urban area, but these measures tend to result in migration of accidents to other areas, reduced motilities and increased fuel emissions in some local residential areas.

Our assessment of TDM measures tends to focus on the potential success of these measures and can therefore overlook many of the potential negative impacts. More careful investigation of the assessment of the impacts of TDM is therefore needed to fully identify the potential outcomes of such measures. The major influence on the success and failure of TDM measures in the future lies with political agendas.

In the UK for example, ten years have elapsed since the publications of the UK White Paper 'New Deal for transport: better for everyone'. In 2008, major local and regional transport improvements are intended through local transport plans and regional funding allocations. The UK Government is strongly supporting local councils in the implementation of congestion charges on motorists entering and leaving cities; unless the cities accepted the congestion charge, they would not get any extra fund for improving their public transport services. These types of policies and political actions will no doubt have an impact on which policies are adopted at the local level as well as their appropriateness and potential impacts, in both the short and long terms.

The dialogue has to continue on the use of TDM measures, their impacts and how best to make use of them. What is needed in order to optimise the utilisation of TDM is vision, concepts and more investigations and experience with TDM measures. *Vision:* is needed to identify potential problems, appropriate solutions, the gaps and opportunities on how best to use TDM measures. *Concepts:* are continuously needed to assess what are available, modelling tools and assessment procedures are needed for predicting implications of TDM measures and gaining confidence and experience for future considerations and applications. Finally more and more *experience* on both national and international levels on TDM will provide more success and less failure with TDM.

Index